CRIMINAL LOVERS

DANIELLE STEEL — bestselling novelist
SUE LYON — internationally famous Hollywood star
MARY P. EVANS — successful attorney
SUE TERRY — mother and grandmother
SANDRA BEEMAN — prison guard

These women have one thing in common: they fell in love with men serving hard time in prison.

Read the shocking true stories of the women who love such violent men as serial killers Ted Bundy, Ken Bianchi, Lemuel Smith, and Richard Ramirez. Some women chose to give up their lives to be near their convict lovers. Some actually married their men in prison, and consented to sex behind prison walls. Others went to jail for trying to break their lovers out. And still others, united with their beloved on the outside, became the final victims of their murderous lusts.

PRISON GROUPIES

**PINNACLE BOOKS AND *TRUE DETECTIVE* MAGAZINE
TEAM UP TO BRING YOU THE
MOST HORRIFIC TRUE CRIME STORIES!**

PRISON GROUPIES

CLIFFORD L. LINEDECKER

PINNACLE BOOKS
WINDSOR PUBLISHING CORP.

PINNACLE BOOKS

are published by

Windsor Publishing Corp.
475 Park Avenue South
New York, NY 10016

First Printing: April, 1993

Printed in the United States of America

CONTENTS

Inside Women

Fatal Affairs

Pen Pals and Cheerleaders

ACKNOWLEDGMENTS

Several people are owed my thanks for their courteous assistance in researching this book about a curious phenomenon in our society which is much more common than most people realize.

Among those to whom I owe a debt of gratitude are Joe Kilcoyne of the *Register-Star* in Hudson, N.Y., Jeff Alderton of *The Times-News* in Cumberland, Md., Joseph Graf of the *Centre Daily Times* in State College, Pa., and Janet Feiler of the *Coeur d'Alene Press*.

Others include police and courthouse employees, as well as busy librarians with public libraries and newspaper morgues who cordially responded to my request for assistance.

Finally, I wish to thank my agent, Adele Leone, for her cheerful support. And most of all, thanks to my editor, Paul Dinas, both for his support and for his patience.

Preface

PRISON GROUPIES by Clifford Linedecker, first appeared to me to be based on a premise too incredible to believe — that large numbers of women from mainstream America would become transfixed and obsessed with men who were habitual criminals and losers. Often the women would become involved to the extent of marrying them even while jailed, committing crimes for and with them, and even dying for them.

Though my work is largely involved with Satanic and ritual abuse, Linedecker was not asking me to explain why women would be drawn to dance with a man in a red suit but rather one with black and white stripes; the former a person believed to be possessed of great power, the latter group too powerless even to leave the lock-up to walk freely and to look up at the stars.

What Linedecker was asking was that I explain to the best of my ability the psychodynamics of such a morbid fascination.

Laughingly, I told him, "Cliff, first you'll have to send me chapters of the book and prove to me that these women exist and then I'll give you an answer if it is explainable dynamically and whether or not I'll do it."

I never expected to be agreeable, but Linedecker's books are so mesmerizing that I felt at least I'd read this one, "on the house," so to say.

Federal Express arrived the next day. I began reading, and all time stopped. I was unable to stop until l had read every line, and thus I found myself agreeing: The book is fascinating, explainable in part, but totally compelling. I recommend it to you all.

As the dynamics are presented they will be discussed in general, not referring to any specific couples as I have not met any members of this amazing bizarre cast of characters and therefore must postulate from facts filtered through the perceptive skill of the author.

Before any student of human behavior can attempt to explain unusual actions, the norms must be postulated. What is a solid healthy basis for sexual attraction and sharing between two people? In my opinion, the sexual bond is a special kind of friendship between *peers* who commit to share the better-or-worse in life together in a mutual fashion with love and concern and a minimum of personal exploitation and manipulation.

As my older son wrote when he was only eight and entering a Hallmark contest to define love: "Love is secretly stealing someone else's problems."

To be able to do so means a common awareness, mutual respect, and a shared value system. Certainly, not a picture painted in current America to sell toothpaste, bring people into the movies, create a basis for families, or sadly, even to sell books.

In addition, for the above to occur, women must feel equal, experience partnership, play an active role in the relationship, to have good self-esteem and self-concepts, and know themselves. Sadly, none of the above is present in any of the women in these stories, regardless of how successful in a man's terms (financially) many of them were and are. Most were reared in dysfunctional families which were not training fields for self-actualization, self-love, or even love of life, but were often lonely, abusive, boring, meaningless, and bottom line: Sad!

* * *

Most of us reading this book certainly will be titillated, we will not act out as these women did, but throughout the book we should frequently stop and examine ourselves and our relationships for equivalents, danger zones, and areas we need to correct.* We have all been reared in a society that does not emphasize the hard work of a love relationship, but one which romanticizes the fantasy of walking into the sunset hand-in-hand happily through eternity; while fifty-two percent enter the boxing ring of divorce.

Why would any woman pursue a relationship with a violent prisoner, and thousands do, even though few become involved? What is it that differentiates those that do?

The Rescuer. The *first* dynamic, one which is in a role that society reinforces, gives to the woman a concept of herself as the nurturer and rescuer. Often men are seen as perpetual little boys whose mommies kiss the "boo-boos" of life and make them all better. How many of us are rescuers and how many of these women act it out to the supreme — several even to die?

The Controller. The *second* dynamic is the need for control. Too many present day relationships are battlegrounds for jousting for control. Many of these women came from families in which control issues were paramount, usually with the female being subjugated and submissive. What could be safer than conjugal rights in a prison trailer — the man remaining locked up, the woman left to pursue life unfettered.

The Celebrity. Third in dynamics is boredom, the feeling of being a nonentity and needing to be known and recognized. A subset of this type of woman is one who has achieved some success, but not enough to fill her craving to be noticed, even if it is through negative attention. Often, early in life she was deprived of praise for her successes, which were taken for granted, and fre-

*The hyperbole of these stories only highlights the dark corners of our own secrets.

quently more was expected of her. In her interactions with men such as these, no one can miss her (i. e. walking together to the conjugal trailer). This subset might be separately labeled *The Attention Seeker,* or the *Exhibitionist,* but the dynamics are so close I have not separated out this class. One moment on the television screen as a celebrity, even if it is paid for by many years' incarceration, is deemed to be worth it.

The Rule Breaker. Fourth is the direct opposite of the above. The person who feels she has had it all, is above it, and does not have to play by the rules. Usually, however, she is smart enough and has sufficient survivorship skills that she does not want to risk-take directly, so she becomes involved with a rule breaker; and if he is eventually freed, she often parades him around to her friends as her "pet freak." His presence adds a new dimension to her already overloaded and overindulged life. Frequently, a woman like this has had everything in life but caring. Her relationships have been materialistically satisfying, but distant and sterile. She feels empty and deficient.

The Starved. The *fifth* is a similar type of woman, but she has not had it all, except for the pain and emptiness. Often she had to parent her parents, and there was never anyone there to parent her. In aligning herself with this type of man, she knows she is needed. She finally *matters* and for that feeling, she may eventually die.

The Russian Roulette Player. *Sixth* is the dynamic of another type of emptiness and boredom. The woman perceives herself as valueless and, much like the adolescent, she needs to prove to herself that she is chosen by fate to survive regardless of the risks. She tempts fate through these alliances.

The Already and Always Guilty. The woman who all her life was labeled the "bad" or "wild" one is the *seventh*. She was constantly blamed for acts or events she did or did not do. Finally, she has a chance to really stand out. Her need is like a repetition-compulsion. We characterize this need in the common vernacular, "I might as well do it, if I am going to be blamed and punished anyway" and do it with a big bang! This woman is overwhelmed with rational and irrational guilt.

The Atoner. Eighth is a very similar woman who feels guilty but does not have the strength to punish herself, but wants society to do so, and therefore she can atone and be forgiven. Her sins may be real or not, but she perceives them as real and needs the authorities to make the final determination; much like patients who want to die but need to be assisted. Both this dynamic and the one before is very common to all women, and is symbolized by the Fall. After all, sex is due to Eve's curiosity, not Adam's passivity.

The Team Player. Ninth is the woman who feels very alone. She has always felt left out, the last one chosen on a team, never class president, attended the senior prom alone or with someone she or her parents asked. She desperately needs to be part of a group. She seldom acts out her fantasies by actually becoming involved with a man, but she lives vicariously through letters, etc.

The Rager. Tenth is a woman who frequently is gender confused, a victim of child abuse, spouse abuse, rape, etc. Like many victims of this, she wants to identify with the perpetrator, not the sufferer. Through her relationship with the criminal she becomes the strong one. She can rage at the world for its injustice and often considers her partner innocent.

The Already Wedded. Eleventh is the woman who may have, as a child, killed for the cults, committed other crimes, worshipped evil and became bonded to the dark side. Her acting out, as described in this book, is a continuation of learned experience.

The Juror. Twelfth is the woman who is a prior victim herself, but who sees the imprisoned man as an innocent, maligned, and unfairly treated person, a victim of society's wrongs, other than a perpetrator. Similar to the rescuer, she is the righter of injustice, the avenger of the miserable. She becomes judge, jury and Supreme Court.

13

The Deviant or *The Identifier. Thirteenth* is the woman who identifies with deviance but does it cautiously and vicariously to avoid repercussions. She is usually more careful in her interactions with the criminal, but usually treats him like the freak she feels she is but has carefully hidden.

The Savior. Fourteenth is the woman who is close in her dynamics to the Rescuer, the Juror, and the Identifier. She feels she alone can teach this man to love correctly, and through saving him she herself can be saved.

I could probably continue outlining dynamics that would make this introduction longer than even this fascinating book. But what I have written above should be sufficient for you, the reader, to now search and speculate on your own for each woman's "whys," an adventure which is more enlightening and fun than to be spoonfed.

However, the glue here is not sex, but power; not romance, but abuse; and finally not love, but self-hate. Truly, Freud was correct when he described the "Death Wish" within all mankind, the compulsive drive for individuals and whole societies to self-destruct. Daily, women are reinforced in their belief in their unworthiness as people, and are designated as second-class citizens.

This book tells the stories of women who knew the dangers, but ran toward the fire, not away from it. Drugged, so to say, by the dance, the music, the evil, and the need to prove they could either perish or survive it — thereby being omnipotent and meaningful.

Let us all enjoy Linedecker's masterful story-telling of these true stories, but also look and learn about ourselves as we read along.

Judianne Densen-Gerber, J.D., M.D.
Westport, Connecticut
October 31, 1992

Introduction

Some of the best men are in prison.

Or so it would seem, because that's the conviction of a growing number of women who look to jails and prisons — even death row — for lovers and husbands.

Yet, most of the women know that they will never spend a single night of intimacy with their jailed boyfriend or husband. And such normal pleasures of married life as sharing a home and parenthood will clearly be beyond reach.

Even though many of the jailhouse Lotharios are drawn from a devil's roster of some of the most ruthless and sadistic sex thrill killers in America, the women they attract are as likely to be alluring, desirable beauties with intelligence and exciting careers, as they are likely to be social rejects like themselves or over-the-hill frumps.

Sophisticated European beauties, college coeds, models, lawyers, corrections officers, television reporters, artists, a Hollywood actress, a best-selling author — even a judge — have succumbed to the dubious romantic charms of long-term prison inmates and serial killers.

In California, Sandra Wix was a member of a jury that helped convict Steven Erickson of the rape murder of a twenty-six-year-old woman. After sitting through the grisly testimony of a gruelling six-month trial that extended into early 1987, she married the convicted killer. Then she asked the California Court of Appeal to overturn the conviction, claiming undue jury pressure on her.

More often, however, women meet convict lovers after becoming pen pals. National magazines, daily newspapers, weekly tabloids and other publications frequently carry classified ads listing pleas from men in prison for female correspondents. And it's not unusual for a convict to be corresponding with as many as from ten to thirty or forty women at the same time while judiciously juggling their visits.

Women also meet convicts as volunteer visitors through religious ministries or other programs, after introductions by relatives or friends, or through their work as lawyers, prison guards or news reporters. And some groupies, especially when the man is a serial killer or otherwise especially notorious, begin their courtship during trials, choosing seats as near to the defendant as possible, smiling, winking or otherwise indicating their admiration and support.

Prison groupies have hijacked helicopters, attempted murder, and died in dramatic attempts to free pen pal lovers from maximum security prisons. They have thrown away promising careers by smuggling guns to killers behind bars, and they have abandoned heartbroken family and friends perplexed by their bizarre obsession with some of the nation's most universally hated violent criminals.

Serial killers like Night Stalker Richard Ramirez,

whose Satanic and cocaine-inspired rape and murder spree terrorized suburban Los Angeles in the mid-1980s, have attracted entire bevies of admiring cheerleaders at their trials.

Lawrence Sigmund Bittaker, who teamed with a former convict pal in the kidnap, rape, torture, and mutilation murder of at least five — perhaps as many as thirty — teenage girls in California, also found love behind bars. A few years ago Bittaker, who with his pal, Roy Norris, cruised for victims in a specially outfitted van they called "Murder Mack" and tape recorded the screams of the agonized teenagers, was married behind bars to a woman identified as a born-again Christian.

Even John Wayne Gacy, Jr., whose homosexual torture and murder spree claimed the lives of at least thirty-three boys and young men, has become a curious love object of women who have publicly announced their intent to marry the former suburban Chicago contractor.

Mass murderer Richard Speck, who slaughtered eight student nurses in Chicago with his powerful hands and a sharp knife during one terrible night of violence in 1966, received hundreds of letters from female admirers after he was imprisoned to serve multiple life sentences. Speck, who is believed to have killed several other people as well as the nurses, was still receiving about a dozen letters a week when he died of natural causes early in 1992.

Other convict Romeos do not share the international notoriety of serial killers, mass murderers, and avowed Satanists, but they nevertheless have little trouble attracting admiring women anxious to abandon careers, husbands, friendships, and respect to become their sweethearts or wives.

Sometimes, after setting up housekeeping with convict husbands who have been released from prison, women have paid with years of physical abuse — or with their lives.

So, why in the world would a normally intelligent woman look on death row, or elsewhere in prison, for that special man she wishes to share her life with? What is the secret of the baffling sexual magnetism of imprisoned serial killers, sadistic sexual psychopaths, stickup men, armed robbers, and other social outcasts who wind up facing execution or serving long terms behind bars?

Most experts who have studied the phenomenon are convinced that the guilt or innocence of the convict is irrelevant. In defending their love choice to others, prison groupies frequently cite excuses such as the purported lack of a fair trial, media prejudice, an unhappy childhood, or say simply that their man is now a different person than he was when he shot down a half-dozen innocent people in robberies, or raped and dismembered a couple of teenagers because he was bored.

Of course, not every woman who falls in love or otherwise becomes infatuated with a violent criminal who is on death row or otherwise serving a long prison sentence has the same motivations.

But psychiatrists, psychologists, and sociologists have come up with some possible answers to the complex puzzle posed by prison groupies. And they range from everything from poor self-esteem, a need to control others, and Florence Nightingale or savior complexes, to sadomasochism and a personal desire for attention — even if it means sharing the notoriety of a Jack-the-Ripper serial sex killer.

One psychologist has described prison groupies as often being the type who adopt stray puppies. They have a pathological or abnormal need to assist or help someone else.

Often the woman is someone who hasn't been able to form significant relationships in her own life, or they have tremendous feelings of guilt about something they believe they have done in the past and must expiate.

A psychiatrist who has testified in trials of several serial killers says that many of the groupies see themselves as saviors: the good woman whose love will salvage the bad man. According to his theory, they feel that their love for an individual, whom the rest of society has given up on or abhors, gives them personal validation and worth. For certain individuals there is some truth to the idea that ladies love outlaws, he says.

It's true that American folklore has always glorified desperadoes, the Jesse Jameses, John Dillingers, Bonnie and Clydes, Al Capones, as being exciting and somehow admirable antiheroes who bravely thumb their noses at society and do things their way.

And some women are apparently willing to go to almost any length to share in the personal publicity and attention that come with publicly linking themselves to especially notorious criminals.

Philadelphia sociologist Netta Gilboa draws a parallel between prison groupies and women attracted to male celebrities such as movie stars and musicians. "The very same reasons a woman is attracted to him (a male celebrity) are the very same reason[s] some are attracted to a well-known criminal," she says. "It's the fame, it's the attention, it's the glamour."

Some of the women are people who want fame at any cost, according to the sociologist. "It may be the only way they will get into *People* magazine," she says.

Ms. Gilboa believes many women who have sought out convicted killers or other men behind bars as husbands or sweethearts were previously victims of abuse, were raised with an absent father, or their mothers were involved with a series of men while they were growing up.

"Their role models and what they have been socialized to be attracted to may in fact be very different from the norm," she explains.

There is no question that women with a history of emotional and sexual or other physical abuse from fathers, husbands, or other males who have been a part of their lives are guaranteed a certain amount of safety in their relationships with men behind bars.

A woman who is restricted to communicating with her husband or sweetheart by mail or telephone, through a thick glass window, or in a crowded visiting room, can't be physically beaten by him. Often for the first time in their lives the women find themselves in control of a relationship with a man. They are the focus of his life, his most important link to the outside, normal world.

The convict may be dependent on them not only for emotional support, and for sexual services in states where conjugal visits are permitted, but for a host of other functions as well. She may provide him with spending money, lobby for his early release, or work closely with his attorneys on appeals. She becomes his voice, and body, on the outside.

And he can't cheat in a physical relationship, at least not with another woman.

Ms. Gilboa, who has a master's degree from Northwestern University and is a member of the Society for the Scientific Study of Social Problems, cautions that people shouldn't underestimate the charisma of some of the criminals who attract prison groupies. She points out that many of them may have gotten away with their crimes for a long time before they were finally caught.

"Someone who is able to manipulate people to get into their car, to let them into their homes, to befriend them, should have no trouble convincing any number of women that he is infatuated or in love with them," she says.

* * *

Long-term prisoners tend to be very good at manipulation, and often learn to use the mail and telephone to lure naive correspondents into behavior that at times appears to be almost unbelievably foolish. They run mail-order con games to obtain money, as well as romance, and often share details of their schemes and courtship techniques with other inmates.

One Florida convict was such a persuasive letter writer that at least two female pen pals he contacted through ads in weekly supermarket tabloids mailed him money, drugs, and photographs of their genitals, according to corrections officials.

Bobby J. Cornelius, another Florida convict, used a pen pal program called "Prison Missions" to strike up a correspondence with a thirty-three-year-old mother from El Monte, California. Cornelius was serving fifteen years for child molestation, and quickly turned the thrust of the correspondence from spiritual affairs to sexual matters.

According to authorities in Los Angeles, Cornelius finally asked the woman to bring her eleven-year-old daughter to the prison so he could molest her. Before the visit could occur, however, prison authorities intercepted a sexually explicit photograph of the girl the woman had mailed to the prisoner and put an end to the disgusting scheme.

Armed robber Kenneth Bean was serving time in a Wisconsin prison when he proposed by mail to six different women. Authorities who charged him with mail fraud said most of the women agreed and complied with his request to send him travel money for a reputed post-release wedding.

The fifty-three-year-old convict con man, whom one newspaper wag referred to as "Wisconsin's romantic jumping Bean," reportedly married one of the women.

* * *

Pat Galloway, an ex-convict who became a prison minister, was quoted in a story in the *Atlanta Journal* and *Atlanta Constitution* as recalling an inmate who convinced his married correspondent that they had been wed by God. Consequently, every time she slept with her husband she was committing adultery. So she left her husband.

Galloway said the same convict had another woman in North Carolina all ready to move out of her home, as well. The prison con man had five hundred years to serve, and was a great manipulator, the minister observed.

My own research has indicated that a happy ending to a behind bars romance is a rarity for prison groupies. And certainly, the phenomenon of prison groupies isn't new.

As far back in this country as the late nineteenth century, legendary gunfighter Buckskin Frank Leslie was serving a life prison sentence in Arizona for shooting his wife to death when a woman named Belle Stowell began writing to him.

Leslie was as handsome as he was ruthless, and despite his appalling history of abusing wives she quickly fell in love with him. One of the lethal gunman's exes was known as "the Silhouette Girl" because his idea of foreplay was making her stand against a wall while he traced her outline with shots from a .45 before making violent love. Leslie and Belle married after his pardon in 1896, but once he was outside prison walls the relationship quickly deteriorated and ended in divorce.

My first recollection of the phenomenon of prison groupies dates back to one of the most notorious and drawn out murder cases of the 1950s and 1960s, that of Dr. Samuel Shephard who was convicted during two controversial trials of the bludgeon murder of his pregnant wife, Marilyn, in a wealthy Cleveland suburb.

Ariane Tebbenjohanns, the glamorous and beautiful twenty-four-year-old blond wife of the heir to a German steel fortune, soon began a trans-Atlantic pen pal relationship with the imprisoned specialist. The relationship quickly blossomed into a long-distance romance, and Ariane joined the growing number of people convinced that Dr. Shephard was really innocent.

He was still in prison when she divorced her husband, left her child behind in Germany, and married him. Their storybook romance was shattered after attorney F. Lee Bailey won Shephard's freedom in 1966. Shephard's new wife complained that he flew into violent rages and she had to flee the house in fear of her life. Finally she filed for divorce and returned to Germany.

Not all prison groupies who eventually meet up outside prison walls with their convict Romeos are as fortunate. Some, including individuals whose stories will be recounted in following chapters, have paid for their dangerous liaisons with gross sexual or other physical abuse, with their own freedom or their lives.

In California a nineteen-year-old school clerk was abducted and raped after initiating an ill-conceived pen pal relationship with a stickup man who was an inmate at San Bernardino County's Prado Conservation Camp next to the more secure California Institution For Men in Chino.

Approximately eighteen months after the teenager began to correspond with the armed robber he escaped, and with the help of a female confederate, marched the girl into a motel room. There she was raped and forced to perform oral sex, then tied to a bed with torn sheets. After enduring a harrowing night of repeated sexual abuse, she escaped when her abductor shot himself up with heroin and dozed off early the next morning.

Queried about the incident by a news reporter, San

Quentin chaplain Harry Howard said that writing to prisoners as pen pals was not recommended.

I concur fully with the good chaplain's advice!

Clifford L. Linedecker
Lantana, Florida

Faithful Spouses

"Apparently prison bars are more appealing to some women than singles bars."

— Geraldo Rivera

Chapter One

Danielle Steel,
Danny Zugelder, and Bill Toth

As petite and energetic as a hummingbird, Danielle Steel is a woman who makes her living writing about the steamy passion and risky pitfalls of love.

But the real-life loves the world's dynamic multi-million dollar queen of romantic novels shared with an imprisoned bank robber and rapist and with a small time thief, drug dealer, and heroin addict are every bit as sensational and titillating as the soul-stirring fictional affairs she creates.

In fact, convict Danny Zugelder claims that two of Danielle's blockbuster novels are based on his own life or on elements of their relationship.

The hulking six-foot-six-inch, 285-pound career criminal has told reporters that he recognizes himself and his five-foot, one-inch, former wife, whose weight hovers around one hundred pounds or less, as the protagonists in *Passion's Promise*.

The romantic potboiler traces the love of a beautiful journalist, Kezia Saint Martin, and an ex-convict named Lucas Johns, who becomes deeply involved in prison reform. The head-over-heels in love heroine unselfishly sets her career aside so that she can follow and support her man.

Zugelder says that there is also a tie-in to his own experiences in Danielle's novel, *Now and Forever*. The story line revolves around a woman whose husband, Ian Clarke, is locked up at the California State Correctional Center at Vacaville after he is falsely accused of rape. But the reputed victim had really consented to sex. Cheryl Ladd starred in a film version of the popular romance novel.

Danielle has not been talking much with the press about Zugelder, or about former hubby Bill Toth. But shortly after publication of her first novel, *Going Home,* she described the theme to a reporter.

"Every woman falls in love with a bastard at least once in her life," she said.

Regardless of the possible truth or inaccuracy of that statement, the incredibly successful romance writer is a woman who has accumulated a vast store of first-hand knowledge about falling in love. She has been married four times.

Her first husband was French-American millionaire banker Claude-Eric Lazard, and her fourth and current spouse is former American shipping magnate John Traina of San Francisco.

But most biographical information about the woman whose first twenty-eight published novels have sold more than one hundred million copies and have been translated into nineteen languages, somehow have little to say about, or completely neglect to mention, the two hardened criminals she wed after her union with Lazard and before her marriage to Traina.

The shocking story of her little known marriages was publicly revealed in late December, 1991 and early January, 1992 when publications in the United States and England published interviews with Zugelder. The supermarket tabloid, the *Star,* first broke the sensational story on this side of the Atlantic. The *News of the World* and the *Daily Mail* informed readers in Britain about the secret lovelife of the popular author.

Approximately six months later *People* magazine published the story; and small items about the blockbuster novelist's murky dalliance with the two menacing criminals at last began appearing in daily American newspapers.

The writer has lived a life that is as dreamily provocative as that of the most alluring of her fictional heroines, and grew up as the privileged daughter of a German father and a Portuguese mother.

Her father was a member of Munich's famous Lowenbrau brewing and banking family. A Bavarian castle with a moat that was as pretty as a fairy tale was among the family properties. Her mother came from a family of diplomats.

Danielle Fernande Schuelein-Steel was born in New York in August, 1947, but spent much of her childhood in Paris surrounded by material goods and all the trappings of wealth and sophistication. She learned to speak several languages fluently.

But she was an only child, and was lonely. She was seven when her parents divorced, and her mother left. Years later she recalled that she enjoyed her father, but he was away travelling for long periods of time and she spent much of her childhood shuttling between New York City and Paris as she was looked after by relatives and servants.

Consequently, she spent much of her time reading, and writing poetry. She attended schools both in New York and in Paris, and graduated from the Lycee Francais when she was fourteen. At fifteen she was studying at the Parsons School of Design and planning on a career as a fashion designer.

After developing a stomach ulcer, however, she transferred to New York University. But health problems continued to plague her. She had surgery for a tumor, and came down with hepatitis before regaining her strength and health.

When she was seventeen, the poor little rich girl married a man who was ten years older than she. But like her, Claude Eric Lazard was a sophisticated continent hopper used to shuttling between Europe and the United States. During their marriage they lived in homes in Paris, New York City, and San Francisco. Danielle was twenty years old when she gave birth to her first child, a daughter, Beatrice.

While the Lazards were living in New York, Danielle joined an all female public relations and advertising firm in Manhattan called Supergirls Ltd. She was hired as a vice president of public relations and new business. The all women firm organized corporate parties and planned public relations campaigns.

John Mack Carter, the editor of the *Ladies' Home Journal* and one of her clients, advised her to become a writer. When the business failed, Danielle headed for her home in San Francisco and wrote her first published novel, *Going Home*. She spent three months at the typewriter.

Although the paperback novel was popular, it didn't make her an instant success. The next five books she wrote were rejected by publishers. Nevertheless, she had been bitten by the writing bug and continued to work.

While her fledgling career as a writer of poetry and womens' romantic fantasies was sputtering, her marriage was failing. She and her husband separated, but writing kept her occupied. She frequently wrote ten hours or more a day, working on her novels, her poetry, and on magazine articles.

In 1972 when Danielle was on the West Coast on assignment to do a magazine story about conscientious objectors who were imprisoned, she was introduced to a career criminal who had nothing to do with the anti-war movement. He was twenty-two-year-old Danny Zugelder, the troubled son of a hard-drinking farm worker who had reportedly walked out on his family when the boy was only three-years-old. According to Zugelder he was serving a sentence at the California State Correctional Center at Lompoc when he volunteered for experiments to determine why astronauts lose calcium while they are in space.

Zugelder proved to be a chip off the old block when it came to his taste for alcohol. He was also a tall, husky boy with a penchant for violence and thievery, and by the time he was in his mid-teens he was a near fulltime hell-raiser who specialized in car theft and bank robbery. Finally, after eight robberies over three years, he was arrested and imprisoned at Lompoc.

Years later he recalled that he was lying naked in his bunk when he first saw the pixyish green-eyed beauty who would eventually become his wife. The muscular convict said he could tell she was attracted to him, and described the meeting as love at first sight. He had the covers pulled up to his waist, and she fell in love with his chest, he said.

Danielle had apparently never met a bank robber before, and she reacted to her meeting with the charming giant with a torrent of chatter and pleasant laughter. People with Zugelder's grim record of crime and violence didn't normally inhabit her sheltered world.

According to Zugelder's story, Danielle repeated her visit the next day. The day after that when she flew back to New York, her telephone rang as she stepped through the apartment door. It was the handsome and ominously appealing convict calling from a prison phone. It was just like a scene that she later penned for *Passion's Promise,* Zugelder would recall.

He said she had already written him a fifteen-page love letter while she was on the airplane.

* * *

31

The relationship quickly flared into a passionate romance, through sensuous phone calls and letters, according to the prisoner. He later suggested that they must have invented telephone sex.

But telephone sex wasn't enough. And after Zugelder was returned to the regular prison population following completion of his role in the NASA experiments, Danielle soon flew back to the West Coast and resumed her visits with him.

In his newspaper interviews, Zugelder said that the first time they had sex, a couple of sympathetic convict pals distracted guards while the passionate couple met for their erotic tryst in a womens' toilet at the visitors' center.

"It wasn't lovemaking," he was quoted in the *Daily Mail*, "just raw sex."

That was apparently good enough. Zugelder said they continued their surreptitious sexual rendezvous for several months until his release. The prison had generous visiting rules, and the big convict said she would come to see him three or four times a week. Sometimes they would sit on the grass and sip *Jose Cuervo* and grapefruit juice that she brought with her to the prison, he said.

When the lusty convict was paroled from his armed robbery term in June, 1973, his diminutive sweetheart was waiting with a car to pick him up. He said they headed for the nearest motel in Lompoc, and for the first time made love together in a bed.

Later they moved into a posh apartment in the Pacific Heights with Danielle's five-year-old daughter, Beatrice. Zugelder got a job with an architectural business. Danielle wrote copy for the Grey Advertising agency, submitted poems to various magazines, and toiled at producing romance novels on her trusty, old, manual typewriter.

During their leisure hours he took her out for Mexican food, on fishing expeditions, and on her first venture to a drive-in movie. She introduced him to the theatre, the symphony, and to society parties, that included a dinner at the French Embassy.

Zugelder claims that his vivacious sweetheart was an exuberant lover, and said he would hurry to her office for feverish lunchtime trysts behind locked doors. "We had sex in restaurants . . . anywhere," he was quoted.

But not all of Danielle's upper crust friends were as excited or as charmed by the personable ex-convict as she was. Nor did they share her seeming conviction that all he needed to straighten out his life was the attention and affection of a loving woman.

Zugelder wasn't comfortable as his wife's reform project, and being shown off to her ritzy friends. When party friends of his wife who didn't know about his background as a robber asked what business he was in, he soberly replied that he was in banking. Few of them suspected that he specialized in large withdrawals at gunpoint.

By his own admission he usually got drunk at the high-class parties they attended together. And he later complained that he was making powerful enemies because of his activities in prison reform — as Lucas Johns would do in *Passion's Promise*.

During those months together, Danielle reportedly had several miscarriages. And their broad differences in background, tastes, and friends added extra stress to the unlikely pairing. Danielle loyally stood by her man, however, when he once more began tangling in new brushes with the law and was accused of some minor crimes. He was never convicted of any of them.

She continued to support him, even when he got into more serious trouble. He was arrested for felony sex offenses after enticing a woman into his car in 1974 and raping her. Zugelder claimed that law enforcement authorities had the story wrong: He was really the victim,

33

he indicated, because the woman had seduced him. But his story simply wasn't believable.

Danielle, nevertheless, continued to support Zugelder throughout the criminal court proceedings, and after he was sentenced for the rape and locked up at the prison at Vacaville. She provided $17,500 for his defense in return for a promissory note. And in an effort to win leniency and participation in a rehabilitation program instead of prison for him, she wrote to the local probation department on his behalf putting much of the blame for his troubles on herself.

In 1975 following Danielle's divorce from her first husband, she and her inmate lover were finally married at the prison. The tiny bride wore traditional white and carried a bouquet for the brief ceremony in the visitor's canteen. The long-haired groom was dressed in simple prison clothes, a white shirt and dark trousers. His uncle, a Baptist clergyman, performed the rites.

More than fifteen years later, an apparently bitter Zugelder would declare that the marriage was important to Steel because she had developed a strong taste for their lovemaking. And only married prisoners were permitted forty-eight-hour conjugal visits every month.

Zugelder explained that a two-bedroom mobile home was made available at the prison for the visits. Danielle brought her daughter with her during every other visit in the trailer, he said.

He ungallantly boasted that he took an insecure, sexual neophyte and turned her into a sensuous swinger.

As Danielle made regular visits to her husband over the next year, she also continued her writing. By the time the couple was divorced on April 14, 1978, she had bloomed into a best-selling novelist.

She had also fallen in love with another troubled man, whose life had been marked by a series of crimes, arrest, and runaway drug abuse. Danielle was in the final weeks of pregnancy on April 15, when she married Bill Toth the day after her divorce from Zugelder. Her son, Nicholas, was born by a caesarean operation about two weeks later. A nanny was hired to take care of Nicholas and his older half sister.

Danielle's newest husband was later described in at least one biographical sketch as an alcohol and drug abuse counselor. (Some writeups left him and Zugelder out altogether.) Lengthy police and prison records, however, drew quite a different picture of her new ruggedly handsome groom. Toth had spent much of his turbulent life behind bars after a dizzying flood of arrests for drug dealing and possession, burglary and grand larceny.

He grew up in San Francisco as the only son of a life insurance salesman and a housewife. After attending local Catholic elementary and secondary schools, he signed up for classes at Santa Clara University. But he never completed college, and during the late 1960s at the beginning of the hippie-era of peace, love and hallucinogens, he dropped out of school and immersed himself into the Bay Area's busy drug culture. He smoked marijuana and hashish, tripped on LSD, and began shooting heroin.

By 1971 he was an addict with a one hundred dollar-a-day monkey on his back. He supported his habit by thievery and selling dope.

The star-crossed couple met in 1977 two years after Toth had entered a San Francisco rehabilitation program and begun working as supervisor of the sponsoring agency's moving company. Danielle needed help moving into a new apartment.

Despite his wasted years on drugs, Toth was a good-looking, masculine hunk, and he and Danielle quickly began dating. When the couple set up housekeeping together about a few months later, she was already pregnant with his child. He was counseling troubled teenagers and still working hard to stay away from drugs and keep his own life turned around.

His discouraging battle to beat drugs and to rehabilitate himself would outlast his ill-fated marriage to the celebrity author. Like Zugelder, Toth would be left with bitter feelings about his doomed relationship with Danielle, and he would eventually publicly accuse her of betrayal.

He peevishly described her in the *People* article as a person who needs someone around she can control.

She was still married to Toth and their son was about eighteen months old, however, when Zugelder was once more paroled from prison. He learned about his ex-wife's latest marriage and the birth of her son through a magazine article.

Zugelder later indicated that bitterness over his failed marriage was at least partly to blame when he went off on a wild robbery, rape, and torture spree along California's northern coast and in Colorado. He said he was driving through his old neighborhood in Pacific Heights when he saw Danielle with her new husband and son, and felt cheated. He realized that he had no wife, no son, and only a one dollar bill and some change in his pockets.

Police captured the brutal rapist in Colorado after he pulled a sawed-off shotgun and a knife on the teenaged daughter of a local police chief, then kidnapped and sodomized her. He was sentenced to eighty years in prison, and was sent to the maximum security Fremont Correctional Facility near Canon City, where he became Inmate Number 45633. He will not become eligible for parole again until 1998.

When he wrote to Danielle asking for five thousand dollars to pay his legal bills, in exchange for promising not to publicly reveal their marriage, she responded by contacting prison authorities. The resentful convict also claimed that a short time later he received a letter from the warden accusing him of blackmail and forbidding him to correspond again with his ex-wife. It seemed that the tiny author with the big heart had given up forever any desire to play a part in rehabilitating the imprisoned robber and sex criminal she once loved.

While Zugelder was contemplating spending more long years behind bars, his ex-wife's new marriage to Toth was also heading for the rocks. She had published her fourth book, *The Promise,* and her career was moving into high gear. She spent much of her leisure time as she had when she was living with Zugelder, busy on the Bay Area's glittering opera, symphony and party circuit.

But like Zugelder, Toth mixed with his wife's society friends about as well as oil and water. He also blamed their enmity for pulling the rug from under their marriage.

Whatever the reason was, it wasn't long before he moved out of their home and into a hotel. For awhile Toth saw Danielle and their son on weekends. Then one day, according to his later account, he showed up at their home and was met by a uniformed police officer who refused to let him inside.

More than fifteen years later when Toth talked about his brief union with the wealthy author, he was still grieving because he couldn't see his son.

By March, 1981 when the courts officially ended Danielle's third marriage she was already becoming one of the most financially successful writers in the world and was earning hundreds of thousands of dollars for her books. Toth wound up after the divorce from his wealthy wife with a mere fifty thousand dollar settlement.

He used the windfall to take off on a self-destructive drug binge. It ended with an arrest for shoplifting, and a ten-month term at California's notorious Folsom prison. For awhile after his release he was permitted to visit with Nicholas. Then Danielle used his record as a drug addict and criminal to win a court order that ended the visitations.

In the meantime, Danielle's bank account was burgeoning, and her name was becoming synonymous with the syrupy melodramas that housewives and schoolgirls buy by the millions to fuel their romantic fantasies. Some of her plots were set in the contemporary world and locations including San Francisco's former hippie mecca, Haight-Ashbury and in Vietnam; others were set in earlier times and other places, including World War II-era Europe. But she also continued to churn out and publish sentimental poems about romance and motherhood.

In 1984 she was one of seven women authors who produced chapters for the popular nonfiction book, *Having A Baby*. In her chapter, Danielle described the pregnancy and birth of Samantha, her third child and first with her husband John Traina.

Critics were sometimes cruel and panned her novels as escapist literature of little or no literary value, or dull and overly sentimental. But there were also good reviews. When *Thurston House* was published in 1983 a reviewer for *Publisher's Weekly* described it as at "the top of the genre."

More importantly even than the plaudit from the publishing industry's most influential journal, readers and fans were buying her hardcovers and paperbacks by the millions.

Her novels were almost routinely selected for book clubs. *Daddy* and *Palomino* became TV miniseries. *Now And Forever* was made into a movie. A few years after her divorce from Toth she signed a whopping sixty million dollar contract to write five books. And in 1986 she made the *Guiness Book of World Records* with an entry noting that she had at least one of her books on the prestigious *New York Times* best-seller list for 225 consecutive weeks. Later, she exceeded even that record.

By then she had married again, this time to John Traina a handsome and successful man with a more appropriate background and lifestyle. By the early 1990s she was the charming middle-aged mistress of a fifty-five-room Victorian mansion with a high gilt-ceilinged ballroom and fifteen bedrooms overlooking San Francisco Bay in exclusive Nob Hill. The imposing home was constructed in 1913 by sugar heir Adolph Spreckles. The Trainases also had a beautiful old farmhouse north of San Francisco, and five servants to help run their busy household.

Danielle was no longer hobnobbing with jailbirds and junkies. She was a twenty-five-million-a-year success story. And when she pulled on one of her Christian Dior gowns to step out with her husband, who mixes chores as her business manager with activities in real estate and investments, it was often to attend a society party, the opera, or to an art or jewelry auction.

The couple is also kept busy watching over a brood of nine children: five daughters and four sons. Danielle's husband had two children from his previous marriage to former debutante of the year cover girl, Dede Buchanan. And since their marriage in 1981, they have become the parents of five more: four girls (including Samantha) and a boy. The youngest of the children, Zara, was born in 1987.

Chapter Two

Carole Ann Boone Anderson
and
Theodore "Ted" Bundy

Carole Ann Boone Anderson would most likely have spent her entire life in relative obscurity — if she hadn't attached herself to one of America's most arrogant and hated serial killers.

But for nearly ten years she shared the spotlight and the notoriety with her bloodthirsty lover, Theodore R. "Ted" Bundy, before fading from public sight shortly before his execution.

A tall, rangy woman who wore glasses with lenses that looked like pop bottle bottoms, and wore her hair shoulder-length, she was already a two-time loser in the marriage stakes and had a teenage son. Carole was wed to Bundy in a bizarre courtroom ceremony hours after he was convicted of the brutal sex murder of a twelve-year-old junior high school girl from Lake City, Florida.

And she bore him a daughter after reportedly coupling with him in a visiting room converted from a cafeteria at the grim Florida State Penitentiary near the town of Starke where he was the most notorious prisoner on death row.

* * *

For years as prosecutors and other legal authorities fought for Bundy's execution, the smirking serial killer and his faithful wife thumbed their noses at the system.

They not only used a crafty legal maneuver to carry out the wedding after corrections authorities rejected their marriage request — and conceived the baby — but Carole also reportedly smuggled marijuana to her lover inside her vagina, and provided him with contraband booze that kept him drunk during important periods of his murder trial for the sex-slaying of school girl Kimberly Leach.

Despite the plethora of allegations of crossing up judicial and corrections authorities and flouting prison regulations, Carole was never charged with committing a crime.

Bundy was as handsome, intelligent, and charming as he was notorious, and the sadistic sex-killer quickly attracted a covey of infatuated groupies who wrote sensual love letters to him while he was behind bars, attended his trials, and zealously defended him to other courtroom spectators and news reporters.

But once Bundy was imprisoned in Florida, there wasn't much of a contest for his affections. Carole had known him in Washington state, long before he was identified as the crazed necrophile who was battering young college-age women to death, then sexually violating their dead bodies in an orgy of mutilation and other abuse. And she staked her romantic claim on him early.

By the time she travelled from Washington for Bundy's murder trials in Miami and Orlando, he had already been identified as the killer of a series of young women in Washington state, Utah, Colorado and Florida. Nevertheless, Carole was staking a solid and binding romantic claim on the accused serial slayer.

In the northwest, Bundy often used crutches or a phony cast on one arm to lure sympathetic coeds away from their friends to his Volkswagen bug where he suddenly attacked them with a tire iron, crowbar, or club. Once the girl was beaten helpless, unconscious, or dead, he shoved them into his car and drove them to isolated wooded areas where he could rape, sodomize, and violate the bodies with everything from sticks to aerosol cans—and chew on their breasts and buttocks with his teeth.

When law enforcement authorities in the Northwest first realized they had a serial killer on their hands who was known to drive a Volkswagen and to introduce himself as "Ted," the press coined an ominous nickname for the mysterious executioner. They called him "Ted The Troller."

"Ted The Troller" is believed to have murdered nearly forty young women, most of them college students, in Washington and Oregon, before he moved his law school studies from the University of Puget Sound to the University of Utah. The murder spree began in 1974 in the coastal states and continued there and in Utah and Colorado through the first half of 1975.

At that time during Ted's summer break from college classes, Ted was working with Carole in the Washington Department of Emergency Services (DES) offices. He appeared at that time to be an up and coming young Republican with a bright future in government and politics. He was also busy juggling relationships with different girlfriends . . . and killing.

When a special homicide task force investigating the serial slayings began disseminating descriptions of the mysterious man thought to be "Ted The Troller," Carole and other workers in the office teased their fellow employee about his ominous look-alike. Even the name, "Ted," was the same. Ted Bundy even had a Volkswagen, just like "Ted The Troller." Bundy's fellow workers may not have taken the good-natured teasing seriously, but time was running out on the deadly masquerade.

The grisly orgy of kidnap, rape and murder ended after a sharp-eyed Utah state trooper chased and stopped a grey Volkswagen he spotted cruising slowly through a darkened subdivision in the Salt Lake City suburb of Granger at about 2:30 A.M. on Saturday morning, August 16, 1975. The driver, who was dressed in dark clothes, produced a driver's license identifying him as Theodore Robert Bundy. The driver's address listed a street in Salt Lake City.

Asked what he was doing cruising around the neighborhood at that time in the morning, Bundy replied that he got lost in the subdivision as he was driving home from the nearby Redwood Drive-in Theatre where he had watched *The Towering Inferno*. Bundy had made a major mistake. That wasn't the movie playing at the theatre that night, and the police officer knew it.

Joined by two other patrolmen, the trooper searched the car and found a crowbar, ice pick, a knit ski-mask, long silk stockings with eye and nose holes cut in them, a pair of handcuffs, and several other items. Bundy was taken in custody on a temporary charge of attempting to evade a police officer, but was quickly tied to a series of murders and other brutal attacks and kidnap attempts on local high school girls.

Then members of a serial killer task force linked him to the baffling string of unsolved sex slayings in Washington and Oregon. And authorities in Colorado filed charges against him for the murder of a pretty Michigan nurse abducted from Aspen where she was skiing with her doctor boyfriend attending a medical convention.

South Vietnam had recently fallen to the Communists, and Carole was working in a resettlement camp in Southern California for Vietnamese refugees when Bundy was arrested and publicly named as a suspected serial killer of young women. Authors Stephen G. Michaud and Hugh Aynesworth later quoted her in their book about Bundy, *The Only Living Witness,* as saying she didn't even remember driving back to her apartment that night, and she sat up until almost dawn drinking tea and scotch and smoking cigarettes.

Other friends and acquaintances of the personable young law student also reacted to his arrest with shock and disbelief. Some of them got together to organize a defense fund to help fight the terrible charges that were being lodged against him and to win his freedom. Carole and other friends had driven to Salt Lake City to visit with him only a few weeks before the arrest, and it was hard to believe that their personable host could have done the terrible things people were blaming him for.

Bundy simply didn't fit the popular image of a sex-crazed killer. And there was no question that he attracted plenty of women, who willingly provided for his emotional and sexual needs. They took care of those needs, even though some of Bundy's sex practices were decidedly kinky. .

Police eventually talked to some of Bundy's former girlfriends, and heard some strange stories. Some were troubling and strange, like his immature habit of waiting in ambush behind bushes or trees, then suddenly jumping out and scaring his girlfriends so he could hear them scream.

There were also more ominous tales, recounted with some reluctance, about uncomfortable anal intercourse, bondage, and near strangulation. Bundy sometimes liked to tie women to the bed with their own stockings or panty hose when he was having sex. One woman told of waking up in the middle of the night and finding Bundy crouched under the covers with a flashlight, intently studying her body.

The woman, a divorced mother of a little girl, was so frightened of her former lover when she talked to police that she made them promise to notify her if he was released from prison and returned to Washington State. But when he was released on bail and drove back to Washington, he moved back into her apartment. And she didn't complain to the police officers she had looked to only a few weeks earlier for protection.

Bundy was back to his old tricks of juggling relationships with women. Another woman he had met in Utah had helped him arrange for a lawyer to defend him and was continuing to stand by him, even as he was moving back in with his former girlfriend.

Despite the loyalty of Bundy's women and other friends, however, he was quickly convicted of aggravated kidnapping in the abduction of a nineteen-year-old Utah girl, Carol DaRonch. He was ordered to serve from one to fifteen years in the Utah State Prison at Point of the Mountain. It was a sentence that seemed surprisingly lenient, in view of the seriousness of the crime.

The young woman barely escaped with her life after Bundy lured her into his Volkswagen by approaching her at a shopping center and claiming to be a policeman. When he tried to handcuff her the spunky telephone operator fought back, preventing him by mere inches from smashing her on the head with a crowbar, and leaped from the little car.

Early in January, 1977, several months after Bundy's conviction in Utah, he was moved to Colorado to face trial in the slaying of the nurse, twenty-three-year-old Caryn Campbell. Her naked body was found dumped in a snowbank near the town of Snowmass thirty-six days after she was abducted from the hotel she had been staying at. Her skull was crushed.

Bundy was locked in the Pitkin County Jail in the basement of the courthouse at Aspen to await trial. In April he was moved to the Garfield County Jail in nearby Glenwood Springs. But he had been driven back to Aspen for a pre-trial hearing, when he leaped from a second floor window at the old Pitkin County

Courthouse and escaped.

Recaptured less than a week later, he was still carrying a photo of a former girlfriend and the young divorcee's daughter back in Seattle. They had once planned to marry, and even obtained a license before Bundy lost his nerve and tore the document up. The relationship, however, had continued almost until his arrest. But soon after Ted was back in custody he heard that she was planning to marry someone else.

Bundy began plotting a new escape. With his former girlfriend now out of the picture, he also wrote to Carole, asking her to mail him health food. She complied, and a spirited correspondence quickly developed. His letters became increasingly romantic, and shortly before the beginning of the new year, she left Seattle for her first jailhouse visit with him in Glenwood Springs.

On December 30, Ted eliminated the possibility of Carole making future visits to him there when he clambered through a hole he had cut in the ceiling of his cell. He crawled a few feet before dropping into a linen closet, then walked unnoticed out the front door of the jail into the chill Colorado night. He had stuffed books and other personal items under a blanket in his bunk to make it look as if he was sleeping, and his escape wasn't discovered until noon the next day.

Bundy had several hundred dollars with him, and early on New Year's Eve he was on a flight from Denver to Chicago. In Chicago he boarded a train and rode to Ann Arbor, where he blended in with students at the University of Michigan. He was comfortable, and felt safest on a big college campus.

On January 4, 1978, he stole a car and began driving south, heading for Tallahassee, with plans to hang out and find work around Florida State University. He got as far as Atlanta, before abandoning the car, and continuing his trip to Florida's state capitol city by bus.

Using an assumed name, he found himself an apartment. But without adequate false identification, he was virtually unemployable. His money was almost gone by the time he reached Florida, and he began shoplifting and breaking into cars to survive. He also resumed his old habit of dressing in dark clothes and prowling at night.

On the night between Saturday January 14 and Sunday January 15, barely two weeks after his escape from the Garfield County Jail, Bundy killed again. It was his first taste of blood in more than two years, and he exploded in a ghastly orgy of violence and rape.

Alcohol and pornography helped set him off on his killing sprees, and he prepared for his night of violence by dropping into Sherrods, a busy disco frequented by students from the university. Bundy guzzled down several drinks while he checked out the girls, and danced once or twice, before the club closed.

Every time he had made a pass at one of the girls in the club, he struck out. He was boozed up and frustrated when he headed off through the darkness toward the university campus and the Chi Omega Sorority House.

Shortly after midnight twenty-year-old Lisa Levy and her twenty-one-year-old sorority sister, Margaret Bowman were brutally murdered as they lay in their own beds. Both were strangled with panty hose. Margaret's head was crushed, bludgeoned so violently that splinters of bone were driven into her brain. Lisa's head had also been subjected to a terrible beating, and her collarbone was broken. A hair spray can had been violently rammed into Lisa's vagina and anus. And her attacker had ripped jagged slashes in her buttocks and breasts with his teeth. Her right nipple was chewed nearly off and clung to her breast by only a paper-thin shred of tissue. The ferocious attack earned the serial sex slayer a grisly new nickname from the press: "The Love Bite Killer."

47

Two other girls at the sorority house were horribly bludgeoned, but survived.

Even the ghastly slaughter at the sorority house wasn't enough to satisfy Bundy's reawakened blood lust, however. Minutes after he ran back into the night, he burst into an apartment building several blocks away and attacked another coed, a twenty-one-year-old dance student from Virginia, in her bed. She was apparently bludgeoned with the same tree limb used to beat the girls in the sorority house, as she slept. The dance student survived, but had to give up her hopes of a career as a dancer because of her injuries.

Almost miraculously, it might seem, Bundy slunk back to his apartment unseen and unrecognized after his night of savagery.

Despite the horror and outrage that swept the nation, and the massive manhunt launched by police, the demons that were eating at the serial sex killer wouldn't let him alone. Even Bundy knew better, however, than to kill again in Tallahassee.

So he stole a white van and began driving east, on the prowl for new victims. On the morning of February 9 in Lake City, about one hundred miles across the panhandle from Tallahassee, he spotted Kimberly Leach. A seventh-grade student at Lake City Junior High School, she was walking from the main building to the gymnasium a few yards away when she disappeared.

Kimberly wasn't found until April 7 when searchers discovered her decomposed remains buried under a hog shed in Suwanee State Park more than thirty miles from the school. Forensic examination indicated that her throat was probably slit. The Florida junior high schoolgirl was Bundy's youngest known murder victim. And she was apparently his last.

By the time Kimberly's body was discovered, her killer had already been in police custody for almost two months. Police caught up with him in Pensacola on February 15 while he was drunk and cruising in a stolen Volkswagen. He was quickly linked to the slaughter at the Chi Omega Sorority House, and held on a series of charges, including two counts of first-degree murder. A few weeks later, murder charges for Kimberly's slaying were added.

This time Bundy wouldn't escape from jail or justice, although it would be more than a decade before he finally paid the ultimate penalty for his reign of terror.

In the meantime, Carole had gone public about her relationship with the accused serial killer, and lost her state government job in Washington. She nevertheless moved to Florida from Washington state with her son, and quickly became Bundy's most regular and faithful visitor. She supported him before, during, and after his trials.

In her book, *The Stranger Beside Me,* author Ann Rule says Ted told her that he gave Carole permission to talk with the press, and advised her to charge one hundred dollars, as well as board and room, for interviews.

The court approved a change of venue from Tallahassee, and Bundy was put on trial in Miami for the murders, attempted murders, and sex offenses committed during his rampage at the sorority house. Ignoring the legal axiom that a defendant who defends himself has a fool for a lawyer, Bundy demanded his right to take an active role in his own defense at the trial and participated in questioning of witnesses.

Carole had thrown herself wholeheartedly into research of the case, determined to turn up evidence that would prove the man she insisted at that time was a close personal friend was not the killer.

And she faithfully attended the trial, but she was only one of several of the cocky serial killer's female admirers who contested for seats in the crowded courtroom. Bundy's groupies smiled and waved at him in court, and sent him mash notes, photographs of themselves, and requests for autographs. Occasionally Bundy rewarded one of his groupies by turning in his chair at the defense table and flashing a boyish grin, but they were no serious competition for Carole. She had laid her claim on him long before the horrendous murders he was accused of committing in Florida even occurred.

When the trial at last concluded it was Carole who sat with Bundy's mother while they were waiting for the verdict. Carole's teenage son joined the two women in the courtroom shortly before the jury announced a verdict had been reached. The panel convicted Bundy on first-degree murder charges for both slayings. Evidence matching Bundy's teeth to the bite marks on Lisa Levy's body had been used with devastating effectiveness by the prosecution.

When he was given an opportunity to address the court immediately prior to sentencing, the convicted sex killer made a fool of himself. Stuttering and snivelling as tears streamed down his cheeks, he continued to claim that he was innocent. The judge was unmoved by the show, and after putting up with a rambling, hour-long statement, sentenced the sobbing killer to death.

Then the first-degree murder charges against Bundy for Kimberly's slaying were moved to Orlando on another change of venue. Court officers tried but were unable to pick an acceptable jury at Live Oak near Suwanee River State Park in north Florida where the schoolgirl's body was found in the hog pen.

Ted's mother didn't travel from Washington to Orlando for her son's second Florida trial, as she had for the first. But Carole, loyal as ever, was there for every day of the proceeding.

She faithfully packed delicious lunches for Bundy and delivered them to an investigator for the defense each morning before the beginning of the day's trial activities. Investigator Donald R. Kennedy testified years later at a federal court hearing on a Bundy appeal that Carole was spiking her sweetheart's fruit juice with vodka. He said he also found pills inside a bag of goodies packed for Bundy during the trial.

According to some press reports, Bundy was swallowing Valium that had been hidden among the health food sandwiches in his lunch.

There is no question that Bundy was sometimes high on booze or dope during much of the trial. But he was sober when the jury returned the guilty verdict against him for first-degree murder.

Hours after his conviction Bundy and Carole thumbed their noses at society, particularly at the criminal justice system, in front of a print and electronic media audience of millions in an especially dramatic way. They were married in a grotesque courtroom ceremony conducted by the groom.

Both had written letters to the Orange County jail chaplain declaring their wish to be married. Ted wrote about Carole's devotion to him. Carole wrote about her teenage son's need for the guidance and advice her death row sweetheart was providing for him. The county director of corrections quickly made it clear that he had no intention of granting the request.

Nevertheless, after carefully researching Florida civil law relating to marriage, Carole obtained a license from the county bureau only four floors above the courtroom where her fiancé was on trial for his life. When Ted signed the license, he listed his post office box number at the prison near Starke as his official address.

And each of the stubborn lovers had the necessary blood tests. For some time they had been wearing matching gold signet rings. Ted had a ring engraved with the letter "C." Carole's was engraved with a "T."

51

When Carole discussed her marriage plans with a reporter for the *Orlando Sentinel,* she declared: "I know what I'm all about and I know what Ted's all about. It's a very private thing, and I simply don't care what people external to our lives think."

Then, on Saturday morning, February 9, 1980, at the beginning of the penalty phase of the proceeding, Bundy—acting as his own attorney—called Carole as his only witness. He was spiffed up for the occasion in a blue blazer with a bow tie sporting blue polka dots. Carole had selected a black skirt and sweater, that later would seem somehow especially appropriate for the occasion. It had been exactly two years since Kimberly Leach's kidnapping and savage murder.

Bundy opened by asking Carole about their relationship. She told about first meeting him in Olympia when she worked for the government agency. Gradually, what had started out as mere friendship evolved into a more serious, romantic relationship, she testified.

"Is it serious?" he asked.
"Serious enough that I want to marry him," she replied.

Continuing, Carole described the defendant as a warm, kind and patient man. She said he was a vital part of her life, and pleaded with the jury to spare him the death penalty. She said she believed that it was wrong for anyone, an individual or an agent of the state, to take a human life.

Turning back to the business of marriage, Bundy asked, "Do you want to marry me?"
"Yes," she responded.
"I do want to marry you," he added in return.

At last the prosecutors were on their feet, protesting the bizarre charade. Bundy huddled with his own attorneys, and apparently got some bad news. Saying they wanted to marry wasn't good enough.

But Carole and the killer-playing-big-time-criminal-defense attorney still had one more chance, during redirect examination. Bundy was still nervous and faltering, but eventually managed to exchange the necessary statements that according to Florida law would constitute a legal marriage ceremony.

"I want to make this very clear — will you marry me?" he asked.

"Yes," Carole replied, with a nervous giggle.

"Then I do hereby marry you," he said with a barely perceptible tremble in his voice.

A notary public who witnessed the exchange of vows from a seat in the spectators' section of the courtroom made the necessary entry on the marriage license. The bride was thirty-two, the groom a year older.

Circuit Judge Wallace M. Jopling, who presided at the trial, was aware the couple wanted to marry, but was caught off balance by the impromptu ceremony. "I was surprised but not offended by it," he later remarked.

Predictably perhaps, Assistant State Attorney Bob Dekle, who was lead prosecutor on the case, was less gracious when he was asked about his reaction to the unexpected courtroom shenanigans. He said the wedding was an obvious attempt by Bundy to gain sympathy from the jury.

Jerry Blair, another member of the prosecuting team, sarcastically referred to the love story retraced on the witness stand by Carole as "a Valentine's Day saga," sparking a wave of laughter from spectators in the courtroom.

But there was nothing funny about the hideous crimes Bundy had been convicted of. And it made it difficult for almost anyone who knew anything about them to be sympathetic to him. The serial killer, nevertheless, tried his best to win the jury's sympathy. He sobbed again when he addressed the panel, asking for mercy.

"You have a hell of a hard job," he said, as tears streamed down his cheeks. "I'm asking you to search your hearts now. . . . The death penalty is a polite way of asking that I be murdered."

Bundy's tearful monologue dragged on for forty minutes, and he broke down before the conclusion, sniffling and struggling hard to force the words out. It was several moments before he wound up his emotional plea for life warning the jury, "If I am killed for the murder of Kimberly Diane Leach and you were wrong, there is no way to correct it."

If Dekle's suspicion was correct about the convicted killer's motivations for getting married, the maneuver failed miserably. Bundy's dramatic marriage maneuver may have been good grist for news reporters, but it obviously had no effect on the jury's decision about the proper penalty for the convicted sex killer of a twelve-year-old schoolgirl. The panel of five men and seven women deliberated only ten minutes before recommending another sentence of death.

Three days later Bundy was sentenced once more to die in Florida's infamous electric chair, "Old Sparky." As he stood and listened to the dread pronouncement, he held a red envelope in his hand. A Valentine card for his bride was inside. The "Love Bite Killer" was still the romantic.

After his murder convictions, Bundy was locked in a six-by-nine-foot cell on Death Row at the Florida State Prison at Starke. Carole found a job as a secretary and moved into a boardinghouse in Gainesville, another university town that a few years later would acquire international notoriety for a shocking series of grisly mutilation murders of students.

On Death Row, Bundy received letters from admirers from all over the country. Most serial killers and other high profile criminals whose crimes have been highly publicized attract groupies and other correspondents, but Bundy seemed to be in a class almost his own. Single and married women wrote that they were in love with him and wanted to have his child. Born-again Christians wanted to become his friend so they could save his soul. He heard from high school girls, grandmothers, and from a few men who were interested in his "life's work."

Carole also exchanged letters with him, and they peppered their correspondence with pet names for each other and saccharine sweet love talk. Bundy sometimes affectionately addressed his sweetheart by her last name, "Boone." Carole was known to refer to him in her letters and in conversation by various affectionate names, but her favorite appeared to be "Bunny."

She supplemented her correspondence with the imprisoned serial killer with regular visits. It was a fast forty-mile drive from Gainesville to Starke, and Carole faithfully made the trip on Saturday visiting days. Sometimes she was accompanied by her son. At other times she made the drive alone and, after pulling into the parking lot, was ushered into an old converted cafeteria equipped with several heavy tables and chairs that had been firmly secured to the floor. It was there that she and Bundy visited, surrounded by other Death Row inmates and their guests, all under the watchful eyes of armed guards.

According to Michaud and Aynesworth, the eyes of the guards weren't always as vigilant as they might have been. In their book, *The Only Living Witness*, the writers claim that the condemned killers and their women sometimes had sexual relations under the tables, behind the water cooler, or in the restrooms.

Carole also reportedly resorted to a classic prison method of smuggling contraband to her lover. The authors wrote that she sneaked marijuana in to him inside her vagina. As other male prisoners learn to do, Bundy transferred it to a classic convict hiding place of his own: his rectum.

Carole, Ted, and a guard were all quoted by Michaud and Aynesworth as saying that Carole and Bundy had earlier "consummated" their relationship while he was being held in a North Florida jail prior to his murder trials.

In October, 1981, Carole gave birth to her husband's baby. Most observers, willing to comment about the event, admitted feeling a sense of relief that the infant wasn't a boy. Ted was also pleased. He had his heart set on a girl.

Being the wife of one of America's most notorious serial killers was an emotionally draining and thankless job. Whether or not Carole tired of the notoriety, or was motivated by concern for the welfare of her son and daughter, she eventually dropped from sight. There were no more interviews with the press to stubbornly reiterate her insistence on her husband's innocence. There were no television appearances, or news photos of her with Bundy's baby.

When time at last ran out on the man once known as the mysterious "Ted The Troller," and "The Love Bite Killer," Carole was conspicuously absent from among the retinue of lawyers and other supporters prominently featured in news stories about his efforts to gain a last minute reprieve from execution.

Right up to the end, Bundy was still receiving letters from enamored groupies who wrote to him on Death Row from the United States and several foreign countries. It was too late, however. Continued manipulation of the lonely correspondents and pitiful cranks might produce a few dollars in gifts for the prisoner, but that was no longer enough. Bundy was in a life-and-death struggle to avoid the electric chair. It was a struggle he lost.

His last minute effort to trade off confessions to more than twenty unsolved murders of young women in the northwest and to help in recovery of the bodies in return for more time was firmly rejected by authorities. "For him to be negotiating for his life over the bodies of victims is despicable," said Florida Governor Robert Martinez.

Shortly after 7:00 A.M., on January 24, 1989, nearly nine years after the kidnapping and brutal murder of Kimberly Leach, the tearful, shaking prisoner was strapped into Old Sparky. A few minutes later he was pronounced dead.

The man who was Florida's most hated killer, perhaps the most reviled serial slayer in the nation, had refused a last meal. When prison authorities cooked steak and eggs with hash browns and coffee for him anyway, he left the food untouched. His last words were, "Give my love to my family and friends."

Outside the prison, hundreds of men and women drank beer, happily chanted, "Burn, Bundy Burn," waved sparklers and frying pans, and hoisted signs advising: "A Small Gift From FPL (Florida Power & Light)"; "Bundy BBQ"; "Roast In Peace"; and "Have A Seat, Ted." After repeated appeals and stays of execution, expenditure of six million dollars in taxpayer money to carry out the sentence, and who knows how many murders, the public had more than enough of the man a judge called "the most competent serial killer in the country . . . a diabolical genius."

Shielded by police, a much smaller and quieter group was assembled a few yards away from the celebration with signs calling on authorities to stop the execution, and criticizing the death penalty. One of them, a forlorn little woman with stringy yellow hair and red-rimmed eyes, who appeared to be about forty, was so choked up she could hardly talk.

She said her name was Wendy, and that she had been waiting all night to provide moral support for the condemned man. She claimed they were soul mates, and that they had been together as lovers in an earlier life.

Chapter Three

Sue Lyon
and
Gary "Cotton" Adamson

It was a storybook romance with a grotesque Hollywood twist, when Tinseltown's sultry Lolita said, "I do!" with a convicted killer serving time in the Colorado penitentiary.

It wasn't screen beauty Sue Lyon's first time out in the marriage race, nor her last time, but it was the most disastrous.

Born into a troubled home, she was still a baby when her father killed himself drinking a combination of whiskey and Seconal.

Left with three small children to support, her mother worked as a cashier in a drugstore, as a nurse's aide, and at whatever other low-paying jobs she was able to obtain. Sue wasn't yet in her teens and money was tight, when she had some pictures taken and began looking for work as a model. She was petite and pretty, and almost immediately she struck paydirt.

In a contest judged by Los Angeles county dentists, she was voted "Miss Smile of 1960." Then pictures of her modeling clothing appeared in the J. C. Penney catalogue, and soon she was doing parts for television productions.

Shortly after that, she got her big break and captured the starring role in Stanley Kubrick's box-office smash, *Lolita*. It was a role already turned down by Hollywood's real-life Lolita of the time, Tuesday Weld. Tuesday later boasted that she didn't have to play the role, because she already was Lolita.

Even with the popular Tuesday Weld out of the race, capturing the movie plum was a stunning feat for the neophyte actress. Kubrick and producer James B. Harris had already interviewed more than eight hundred girls, experienced actresses and newcomers, without finding just the right teenager for the role. When Kubrick spotted Sue making an appearance on television's "Loretta Young Show," he summoned her for an interview. That was quickly followed by a preliminary screen test, then a second with James Mason, who would ultimately play opposite her as the dirty old man, Humbert Humbert.

No fictional female had stirred up such a fire storm of controversy since Lady Chatterley. Vladimir Nabokov's daring novel, and the subsequent blockbuster movie, about the forbidden love of a middle-aged man and the fetching twelve-year-old introduced Lolita as a new adjective for child seductress into the English language.

Demands to ban the film were called for in several countries, including Britain and France. Kubrick however won a bitterly fought contest against officials charged with protecting American morals at that time by enforcing the U. S. Motion Picture Production Code, and the film at last opened in June, 1962.

Judged by contemporary standards, it might seem that there was much fuss over nothing. There was no dirty talk, no nudity, and no violence. Yet in most countries where it was shown, viewing was restricted to filmgoers who were at least eighteen years old.

Meanwhile Sue was captivating moviegoers with her erotic performance as the pre-teen tease. Few early 1960s American moviegoers had ever seen such a bold film on such a forbidden subject. Suddenly, she was a star.

The first public awareness of trouble in the pretty teenager's off-screen life and career occurred when she travelled to Puerto Vallarta, Mexico, to film *Night of the Iguana*. Newspapers reported that director John Huston had tossed her boyfriend, Hampton Fancher, III, off the set. In December, 1963, shortly after she returned from Mexico, however, she married the struggling actor. She was seventeen, and already internationally famous. The marriage lasted a year while she partied, although the relationship continued for some time after that. Fancher later became a successful screenwriter with dazzling credits, that included the blockbuster science fiction hit, *Blade Runner*.

Within days of Sue's divorce from Fancher, her youngest brother, Mike, committed suicide in Mexico. Then she and her mother were driving together outside Los Angeles when their car was hit head-on by another. Although her mother escaped serious injury, the young actress suffered a broken leg and a badly damaged knee.

After her recuperation, she became involved with Roland Harrison, a former fullback with the San Diego Chargers. A black man, Harrison was working as a school custodian and freelance photographer at the time. Sue risked her career by marrying him.

She had carried on a steamy pen pal relationship with a soldier in Vietnam and was pregnant with Harrison's daughter, Nona, when the marriage broke up. She and the soldier eventually became engaged, but that relationship too, went down the drain.

After she was swept off her feet by Gary "Cotton" Adamson and followed him to Colorado, however, her movie career quickly went into a suicidal tailspin. Sue left Los Angeles behind and moved into a noisy motel room close enough to the penitentiary in Canon City to see the watchtower, and got a job as a cocktail waitress to support herself.

Adamson was a sweet-talking career criminal and heroin junkie who was serving forty years after convictions for second-degree murder and armed robbery.

The odd couple first met when the bleached blonde twenty-six-year-old cinema queen was doing volunteer work for the Federal Public Defender's Office in California. With no training as a paralegal, she functioned primarily as a gofer, visiting prisoners to keep their morale up, running errands, and doing what she could to save time for the hard-pressed professionals.

Sue was working with a prisoner named Kenny who was locked in the Los Angeles County Jail on drug charges when Adamson was moved into the same cell. He had escaped from jail in Colorado, and fled to California where he robbed some banks and fed his heroin habit. Locked up without access to the narcotics his body craved after his apprehension by federal law enforcement officers, the twenty-nine-year-old bandit was kicking the habit cold turkey and was in terrible shape.

The actress later told an interviewer that Kenny suggested Adamson get in touch with a girl he knew, who would visit him, run his errands, and help his public defender. Adamson wasn't intimidated when he learned the errand girl was an internationally known actress, who was only fourteen-years-old when she launched her big screen career starring opposite James Mason in producer-director Stanley Kubrick's blockbuster 1962 film *Lolita*.

By the time she crossed paths with Adamson, almost twelve years after her movie debut, she had completed a leading role in *Night of the Iguana* with Deborah Kerr, Ava Gardner, and Richard Burton; *The Flim Flam Man* with

George C. Scott and Michael Sarrazin; *Tony Rome* with Frank Sinatra and Jill St. John, and played juicy parts in several other popular films. She was earning as much as seventy thousand dollars per role, an enormous salary for the 1960s and early 1970s.

Adamson wrote his first letter to her, and the actress was soon running his errands, visiting him, and helping his public defender. They continued exchanging letters on a near daily basis after Adamson was sent back to prison in Colorado, and Sue flew to Spain to work on a couple of Spaghetti westerns. It was two years, however, before she first visited him at The Colorado Territorial Correctional Facility.

As she later described the romantic moments in a Hollywood magazine story, they were sitting together on a rock formation in the visiting yard at the prison when they decided to get married.

The love-struck couple didn't have an easy time of it however. They were faced with a storm of opposition. Sue would later claim that her agent told her she had been lucky to get away with marrying a black man, but that she could never salvage her career if she married a convict.

Nevertheless, a few weeks later, Sue married her sinister convict paramour in a tender ceremony attended behind the walls of the old maximum security prison by a few members of Adamson's family, a couple of the actress's friends, and a sprinkling of stickup men and other prisoner pals of the groom. Nona, her daughter, was the flower girl. Wearing a simple cream-colored dress and a veil, the bride carried a Bible and bouquet.

A reporter from the *National Enquirer* attended the ceremony. Dozens of newspaper and television reporters from the conventional press meanwhile gathered outside the penitentiary clamoring for news of the bizarre wedding of the movie queen and a killer convict serving a twenty-to-forty-year prison term.

The groom and his convict pals were locked up again after sharing wedding cake and soft drinks with the bride and the other guests. Adamson still had a minimum of about four years to serve on his sentence, and it would be two years before the couple was able to consummate the marriage.

In the meantime, Sue rented a cottage for herself and her daughter in Canon City close to the prison. As her agent had predicted, the offers of movie roles quickly dried up. Years later she would complain to reporters that she was blackballed by the film industry because of her controversial marriage.

But for the time being she had what she wanted. She was close to her man, and almost every chance she got, she made the trip to see her husband at the prison, where they talked for hours among the babble of other couples and family members inside the visiting areas.

The first rosy blush of their post-wedding bliss didn't last however, and according to Sue, she learned that her new lifemate was still using heroin he obtained inside the prison. She said he pestered her for money to support his habit, and once nearly died of an overdose. Then he quit, cold turkey.

About two years after the nuptials, Adamson was granted a furlough and they were at last able to spend their first night together in the cottage. For the next couple of years, there were a few other periods of carefully restricted freedom, as well. Then Adamson was assigned to the drug program at the Colorado State Hospital in Pueblo.

Sue was also having serious thoughts about that time of returning to Los Angeles and attempting to revive her movie career. Adamson wanted her nearby, and was against her leaving Colorado. But she left her self-imposed exile in the isolation of the prison city for Los

Angeles anyway. He walked away from the state hospital, and fled to Indianapolis.

The next time the couple got together, Sue visited him in an Indiana prison where he was being held after robbing an Indianapolis bank. By that time she had already filed for divorce, citing grounds that her marriage had irretrievably broken down, but she did her best for him. As she had done before when she first met him at the Los Angeles County Jail, she contacted his public defender. Five years after their wedding, the union at last ended.

Shortly thereafter, Sue dived back into her film career with a big splash, appearing in five movies and television shows the first year.

Curiously, after the first rush of activity, the movie and television jobs became scarce again. After being reduced to living with her daughter, her dog, and her plants in a cheap apartment in East Los Angeles and driving a pickup truck, she went to work in a men's clothing store. Then, with her once brilliant film career still in the trash can, she found a job as a teacher's aide in a nearby elementary school.

Even that job ended, however, and by 1983 she was still living in crime-ridden East Los Angeles, dating a plumber who lived nearby, and working as a two hundred and eighty dollar-per-week secretary. Then she lost that job to a computer.

For a time the job in the elementary school had reawakened an old desire, and she started a course in Spanish and began considering the possibility of becoming a teacher.

After years of psychoanalysis, Sue was diagnosed as a manic depressive. She began taking Lithium to stabilize her moods, and gradually dropped from public sight.

When she surfaced once again, she was quoted by writers, specializing in the Hollywood scene, as charging that her role as the sexy child seductress had ruined her life. She complained that her sudden stardom and wealth had exposed her to a fast life and temptations that no girl her age was equipped to handle.

In the mid-1980s she began putting her life back together again. She married her fourth husband, this time she chose thirty-seven-year-old Richard Rudman, a radio station engineer. She met him while she was working as a secretary for radio station KFWB in Los Angeles.

By early 1992, they had been married for seven years and were living a quiet life in the Hollywood Hills where she was busying herself gardening and with homemaking chores.

Chapter Four

Kristin Joan Svege Watson
and
Charles Denton "Tex" Watson

Life has been full for Charles Denton "Tex" Watson, since the notorious Manson family assassin was sent to prison for his leadership role in the slaughter of seven people nearly a quarter of a century ago.

After wooing a German beauty from behind the walls of the maximum security prison at San Quentin and the California Men's Colony at San Luis Obispo for years, he married Kristin Joan Svege, an attractive young woman from New Jersey and fathered three children.

His wife, the former Kristin Joan Svege, journeys to the prison for regular conjugal visits.

California is one of eight states that permits conjugal visits for most well-behaved prisoners, and every two months Kristin is permitted a forty-eight-hour lovefest with her notorious husband in a two-bedroom trailer apartment on the prison grounds.

Nine trailers have been set aside at the prison for inmates and their families, and they are equipped with kitchens, living rooms, bathrooms, and outdoor picnic tables and playground equipment for children.

Visiting regulations permit women to load up their cars with food and drive to the sprawling, attractively landscaped prison for two days of private or family time with their convict husbands. Prisoners at San Luis Obispo wear civilian clothes and are given considerable freedom of movement even when not entertaining visitors.

Lawns are dotted with flower beds, and during regular nonconjugal visits, inmates are allowed to entertain their guests in a lounge outfitted with sofas and comfortable chairs. Inmates are permitted to keep typewriters or computers in their cells.

Security considerations rule out permitting conjugal visits for Death Row inmates at California's grim prison at San Quentin, and for other convicts considered to be especially dangerous.

After leading four Manson Family women on a ghastly two-night murder spree, Watson was sentenced to die in California's gas chamber. He personally killed four of the seven victims.

But he and other condemned prisoners from all over the country escaped paying the ultimate penalty for their crimes when the U. S. Supreme Court temporarily wiped out capital punishment statutes on constitutional grounds in a narrow 5-4 landmark decision in 1972. Watson's death sentence was automatically commuted to life in prison.

By the time new Supreme Court rulings permitted individual states to restore restructured capital punishment laws, Watson had been transferred to San Luis Obispo. He became a model prisoner there, continued an industrious correspondence with supporters and admirers, and developed an impressive knowledge of the Bible.

Watson met Kristin after carrying on a long affair with a beautiful young German woman who had pursued him since the beginning of his multiple murder trial. She was the most prominent of a phalanx of groupies, who smiled, nodded, and fawned over him during the grim proceeding.

Soon the cameras of the news media were recording their exchanged smiles and waves. When the multiple killer's dark-haired admirer wrote to him at the Los Angeles County Jail where he was being held during the trial, he wrote back. That was the beginning of an exchange of letters between the couple.

Although she returned to Germany for awhile after his conviction, they continued their correspondence. She mailed him photographs and clippings, and wrote of her plans to return to the United States so she could visit with him. Soon after she obtained a new American visa she began visiting him at San Quentin.

The visits didn't end until a couple of years after Watson was transferred to the California Men's Colony. The German woman had rented an apartment in Los Angeles, and hitchhiked the roughly four-hundred-mile round-trip between the city and the prison for weekend visits. But she didn't share Watson's growing interest in born-again Christianity, and eventually returned to Germany.

In *Will You Die For Me?*, a book Watson wrote with Ray Hoekstra, a prison ministry chaplain, the convicted killer said his German admirer had obtained a lifetime American visa and was talking about marrying him before the falling-out.

Then Kristin read Watson's book, which was filled with accounts of his return to Christianity and his newfound spirituality. She was living in the southwest when she wrote to him at the prison. He invited her to visit, put her on his visitors' list, and she hurried to San Luis Obispo for her first meeting with the man she was to eventually marry.

According to Bill Nelson, a West Coast radio talk show host and producer who has spent much of the past decade chronicling the affairs of the former Manson family members, the convicted killer provided her bus fare.

When Kristin struck out for California to meet Watson, she left a boyfriend behind. He followed her to San Luis Obispo and in an emotional confrontation in front of the house where she was renting an apartment made a desperate last-minute plea to salvage their old romance. She turned him down.

Seven years after he was moved off Death Row, he married Kristin. The bride wore an ankle-length gown in traditional white, with matching white shoes, and carried a bouquet and a Bible for the ceremony.

The happy couple honeymooned in a trailer after their marriage in the prison chapel on September 7, 1979. A clergyman from the Assemblies of God, the Rev. John S. Milton, performed the ceremony.

Watson was a few weeks shy of his thirty-fourth birthday when he was married. He listed his occupation on his marriage registration certificate as minister and his place of business as the prison chapel.

Kristin was twenty and listed her latest job as employment at a home for the handicapped in San Luis Obispo. Spokesmen at the home told reporters, however, that she was no longer employed there and had held the job only a short time.

Despite the demands of their domestic duties, the couple have made time in their busy lives to set up a mail-order prison outreach they call Abounding Love Ministries. Established as a nonprofit corporation, the ministry has the appropriate acronym, ALMS.

With the assistance of loyal friends, the industrious couple has turned the program into a thriving enterprise that has enabled them to collect thousands of dollars. ALMS has operated with a mailing list of five hundred names, and accepts donations for tapes of Watson's sermons, and religious songs sung by Kristin.

Kristin also helps to keep interest in the family and the ministry high by appearing at area churches and on radio shows to talk about her husband's life behind bars and to give Christian testimony. The couple also published an occasional report on their communal activities, which they labeled *The Watson Family Newsletter.*

Referring to themselves and the children as "bears" and "cubs," the authors fill the newsletter with chatty tidbits about such things as family visits with "Papa Bear," in one of the prison trailers.

In one newsletter, a typical visit was described as including family time spent with "Daddy Bear" who busied himself cooking, washing dishes, cleaning crumbs and fussing over "Mrs. Bear" and the "Cubs." Time was also made however for talks, Bible studies and prayer, readers were assured.

Some of the items mention "Hiromi Bear." A young woman of Japanese descent, Hiromi Higashi moved into Kristin's home in San Luis Obispo in 1989, and quickly began helping with everything from child care and errands to stamping mailings for the newsletter and for ALMS. By the early 1990s she was listed on ALMS mailings as "secretary." Tex was president, and his wife vice president-treasurer.

Meanwhile, as the California Corrections Department pays the bills for her husband's room, board and education, Kristin and her brood have relied on money from his family, the boarder, the ministry — and taxpayers — for their support and care.

According to Nelson, who wrote and published *Tex Watson: The Man, The Madness, The Manipulation* (Pen Power Publications), although Kristin was not on welfare, when she gave birth in the San Luis Obispo General Hospital, California taxpayers helped pick up the bills through its Medi-Cal program. Medi-Cal was established to provide for the health care of low-income and other needy residents of the state.

Joshua Denton Watson was born on March 21, 1982, Benjamin Charles Watson on Christmas day, 1983, and Mary Elizabeth Watson on February 19, 1989.

At one of his parole hearings, Watson told board members that having children was "the Christian thing to do."

A couple of years before her death early in 1992, Sharon Tate's grieving mother, Doris Tate, talked about the revulsion she felt at the knowledge that Watson was permitted to father children.

"He took my daughter and her unborn son, and now he has three babies of his own," she complained. "It's not fair to anyone. The kids don't have a full-time father—and the father they have is a killer."

Before her death, Mrs. Tate faithfully attended each of Watson's parole hearings, to voice her opposition to his release. At a hearing in 1987 she criticized his use of ALMS to peddle tapes of his sermons and his book.

"Not only was my daughter murdered by you, Mr. Watson, but I have to live with the fact that you make money out of the tortures you have inflicted on her," Mrs. Tate told him. That appeal for parole, like earlier appeals, was turned down.

Although Kristin and members of Watson's family and friends, where he grew up in the small north Texas town of Copeville, are his most loyal supporters, he has also attracted a sympathetic following through his mail-order ministry. Some of his correspondents and donors write to the California Parole Board pleading for his release so that he can talk to young people about the evils of drugs.

Watson's reputed potential as an evangelist and fighter against drug abuse are subjects frequently referred to in the newsletter and in ALMS mailings. In a letter to the board from Kristin, she wrote: "I feel the state of California and this nation needs to hear from Charles on the issue of drugs. What better example of the fruit of drug abuse do we have?"

Watson reportedly hopes to eventually return to Texas and become a television evangelist.

Despite his generally good behavior in prison, however, the savagery and grisly nature of his crimes have worked against him. Soon after his transfer to the Men's Colony he began working as a chaplain's assistant, helping at the chapel, teaching Bible classes and delivering sermons.

But he and Bruce MacGregor Davis lost their jobs at the chapel a few years ago after newspaper reports that other inmates complained the former Manson Family pals were misusing their position and intimidating other convicts. Watson was reassigned to a job cleaning cells.

And late in 1991 Watson and his wife both wound up with explaining to do, when authorities obtained search warrants and seized financial records for the couple's business from his cell at the prison and from her house in Laguna Lakes. Nelson had tipped authorities off that he believed Kristin was violating Medi-Cal regulations, and provided documents showing she had given conflicting answers to different agencies about her personal income and income from the nonprofit ministry.

State investigators told reporters that they believed Kristin had failed to report income from the nonprofit business she and her husband ran, according to Medi-Cal regulations. Investigators said in court documents that she was an officer of the corporation and received an annual salary of twelve thousand dollars. But that income was not reported on a Medi-Cal status report or on a Medi-Cal renewal questionnaire, as required, investigators stated in court documents. A little more than four thousand dollars in benefits was at issue.

Sales of Christian tapes and other merchandise through the ministry reportedly generated between five hundred dollars and two thousand dollars per month. At this writing the investigation was continuing.

Escapes

Chapter Five

Barbara Oswald, Robin Oswald,
Karen Wibbenmeyer Trapnell,
and
Garrett Brock Trapnell

Garrett Brock Trapnell is a smooth talking convict and lifetime adventurer who can charm women into giving up their family, going to prison — or dying for him.

The handsome, six-foot, blond, blue-eyed skyjacker and career criminal once told a judge that any man sentenced to life in prison "has an inherent right to escape."

He didn't tell the judge, however, that he was going to sweet-talk a love-addled mother and her teenage daughter into putting their lives on the line to break him out of America's most secure federal prison in two separate escape attempts.

Trapnell was locked in the federal penitentiary near Marion, Illinois, after a conviction for hijacking a Trans World Airlines (TWA) Boeing 707 enroute from Los Angeles to New York on January 30, 1972.

The early 1970s were a bad time for skyjacking in the United States. For awhile it seemed that almost every other week, a domestic terrorist of one stripe or another was boarding a jetliner, then pulling a gun or bomb and ordering the crew and passengers to Cuba, Morocco,

Algeria, just about any place they thought the government might accept someone who claimed to be a fugitive from injustice in America.

Trapnell had a political motive in the quixotic grab bag of demands he made after ripping open a fake plaster cast on his arm and pulling out an automatic pistol as the 707 was flying over Iowa. Moments later he summoned a stewardess and handed her a note for the cockpit crew. The skyjacker was bleeding profusely from a cut in his arm inflicted as he sliced open the cast with a razor blade.

When he commandeered the transcontinental flight, his demands included freedom for Angela Y. Davis. The Black radical was accused (and was later declared innocent) of helping plot an escape attempt in August, 1970, in which a judge, two prisoners, and a teenage boy accomplice were shot to death at the Marin county courthouse in California.

Trapnell also wanted the release of a friend who was in a Dallas jail charged with armed robbery; an opportunity to talk with a lawyer and a psychiatrist; a private chat with President Richard M. Nixon; and clemency for air piracy. But he was most insistent on a demand that he be paid a ransom of $306,800 for the aircraft, ninety-four passengers, and seven-member crew of the 707. That was exactly the value of a luxury yacht he lost possession of in a federal district court case the previous year in Miami.

Complying with Trapnell's orders, the crew landed the 707 at John F. Kennedy International Airport in New York, where he talked with a psychiatrist by telephone. He rejected the doctor's pleas to surrender, and demanded that a lawyer be flown from Miami to New York to talk with him. An attorney, who had represented him in the federal court case over ownership of the yacht, talked with him by radiotelephone.

Listeners throughout the New York metropolitan

area listened to the skyjacker's chillingly erratic demands broadcast via a hookup with a local radio station, WCBS. At one point in the bizarre broadcast, Trapnell threatened, "I'm going to tell you one thing. If those Texas cowboys come out shooting and try to board the craft, I'm gonna' shoot the crew and ram everything on the runway." The skyjacker knew how to fly, and FBI agents and other authorities at the airport were aware of his ability to pilot an aircraft.

Despite his threat to slaughter the crew, the skyjacker permitted ninety-three passengers to disembark from the 707. Trapnell eventually became worried that FBI agents would try to seize the aircraft and ordered the pilot to take off and circle the airport.

Then he ordered the pilot to land, and demanded that the jetliner be refueled and a relief crew be supplied for a flight to Dallas. His decision to permit a relief crew aboard was the break law enforcement authorities were waiting for. Eight hours after the tense standoff began, an FBI man disguised as a member of the relief crew got the drop on the thirty-two-year-old skyjacker and shot him.

The original crew was still on the aircraft when the relief group began to file aboard. Trapnell stood at the doorway of the cockpit with a pistol in his hand. As the first two men boarded, they were searched by one of the original crewmen, complying with orders from the gunman, and ordered to sit in the lounge with their hands on a table.

But the third and fourth men to file aboard were FBI agents, both qualified pilots, dressed in TWA flight uniforms. As Trapnell's attention was directed at the first of the agents and slightly lowered his gun hand for a moment, the second FBI man fired.

"I'm shot," the hijacker screamed. Minutes later he

was being loaded into an ambulance, and rushed to Queens General Hospital. FBI agents who searched the injured skyjacker found he was carrying $2,174 in cash.

Trapnell was struck in the left shoulder and left hand, but survived the injuries. When police questioned him, he said his name was Gary Trapanelli. Officers said he had used about twenty-five different aliases at varied times. But the FBI and other law enforcement officers quickly determined his true identification.

The accused skyjacker's arraignment at the federal courthouse in Brooklyn was a circus. It was Trapnell's thirty-fourth birthday when he appeared before U. S. Magistrate Max Schiffman. A member of the U. S. attorney's staff had barely begun advising the judge that Trapnell's family in Miami had hired Nathaniel L. Barone, Jr., to represent him, when the defendant began shouting, "I didn't retain Mr. Barone. There's no need for a grand jury indictment against me, no need to drag this on any further. I'm the one who committed this crime."

The state's attorney told the court that Trapnell's arrest record extended back to 1958. And he said the defendant had been treated at nine psychiatric hospitals after arrests for offenses including airplane theft, kidnapping, and bank robbery.

Despite repeated warnings from the bench, Trapnell wouldn't shut up, and he wouldn't accept the suggested assignment of a Legal Aid Society lawyer to represent him. After the raucous arraignment was at last concluded, another federal magistrate ordered him remanded to Bellevue Hospital for a thirty-day psychiatric evaluation.

Trapnell eventually wound up with a life sentence in federal prison. It could have been worse. The most severe sentence on federal charges of air piracy was execution. Nevertheless, instead of sailing the high seas in the sixty-foot yacht, Trapnell wound up in a prison cell.

After the TWA hijack, the Massachusetts native became the subject of a biography called *The Fox Is Crazy, Too*, that detailed his life of crime. In the book, written by Eliot Asinof, Trapnell was pictured as a roguish schemer who was spending his life doing everything he could to cross up the establishment.

He was one of those bright but twisted individuals who loved to joust with society, and who occupied his facile mind thinking up con games, scheming prison breaks, and pestering the courts with frivolous law suits filed from behind bars. He was a shameless manipulator, who used the Constitution, the courts, mental health professionals — and women — to get his way.

Trapnell was said to have once been the Royal Canadian Mounted Police agency's most wanted criminal, and the FBI, Interpol, the Policia Secreta de Panama, and law enforcement agencies in several U. S. states had files on him. He also had an unusually high IQ of about 130, and was said to have been married six times.

In October, 1977, Barbara Oswald watched a segment about Trapnell on the popular television program, "60 Minutes." Then she read the book, and knew immediately that she had to meet the roguish convict.

A forty-three-year-old divorcee, the former Barbara Annette Brown had already packed more heady adventure into her life than most women. She was fourteen-years-old when she ran away from a Lutheran home for children. And during the early and mid-1960s she was arrested several times for prostitution, although there is no indication she was ever convicted. Nevertheless, police, tricks and other whores in the St. Louis area knew her as "Bobbie," a good-looking hooker who liked to talk.

After joining the Army in 1968, she seemed to get her

life back on track. She was bright, knew how to take care of herself, and took to the discipline of the military. She was sent to a military school in Biloxi, Mississippi, and became an air traffic controller. She also worked as a recruiter in St. Louis for awhile, and was eventually promoted to staff sergeant. But after a motorcycle accident, she left the service. Much later she confided to friends that she enjoyed fooling the military about her past. She loved to talk, and could be good company when she wanted to be. But acquaintances later recalled that she also had a sarcastic streak that surfaced from time to time. Even in middle age, she still retained traces of the tough runaway and "working girl."

She had been married for several years to Robert S. Oswald and was the mother of five children. But the marriage soured and by the spring of 1978 she was divorced and only a couple of courses short of earning her master's degree in the rehabilitation of convicts at Webster College outside of St. Louis. Barbara had always wanted to become someone important, however, and she dreamed of fame. Once she even tried to sell her life story to newspapers in St. Louis, but the editors weren't interested. She hadn't yet played out the most dramatic chapter in her life.

She started that chapter when she got herself on Trapnell's visitors' list and began making regular treks to the fortress-like prison in southern Illinois. She also kept up a spirited correspondence with the articulate convict by mail, and accepted his collect telephone calls. Sometimes she took her youngest daughter, Robin, with her on the prison visits. Robin was a cute and perky, strawberry blonde with frizzy hair, who was on the pom-pom squad at Clayton High School in suburban St. Louis. She soon began writing to Trapnell, as her mother did.

Meanwhile, Barbara was agreeing to a bold scheme worked out with the lifer for her to hijack a helicopter and rescue him and two of his prison pals from the exercise yard. If Barbara managed to successfully carry off the daring prison break, it would become the first ever from the maximum security penitentiary.

The Marion Federal Penitentiary was opened in 1964 to replace the infamous prison at Alcatraz, as the nation's most escape proof lockup for its most dangerous and incorrigible criminals. Although he had never been accused of murder, Trapnell was one of the prison's most notorious inmates and was known by corrections authorities for his escape attempts.

On May 27, 1978, Barbara climbed out of bed early and drove from her home to the St. Louis Municipal Airport. Two nights earlier she had telephoned a policeman acquaintance and asked to borrow one thousand dollars, so she could fly to California and bring a couple of her children home for a visit. He told her he didn't have that much money around the house.

But Barbara wasn't planning a flight to California. She had her mind set on a shorter flight, on a helicopter. At the airport she told the chopper pilot, Allan Barklage, that she wanted to look over some flooded property along the Mississippi River south of St. Louis, and paid a five hundred dollar deposit.

A few minutes after they were airborne, she pulled a .44-caliber pistol and ordered the pilot to fly to the prison. The helicopter was almost over the prison when Barklage grabbed for the gun. The helicopter bobbed and weaved through the sky as the man and the woman struggled desperately for the weapon. Then three shots were fired, and slammed into the head and body of the forty-three-year-old divorcee.

When the shaken pilot landed the helicopter a few yards outside the main walls of the prison a few moments later, Barbara Oswald was dead.

FBI agents later found her station wagon parked about forty miles from the prison at the Perryville Municipal Airport in McBride, Missouri. The 1974 vehicle was packed with changes of male clothing, a shotgun, a rifle, two pistols and ammunition.

The slain skyjacker's family gathered to bury her and mourn their dead. But Barbara Oswald's violent death didn't weaken Robin's loyalty to the convict her mother had died trying to rescue. She continued writing to Trapnell at the prison, and after completing her sophomore year at Clayton High she didn't bother returning to classes the following fall. A school friend later told a news reporter that Trapnell was like a father to the girl.

Robin stayed with friends for a few weeks after her mother's death, then moved in with an older married sister in the St. Louis suburb of Maplewood. She found herself a job in a restaurant — and she continued her friendship with Trapnell.

During a federal court trial for Trapnell and one of the other convicts charged in the deadly breakout scheme thwarted by the plucky helicopter pilot, Robin testified as a defense witness. The seventeen year old's testimony appeared to add little to the defense, but she took advantage of an opportunity to talk privately with Trapnell for a few minutes before she was called to the witness stand. Court authorities were later quoted as saying her testimony indicated she thought of the career criminal as a father figure.

Arrogant and self-important as always, Trapnell had insisted on acting as his own attorney.

Trapnell and thirty-four-year-old Martin J. McNally, who was also imprisoned for an aircraft hijacking attempt in 1972, were charged with attempted escape, conspiracy to escape, aiding and abetting aircraft piracy, and aiding and abetting a kidnapping. The third convict accused in the failed breakout was James K. Johnson. He was a slick character who was serving sentences for bank robbery, kidnapping, and two prison escapes. He had pleaded guilty to criminal charges in the latest escape attempt a few days earlier.

While the federal court jury in Benton, Illinois was hearing final summations and beginning its deliberations in the attempted prison escape case on Thursday, December 21, 1978, a shocking new chapter in the saga of the strangely charismatic Trapnell was being played out a few miles away. And seventeen-year-old Robin Oswald was the unlikely star of the bizarre drama, with support from an unwilling cast from the crew and passengers of another TWA jetliner.

As jurors filed into the courtroom for the beginning of the last day of the trial, deputy United States marshals, sharpshooters, and canine officers with dogs were stationed around the Williamson County Courthouse. All spectators were banned from the courtroom, except for two handpicked reporters and a sketch artist.

Barely twenty miles south, Robin was holding eighty-three passengers and four crew members of TWA Flight 554 from Louisville to Kansas City, hostage.

The determined teenager had boarded Flight 554 in Louisville, and quietly sat through a stop in St. Louis. She chatted briefly with the man sitting next to her, then loaned him one of two newspapers she had carried aboard. A prominently featured story in the newspaper dealt with the trial of Garrett Trapnell, and Mrs. Oswald's deadly attempt to break him out of prison.

The DC-9 had nearly reached its destination and was about to begin its descent before Robin peered out the window at the urban sprawl beneath them and asked her seatmate, "Is that Kansas City?" He replied that it was, and she left her seat two rows from the rear of the airplane and walked into the restroom.

After she returned to her seat a few moments later, she asked the passenger next to her to help her work the call button overhead. A stewardess responded a few moments later, and Robin handed her a folded note. "Oh, my God, no," the stewardess gasped as she looked at the note. Her face paled as she glanced briefly at the grim-

85

faced girl in the baggy brown pantsuit with the sweater and down ski jacket, then she turned and hurried on shaky legs toward the pilot's cabin.

It was about 10:00 A.M., and the beginning of a tension-filled ordeal that was every bit as dangerous as the desperate skyjack attempt that had led to the death of Robin's mother a few months earlier.

A passenger from New York City, who boarded the aircraft in St. Louis and took a seat directly across the aisle from the girl, later recalled that he had noticed she was holding her side and thought she was sick. Instead, she was clutching three ominous cylinders strapped to her waist. She told crew members of the aircraft that the cylinders were sticks of dynamite, and she threatened to blow herself and everyone else out of the sky if they didn't follow her orders.

Gripping a device with a button in one hand, she ordered the jet turned around and flown to Marion. From all appearances, the desperate girl had wired herself as a human bomb with dynamite strapped to her waist and a detonator in her hand. Wiring extended from the cylinders, and up one of her sleeves. Faced with a skyjacker and a planeload of innocent people aboard, the pilot had no choice. He wheeled the aircraft around, and flew east, back across the state of Missouri to Illinois.

Complying with the young skyjacker's orders, he set the aircraft down at an isolated airstrip about ten miles northeast of the penitentiary, and twenty miles from the courthouse where Trapnell and his prison buddy were on trial. It was the Marion-Williamson Airport. The pilot taxied the DC-9 to an area several hundred yards from the terminal and hangars, and brought it to a stop.

A few minutes later, however, she ordered the pilot to turn the DC-9 around, so they would be ready in case they needed to make a fast takeoff.

* * *

Then the negotiating began. Robin remained near the rear of the aircraft, from where she passed notes to a stewardess for the crew in the cockpit, and talked by a specially rigged radiotelephone with law enforcement authorities. She was surprisingly calm and polite, considering her age and the tense situation she had gotten herself into. She showed no more nervousness than she might if she was preparing for a high school history test.

She never raised her voice or swore, and her conversation was grammatically correct and courteous. She said "please" and "thank you." And during one exchange with a stewardess, she smiled and asked, "Aren't I the nicest hijacker?"

She backed up that observation about her behavior by permitting a few older passengers and mothers with small children to disembark. And she let the women use the bathroom, but refused to permit any man to leave his seat.

Several passengers nevertheless recalled later that they could hardly believe the petite, polite teenager was really a skyjacker and that they were really involved in the frightening drama. "This is the kind of thing that happens when you're flying to Beirut," one man marvelled. "It's not what you expect when you're travelling to Kansas City."

But the skyjacking was for real, and Robin was deadly serious. She refused to talk by radiotelephone with two of her sisters and a brother. Federal and local authorities had rushed her siblings to a control room at the airport, less than a mile from the parked DC-9 as soon as her identity was learned. They were hopeful that the girl's family members could talk her into ending the siege and giving herself up.

But the petite skyjacker didn't want to talk to them about surrendering. A fellow passenger later recalled that she said she hated them, in fact she said she hated everyone, he related. She insisted she didn't want to meet with anyone but Trapnell.

She also said she knew that the penalty for skyjacking was ninety-nine years to life in prison, and stubbornly insisted that she would never surrender. Robin tried to make several outside calls, but each time the operator told her the number was no longer working. Nervous passengers could hear the conversations over a speaker.

Anti-hijacking experts, including a specially trained mediator from Louisville, kept her busy talking however. They said that they couldn't get to Trapnell because he was tied up at the courthouse.

The girl's good humor began to erode as the tense standoff dragged on and nightfall approached. The airplane had exhausted its fuel, and with no electrical power or air conditioning, it became hot and muggy inside. The steely-eyed skyjacker began to show signs of fear and anger. By 6:00 P.M., she was losing her patience, and threatened that if her demands weren't met soon she would blow everyone aboard off the face of the earth.

But she consented to pleas by negotiators and fellow passengers to permit members of the crew to open one of the doors in front so that the stagnant air could circulate. One-by-one, passengers began sneaking through the gloom in the darkened aircraft and out the door onto the chill, windswept runway.

It wasn't clear to the passengers if Robin was aware that her hostages were taking advantage of the deliberately long and drawn-out negotiations to gradually empty the aircraft. As passengers near the rear of the aircraft blocked her view by leaving their seats to go to the bathroom, or to rummage around with overhead luggage, others near the front took the opportunity to slip out the open door.

By 8:00 P.M., only about a dozen passengers and crew members remained aboard the night-shrouded aircraft with the girl. At last she agreed to surrender, and walked off the DC-9 into the waiting arms of FBI agents. The lawmen quickly unstrapped the cylinders she had attached to her waist. They weren't dynamite, as she had threatened, but relatively harmless railroad flares. The "detonator" was a button from a doorbell.

The ominous appearing cylinders had looked enough like dynamite, however, to stretch the siege over nine hours.

FBI spokesman Edward Haggerty announced to the crowd of journalists, relatives, and airline employees gathered in the crowded terminal that the ordeal had ended.

"I think she finally came to her senses and decided that she did not want to end her life in any way, and that during the course of the evening she decided she did not want to hurt the passengers," Haggerty explained.

Relieved passengers were flown to St. Louis and to Kansas City. "She had it all together," a woman on her way from Ohio to visit a brother in Kansas City during the Christmas holidays, told waiting reporters before re-boarding the same DC-9 where she had been held hostage. "I felt she really knew what she was about, knew what she wanted."

Federal law enforcement officers briefly questioned Robin, then transported her to the juvenile section of the St. Clair County Jail in Belleville, a few miles from east St. Louis.

Officials had decided to hold her there until it was determined whether federal or state authorities had jurisdiction over the case. She was a few weeks past her seventeenth birthday, and was considered an adult according to state law. But according to Federal law she was still considered a juvenile offender.

At just about the time the girl was driven to the juvenile lockup in Belleville, the federal court jury of nine men and three women at the courthouse in Benton were returning guilty verdicts against Trapnell and McNally.

The jury took twelve ballots during seven-and-one-half hours of deliberation before reporting the verdicts at 8:45 P.M., convicting the convicts on all four counts against each of them.

Trapnell had tried earlier to get the trial recessed, complaining that he was in a very emotional state. The request was denied.

Informed after reporting the verdicts, about the sky-jack attempt, one juror said they were totally surprised. "It proves something about Trapnell," the juror added to a reporter.

News of the skyjacking sparked widespread speculation among court watchers that the escape effort may have been set up when Robin and Trapnell talked after her testimony at the trial. Federal Judge Harold A. Baker ordered the two convicts returned to the prison at Marion, pending sentencing.

After serious consideration of Robin's background and the crime she was accused of, authorities decided to put her on trial under the federal juvenile code. Consequently the hearing at the U. S. District Court in Benton was closed. In December, 1980, after serving a period of time in juvenile custody, she was paroled for good behavior. According to terms of the agreement she was to be kept under parole supervision until her twenty-first birthday.

Meanwhile Trapnell had settled back into prison life. Less than a year after Robin's aborted attempt to help him escape, he announced his candidacy for the presidency of the United States, reputedly under the banner of the National Christian Democratic Party. Campaigning from prison, he demanded protection from the U. S. Secret Service and the right to solicit funds to support his candidacy. He didn't get the Secret Service protection, or the campaign funds. And he and Democratic candidate Walter F. Mondale both lost the 1980 race to Ronald Reagan.

Trapnell was better dealing with women than he was at politics. And if attractive women didn't find him, he knew how to find them — even from his jail cell.

About the time he was running his low-key presidential campaign, a pretty television reporter for KFVS-TV in Cape Girardeau, Missouri, mispronounced a word during a newscast. Cape Girardeau is a city of about 31,000 people hugging the state line near the southern tip of Illinois, and KFVS was the station Trapnell listened to and watched at the prison.

He wrote to Karen Wibbenmeyer and corrected her pronunciation. It was the beginning of a correspondence between the two that became increasingly personal, then romantic. Trapnell courted her by telephone, with roses, and with long letters that he illustrated with doodles and saccharine sketches of her. And he coined a pet name for his new correspondent, "Wabbit," as he pursued her with all the apparent starry-eyed passion of a sixteen year old.

The vivacious TV reporter fell hopelessly in love with the amorous convict charmer and, after a courtship of two years, she married him.

Karen's improbable love affair, then marriage, to the Rasputin-like career criminal carried a heavy personal price tag. According to a 1984 story in *US* magazine, she wound up estranged from her family, and virtually destroyed her career in television while following her convict husband around as he was transferred from prison to prison.

Trapnell was transferred to a federal prison in Pennsylvania, before being shifted to Leavenworth. He was in the federal prison in Atlanta at the time of the magazine interview with his wife, and she was working as a waitress. Later, he was moved once more back to the prison at Marion.

Karen had gotten a job with WNEP-TV in Wilkes-

Barre, Pennsylvania, after her husband was transferred to the nearby federal prison. Then station management heard that a helicopter escape was being planned at the prison. The station owned a helicopter. According to the account in *US,* managers told Karen they had decided there wasn't a position available on the staff for her after all.

Karen conceded to the magazine reporter that her domestic life was less than ideal, and that she is sometimes plagued by self doubts that she deserves better. They had never been permitted to spend any time together, except when they were under the watchful eyes of guards.

She was quoted as saying, nevertheless, "It's been worth it."

Chapter Six

Joyce Bailey Mattox
and
Jesse Glenn Smith

Joyce Mattox was a hardworking, hard loving woman who simply couldn't seem to find the right man. Perhaps it was because she didn't look in the right places.

Although she sang in the choir of her Baptist Church in Spartanburg county, a few miles outside Greenville, South Carolina, and consumed romance novels by the stack, by the mid-1980s she was the veteran of three failed marriages.

Joyce's life could have been a model for the lyrics to some of the hard-core country music songs she loved to listen to. Since she was a little girl she had dreamed of doing something that would make her famous. But by the time she observed her fortieth birthday, she was working in a dead-end job on a night cleanup crew at a textile mill in Startex.

It was early in 1985 when a friend arranged an introduction for her with a man who couldn't booze, run around, or beat her. Thirty-six-year-old Jesse Glenn Smith was serving a life sentence in the Perry Correctional Institution a few miles outside Greenville.

The prison had been constructed less than three years earlier as a maximum security facility to hold 1,150 of South Carolina's toughest, most dangerous convicts. Perry was surrounded by double fences topped with coils of razor wire, and the entire facility, inside and out, was swept constantly by the latest in high-tech electronic equipment and cameras. It was a thoroughly modern institution, that cost the taxpayers of South Carolina nearly twelve million dollars to construct, and it was about as escape-proof as a prison can be made.

Joyce wasn't intimidated by the institution, or by the hardened criminals who were sent there from all over the state. The short, big-busted, stringy-haired, strawberry blonde was a lonely, romance-hungry woman, and she was soon writing love letters or talking by telephone on an almost daily basis to the exciting new man in her life. On Sundays she drove the short distance from her cramped rental trailer near the mill in Spartanburg county where she worked, to the prison for "contact visits" which permitted inmates to hold hands and exchange kisses with their female guests.

Smith was a local desperado whose hell-raising had kept him in trouble all of his adult life, but he was as much in love with romance as Mattox was. He was serving an eighteen-year sentence for armed robbery following a 1973 conviction, when he busted out of jail to marry his childhood sweetheart.

By 1984, Smith was free on parole when he pulled a gun and plugged a bartender at the Mustang Lounge in Greenville. Then he took off in his pickup truck at the head of a fleet of police cars in a crazy chase through the city before he landed back behind bars for another long prison term.

Joyce knew all about her new boyfriend's wild and wooly reputation, but somehow she decided that he was the man she had been seeking for so many years. He was handsome, masculine, exciting, and she would confide much later — he never lied to her.

One Sunday while she was visiting with him at the prison, Smith's wife, Doris, showed up. According to Joyce's account, Mrs. Smith hadn't been visiting her husband for some time. And he told his wife that he was in love with Joyce and she would be doing the visiting.

During the Sunday visits and telephone calls, Smith did a lot of joking about breaking out of the maximum security prison. When he brought the subject up during a December 13 visit, eight months after the romance had begun, he made sure that Joyce knew he wasn't joking anymore. He told her he wanted her to hijack a helicopter, set it down in the prison exercise yard, and lift him and two convict pals to freedom.

His pals were forty-two-year-old William Douglas Ballew, and twenty-year-old James Rodney Leonard. Ballew was a stickup man who was serving a twenty-three-year term for armed robbery. Leonard was a killer, serving life for murdering a high school teacher. He had already been caught making one escape attempt from a local jail. Like Smith, both his coconspirators inside the walls had long police records for violent crimes.

Although Joyce didn't know anything about guns, helicopters, or prison breaks, and had been in trouble with the law only once before over a bad check she blamed on one of her husbands, she thought she could carry off the daredevil caper. Smith provided all the reinforcement she needed with telephoned reassurances three or four times per day.

Smith told her that another married woman named Wanda, who was sweet on Ballew, would also be going along on the caper.

Joyce had recently lost her job cleaning up at the mill. She nevertheless withdrew her life savings from the bank, seven hundred eighty dollars, and began making arrangements for the breakout.

* * *

One of the first projects was the purchase of a .32-caliber pistol at a pawn shop in Spartanburg. The pawn-shop clerk loaded it for her, because she didn't know how. On Wednesday, December 18, the day before the planned escape, she telephoned Palmetto Helicopters and arranged to pay $165 for an hour-long sightseeing ride on Thursday. She explained that she had never been for a helicopter ride before.

As other residents of the area were winding up their Christmas shopping, she bought some men's clothing, and loaded them along with some of her own, in her 1974 Chevrolet Nova. She drove the car to a field about four miles from the prison, near the town of Fork Shoals, and parked it. She gave a neighbor twenty-five dollars to leave another vehicle, a Dodge Aspen, a few miles there near a convenience store. She didn't tell him what was going on.

Smith telephoned her collect on Wednesday night and again on Thursday morning to remind her that he loved her and would be waiting.

After a near sleepless night, she roused herself out of bed early Thursday morning, cleaned up, slipped into blue jeans, a blouse and a red jacket, then pulled on a comfortable pair of cowboy boots. After exchanging a few last-minute words with her lover by telephone, she stepped out of the house and into the most exciting and dangerous adventure of her life.

This time her imagination wasn't linking into some fictional bodice ripper dreamed up by a romance author. The chunky, five-foot, two-inch, 140-pound backwoods beauty would be living the real thing.

If there had indeed been another woman, she got cold feet, because she never showed up. It was up to Joyce to hijack the helicopter and force the pilot to land it in the prison yard by herself. But she was up to the job.

* * *

At about 9:45 A.M., she climbed into a blue-and-white Hughes 300C helicopter. Pilot Larry Green had faced danger before as a two-tour veteran of Vietnam, but when he lifted off in the chopper that morning it seemed that there was no reason to believe that it wasn't the beginning of a routine flight.

The skids of the aircraft had barely left the ground, however, before all that changed. The big woman with the bulging breasts who was his passenger pulled a pistol from one of her cowboy boots and pointed the barrel straight at his ear.

Without the slightest hesitation, or a hint of nervousness, she ordered, "Take me to Perry." Green tried to talk her out of it, pointing out that they were sure to be fired on by armed guards at the prison. Joyce refused to be talked out of the plan, and ordered the pilot to take off his headset so that he couldn't tip anyone off about what was going on. Jesse had warned her about the headset.

She also calmly explained that Green didn't have much of a choice. He could take his chances on the marksmanship of the prison guards, or get shot right there at the controls of his helicopter.

Exactly at 10:00 A.M., in accordance with the determined woman's orders, the chopper skimmed over the fences and wall at the prison and set down in the exercise yard where some two hundred convicts were milling around. There was a frenzied scramble, and five convicts managed to duck under the rotor blades and squeeze into the cabin of the aircraft. During the melee, a guard, William T. Wade, was shot in the mouth as he tried to pull the convicts from the helicopter. The shot came from inside the chopper, although guards were also shooting from a tower and from other positions nearby.

Inside the aircraft it was so crowded that Smith, who was a small, wiry man with the name "Cindy" tattooed across his left hand, perched on the big woman's lap.

97

The gun was pressed into the pilot's ear again, and one of the convicts snarled an order to get going if he wanted to continue living. The pilot revved up the engines, but the two-seater helicopter was so overloaded that it wouldn't budge. The man sitting on the hijacker's lap shouted for his buddies to help get the hitchhikers out. Two men were ejected after a brief struggle, and the helicopter, still overloaded, lurched into the air. It barely cleared the twelve-foot fences surrounding the prison.

Continuing to follow the woman's orders, the reluctant pilot flew his menacing passengers to the field near Fork Shoals and set the helicopter down near the cars. One of the men leaned over and grabbed the keys out of the ignition. Joyce leaned over and stuffed $165 in Green's pocket, payment for the ride. Then he was ordered to get out and start walking, as the convicts and their female accomplice leaped from the helicopter and ran for Joyce's Nova. Jesse jumped behind the wheel, while Joyce squeezed into the front passenger seat beside him.

While the fugitives scrambled into the old car, corrections officers, along with state and local police departments throughout western and central South Carolina were already launching one of the biggest manhunts in the history of the state.

Inspection of visitors' records at the prison helped corrections officials to quickly zero in on Joyce as the mysterious woman hijacker. The records disclosed she had been a frequent visitor of Smith's and had last signed the visitors' log at the prison only six days before the breakout. Employees at the helicopter service confirmed the identification. Joyce's description and a description of her car were broadcast to police agencies.

Police set up roadblocks, dispatched helicopters and small fixed-wing aircraft with officers riding along as spotters, and called out teams of armed lawmen in cars and on foot with tracking dogs to press the search.

"They are extremely dangerous individuals," Sheriff Johnny Make Brown of Greenville county cautioned. "They will not hesitate to use violence." But the sheriff had a grim warning of his own for the fugitives. "We don't want to get violent, but I can assure you that we will meet violence with violence," he stated.

Shortly after the escape, a clerk at a convenience store, located a few miles from the field where the helicopter landed, telephoned police and told them he had just seen a woman and three men climbing into a Dodge Aspen. He said the vehicle was parked by the store when he arrived at work that morning. An old Chevrolet was abandoned by the fast-moving group.

The store clerk hadn't noticed the number of the license plate on the Dodge. But he told searchers that he was certain the men he had seen were wearing civilian clothes.

State warrants were sworn out for Joyce and her convict companions on charges of escape, or aiding an escape, and on charges of assault and battery with intent to kill, in the wounding of the guard. Authorities charged all the fugitives in the shooting because they were unable at that time to determine who did the shooting. Wade's jaw was broken by the gunshot, but he eventually recovered.

The FBI moved into the manhunt when Joyce was charged in a federal warrant with air piracy. Authorities also distributed photos of the convicts and a description of Joyce to police agencies. The FBI warned that the men might try to finance their escape with stickups of convenience stores or service stations.

The nationwide manhunt continued on through Friday and Saturday with no trace of the fugitives. As

Smith's wife went on television and pleaded for him to give himself up, the fugitives were living on beer and hamburgers and putting as many miles behind themselves and the prison as they could.

Although there was a possibility the group was hiding out somewhere in South Carolina, there seemed to be a good chance that they had fled across state lines into Georgia, North Carolina, or beyond. The search effort became nationwide.

A few hours before dawn on Sunday morning, county sheriff's officers in Mobile, Alabama, logged in a report from a motorist who said his car was stolen by a gang of escaped convicts and a woman. He reported he was driving along Interstate 10 a few miles outside the city when he stopped to help two men standing beside a broken-down car.

He quoted them as saying they had blown their engine, and asked him to drive them to a Motel Six. The motorist said another man and a big woman were waiting in the hotel room when he accepted an invitation to come inside for a few minutes.

According to the motorist's story, they were friendly, and as soon as he walked into the room one of them asked, "Do you know who we are?"

"Hell no, I don't," he said.

So they told him. They said they were on the run after breaking out of a South Carolina prison in a helicopter. And they said they would have to take his car. Asked by police to describe the woman, the motorist said she was wearing blue jeans, a red satin jacket, and cowboy boots, and was unusually buxom.

A few minutes after the motorist's call, a new alert was being broadcast for the escapees and their companion, along with a description of a stolen light blue 1979 Pontiac Bonneville with Alabama plates. Police who checked out the Dodge abandoned along I-10 found the escaped convicts' discarded prison uniforms in the backseat. And just as the two men had told the unlucky Good Samaritan who stopped to help, the engine was blown out.

Time was beginning to run out on the escapees when the motorist reported his car stolen.

Almost exactly twenty-four hours later the missing vehicle was parked at a Welcome Center operated along Interstate 95 by the state of Georgia about a mile north of the Florida line. Visitors can stop there for maps, directions, information about tourist sites, water, or to use the bathrooms. Sometimes weary drivers simply pull into a parking space and catch a few quick winks, especially at night.

It was about 3 o'clock Monday morning, December 23, when a Georgia State Police Trooper Joe Cunningham and Sgt. Charlie Easterling of the Camden County Sheriff's Department, who were checking out a report of a possible burglary, noticed a blue Pontiac with Alabama tags parked in one of the visitor spaces. People were sleeping inside.

The officers confirmed that there was no burglary, but decided to ask for a routine check on the state police computer of the license tags on the parked Bonneville. A few minutes later Cunningham was notified by radio that the tags belonged on a stolen car that was believed to be occupied by escapees from a South Carolina prison. Cunningham and Easterling were warned that the fugitives were believed to be armed and dangerous.

Backup officers were on the way in minutes, and they cruised into the rest area with their lights off and their sirens silent. Quickly and quietly they blockaded the entrances and exits with their squad cars. With guns drawn, the officers took up positions behind their vehicles.

At a signal from one of the state police troopers the headlights and some of the sirens on the police cars were all turned on at once. Police used a loud speaker to order the fugitives to leave their car with their hands in the air.

"Come out! You're surrounded!" the police officers ordered.

Two sleepy-eyed men slid out of the backseat and stood beside the car in their stocking feet, with their hands held high. Moments later a man and a woman struggled groggily out of the front seat and hoisted their hands into the air. The woman's clothes were rumpled and her hair was tangled and stringy. She looked exhausted.

Police confiscated a .32-caliber pistol and several knives from inside the car. But the arrests had been made without firing a shot.

The prisoners were locked briefly in the Camden County Jail in Woodbine. Then federal law officers drove them north to Savannah, Georgia, on the South Carolina border, and were locked in the Chatham County Jail. Later that day they were arraigned before a U. S. magistrate on the federal charges of air piracy.

They all waived extradition, and were driven across the state line to Greenville. There, they were arraigned on state charges. Joyce was charged with assault and battery with intent to kill, aiding and abetting an escape from prison, and carrying a pistol. The three convicts were charged with prison escape, and aiding and abetting air piracy. The men were also charged in Alabama with auto theft.

A couple of weeks later a federal grand jury in Columbia, the state capital, returned new indictments against the former fugitives for air piracy, and using a firearm during a crime of violence.

Joyce was in about as much trouble as it was possible to get involved in. But she had packed a lifetime into four exciting days, and she told police that no matter what happened to her, those memories could never be taken away.

She was sentenced in federal court to a forty-year prison term. A few weeks later she and her former companions appeared before Judge C. Victor Pyle, Jr., at the county courthouse in Greenville and entered guilty pleas to a battery of state charges tied to the escape. Joyce and the men were brought to the courthouse in handcuffs and chains. Responding to the judge's invitation to make a statement before sentencing, Joyce said she was sorry.

When Smith was given the same opportunity, he told the court that it was his fault Joyce had become involved in the scheme. "If you put her on the street today, you'd never have to worry about her committing another crime," he said.

Tears were streaming down Joyce's face when Judge Pyle ordered another forty-year prison sentence for her. But she would become eligible for parole in ten. Lengthy sentences were added on to the terms her companions were already facing, with the result they were expected to remain behind bars for life.

On February 12, 1985, she and her fellow inmates watched CBS television's movie of the week based on Joyce's escapade, *The Outside Woman*. Actress Sharon Gless played her part in the movie. It was as romantic and exciting as anything Joyce had ever read in the bodice rippers she had loved so much.

Chapter Seven

Diane Brenda Brodbeck
and
Jon Evans Yount

When forty-three-year-old Diane Brenda Brodbeck told her husband, Chester, that she and one of her women friends were going to take a weekend bus trip to Williamsburg, Virginia, there didn't appear to be any reason for him to worry.

The slender beauty parlor receptionist and grandmother seemed to have her feet firmly planted in the picturesque York county, Pennsylvania Dutch farm country that was her home.

She was an active church woman, who took her religion so seriously that for several years she had been visiting convicts as a prison ministry volunteer with the Lutheran Social Services in Harrisburg.

And she had formed an especially close relationship with a prisoner who was serving a life sentence for one of the most perverse and sadistic murders in the recent history of the farming and coal mining communities of south central Pennsylvania.

The convict was Jon E. Yount, who had already served twenty years of a life sentence for the grisly sex slaying of a high school girl from Luthersburg in rural Clearfield county.

Yount was twice convicted of the savage knife slaying of eighteen-year-old Pamela Sue Rimer, after laying in wait for her at an isolated school bus stop about a quarter of a mile from her home. It was April 26, 1966, only a few weeks before the girl and her classmates were scheduled to graduate from the DuBois Area Senior High School.

Investigators concluded that the pretty teenager was carrying an armload of schoolbooks when she was attacked and smashed on the head with a metal wrench with such brutal force that her skull was fractured. But somehow she remained conscious and began running through a woods toward a busy road, before she stumbled and fell down a steep hill.

Her killer caught up with her there, ripped off one of her stockings, and strangled her with it so hard that the capillaries in her eyes burst. Then he slashed her throat, cutting through the veins of her jugular and her larynx, and nearly severed her fingers as she vainly fought to defend herself.

When the teenager's pitifully mutilated body was found, she was lying facedown under a large tree. She had drowned in her own blood. Sperm found in her body during the autopsy confirmed that she was raped.

Incredibly, Pamela Sue's killer was the instructor in her advanced mathematics class.

The high school senior had complained earlier to her mother about her teacher's weird stares. And she was uneasy because she had seen him drive by her house on several afternoons.

His behavior was so odd and frightening that the friendly honors student told her mother she wanted to transfer out of his class even though there were only a few weeks left in the school semester. After graduation, Pamela Sue planned to enroll at Penn State University in State College on a scholarship.

Instead, shortly before her classmates gathered for

their high school commencement, she was buried in her prom dress. Her classmates laid the tassels from their graduation mortarboards on her grave.

Pamela Sue's ghastly murder was the second in a series of tragedies that stalked her family for more than a decade. Her only sibling, a ten-year-old brother, was killed three years earlier in a tractor accident. And her father died in 1976. Mrs. Rimer later wrote that he became mentally ill after their daughter's murder.

When police took the twenty-eight-year-old schoolteacher into custody a few days after the slaying, he told them that it was all the result of a terrible misunderstanding. He explained that he was driving near Pamela Sue's home looking for property to purchase when he saw her walking near the bus stop, and offered her a ride.

Yount claimed she mistook one of his remarks as an improper sexual overture, threatened to tell authorities, and tried to scramble out of the car.

The schoolteacher's memory mysteriously began to falter after that point. He told investigators that he dimly recalled striking the girl with a wrench. But he couldn't recall stabbing her with his pocketknife.

If Yount's story was believed, the lack of premeditation would rule out a charge or conviction for first-degree murder. Conviction for second-degree murder, the most serious possible charge for unpremeditated murder, carried a maximum sentence of from ten to twenty years.

He was convicted in 1966 by a Clearfield county court of first-degree murder and rape and sentenced to life in prison.

Although Yount was a well behaved prisoner and stayed out of trouble, he kept busy with his legal counsel appealing his conviction and seeking a new trial.

In 1970, the Pennsylvania Supreme Court overturned his conviction on grounds that he wasn't advised of his right to free legal counsel after he was picked up as a suspect in the crime. His new trial ended with the same result as the first, however. Once again he was convicted of first-degree murder.

Yount responded by filing new appeals. After making their way through the state and federal systems, they eventually reached the U. S. Supreme Court, where he was again rejected.

But Yount was persistent. While pursuing his appeals, he also made nine appearances before the Pennsylvania State Pardons Board, seeking early release. Each time Pamela Sue's mother, Mrs. Lavonne Rimer, campaigned against his release, contacting state officials and gathering signatures on petitions opposing commutation of the life sentence.

While working tirelessly for his release, Yount found time to head a prison Jaycee chapter and to continue his education. He learned computer programming, earned a master's degree in education, and eventually was permitted to travel to various prisons and perform as an organist.

He was an inmate at the Pennsylvania State Prison at Camp Hill and was still busy seeking to win his release through legal avenues when Mrs. Brodbeck first met him in 1983.

Early conversations between the York county homemaker and the convicted rapist-murderer may have revolved around the gospel and other spiritual affairs. But at some point in their relationship, the talk turned to more earthly and personal matters.

Mrs. Brodbeck visited often with the curly-haired, bespectacled killer. Soon, they were exchanging letters between visits.

When Yount was transferred to the Rockview State Correctional Institution in September 1985, the correspondence and visits continued — although the move had added nearly two hundred miles to the loyal woman's round-trip drive.

Yount mailed his letters to Mrs. Brodbeck to a post-office box she rented in Lewisberry, Pennsylvania. Using her middle and maiden names, she rented the box as Brenda Warner.

At Rockview, Yount was assigned to a farm detail where supervision was intermittent. Some convicts were permitted to work for hours on their own without the presence of a guard or other prison employee. But after twenty years of good behavior, it seemed that Yount had proved he could be trusted.

Then in December 1985, Yount's petition for a third trial was rejected by the courts. He was forty-eight years old, had spent twenty years in prison, been turned down nearly a dozen times by the Pardons Board, and had just about exhausted every possible legal method to win his freedom.

It was a few minutes after lunch on a brisk early spring day on April 5, 1986, when Yount was dropped off about a mile from the prison and began walking toward a tractor he had been assigned to drive plowing a field. The field was about a mile from the prison, and outside the fence surrounding the institution.

About forty-five minutes later an off-duty guard saw Mrs. Brodbeck driving away from the prison, apparently heading toward the town of Axemann. He recognized her from her frequent visits there to see Yount.

It was 3:30 P.M. before Yount's foreman checked up on him and discovered that the convicted killer was missing. A check of the fugitive's visitors' list, and disclosure by the guard that he had seen Mrs. Brodbeck driving near the prison, quickly led corrections officers, local and state police to focus on the rural Wellsville housewife as a possible accomplice in the escape.

Her husband told police that he believed his wife's relationship to the escapee was solely religious. He also said he hadn't known that Yount was transferred to Rockview the previous fall.

But investigators tracing her recent movements and activities uncovered curiously suspicious behavior. They learned:

* She never showed up at her friend's home in the Northumberland county community of Elysburg for the reputed drive to Virginia.

* Letters she left behind from Yount were filled with sexual innuendos.

*She had withdrawn $7,410 from a secret seven-thou-sand-five-hundred-dollar bank account, three months after her prison paramour's final appeal was rejected.

* She had rented storage space in Harrisburg and left a light blue car there. Approximately a month after the escape, police found her tan 1978 AMC Concord abandoned in a Howard Johnson's parking lot in suburban Harrisburg. Detectives said they believed she had picked up Yount and driven with him to Harrisburg, where they swapped cars.

By that time there was little doubt, if any, that the missing grandmother had helped the dangerous sex criminal escape.

She was charged in the District Court of Justice Robert May with escape, conspiracy, hindering the apprehension or prosecution of a criminal, and aiding in a crime.

A warrant was also issued for her arrest, describing her as forty-three years old, five-foot, seven-inches tall, about one hundred pounds, and with sandy blond hair and blue eyes.

Yount was described in a similar warrant and in

wanted posters as five-feet, ten-inches tall, 175 pounds, with brown eyes, and brown curly hair and a beard that was flecked with grey. He was wearing brown twill institutional clothing when he fled.

After tracking the fugitives to Harrisburg, investigators lost their trail.

Pamela Sue's mother had learned of the killer's escape through an anonymous Saturday night telephone call. And Trooper Raymond Fratangelo, an investigator with the State Police in DuBois, where Yount had once taught mathematics to the victim, disclosed that the woman had moved temporarily out of her home.

Mrs. Rimer had put up a dogged fight against Yount's efforts to win release from prison, lobbying state legislators, gathering thousands of names on petitions opposing his pardon or commutation, and appearing before the Pennsylvania State Board of Pardons.

At a hearing in 1979 where his lawyer argued that Yount had been rehabilitated and had a computer job waiting for him in California, Mrs. Rimer declared that she and other people in the community were afraid of him.

"I live alone. I would be fearful and I know these people would be too," she testified, pointing to an envelope filled with signatures opposing commutation.

But there was no indication that Yount, or his suspected companion, wasted any time fleeing from central Pennsylvania after the escape.

Sightings of Yount, sometimes including a vague description of a woman companion, were reported as near as State College, about five miles from the prison, and as far away as Montreal.

A few days after the escape, a former school friend reported spotting Yount in the State College downtown area. Several months later, a supermarket checkout clerk in Maryland told police she recognized him as a former customer. She said she remembered his permed hair. At about the same time, investigators checked out reports that Yount was hiding out in Canada. Later reports indicated they were in Rock Springs, Wyoming.

When police learned that a book with the intriguing title *Vanish: Disappearing Through I. D. Acquisition* listed the author as "Johnny Yount," they thought they might have a lead on the missing killer's location. But when the FBI and local police checked with the publisher, Paladin Press, of Boulder, Colorado, they learned that the name was a pseudonym and that the real author was a writer from Los Angeles. The book had nothing to do with the fugitive sex-slayer.

For months after the escape, police and members of Mrs. Brodbeck's family worried that she might be murdered by the convicted killer. It seemed that there was always the chance that when he no longer needed her help, he might decide that she was in the way and he could more easily avoid discovery if he was alone.

Trooper William F. Madden, who was in charge of the manhunt, described Yount to reporters as a manipulator, who may have had some sincere feelings of affection for Mrs. Brodbeck.

"If he was manipulating her and used her only as a means for escape, then she's dead somewhere," the state policeman was quoted as saying.

Madden's fears for Mrs. Brodbeck's safety were unfounded. They were on the run together, and they headed west.

Then on May 18, 1985, more than two years after Yount walked away from the prison farm, the search for the fugitive killer and his companion was featured on a segment of NBC-TV's "Unsolved Mysteries." More than twenty-four million viewers were believed to watch the popular show.

Over the next few days, the Pennsylvania State Police barracks at Rockview were flooded with telephone calls from people who thought they knew something about the fugitive couple's whereabouts. Other tipsters telephoned the FBI.

The calls came from all over the country, and some were more credible than others. One anonymous caller claimed that a photograph of a man who looked like Yount was printed in a recent issue of *Sports Illustrated*. Two other tipsters, one calling from Indiana, the other from Texas, reported that they believed Yount had recently been a contestant on a popular television game show.

One of the telephone calls to the FBI was from a resident of Boise, Idaho, who claimed to have recognized Mrs. Brodbeck from the telecast. The tipster said the woman had worked in Boise as a secretary for a lawn service.

A few hours later FBI agents had confirmed that a woman fitting the description of Mrs. Brodbeck had worked for the company, but had already left. Amazingly, the woman wore the same hairstyle and had the same color hair as Mrs. Brodbeck when she had dropped from sight more than two years earlier.

The federal lawmen quickly tracked her and her companion approximately 350 miles north of Boise to Coeur d'Alene on the Washington state border. She was traced through driver's license records after becoming involved in an auto accident in Kootenai county in early June.

Mrs. Brodbeck had her car registered under the name of Mary Katherine Kermer, an alias she used. She also sometimes altered the spelling of the last name slightly and identified herself as Mary Katherine Kermen. Yount used James Marvin Forsgren as his alias.

Early on a Wednesday night, June 15, 1988, several

FBI agents walked up to Yount as he was quietly working in his garden outside a rented basement apartment in the far northwest Idaho city and took him into custody without a struggle.

Unlike his fellow fugitive, he had changed his appearance. He had swapped his glasses for contact lenses, cut his permed hair short and straight, and grown a full beard.

A couple of hours later, at about 9:30 P.M., agents arrested Mrs. Brodbeck as she returned home from her new job with a chimney sweep firm in nearby Spokane, Washington. The fugitives confirmed their identities but refused any additional comment, and were locked up in the Kootenai County Jail.

Investigators learned that the couple had lived quietly in Boise for nearly two years before they moved to Coeur d'Alene the previous March. Yount was unemployed during the couple's two years on the run, and the couple lived off Mrs. Brodbeck's earnings.

Their landlady in Coeur d'Alene, who lived above the Dalton Gardens basement apartment, later described the couple to reporters as nice people who were very ordinary. She said the woman was quiet and didn't make a habit of visiting with neighbors, but the man was more outgoing and was a charmer. She said he had even offered to take her fourteen-year-old son fishing, but she declined.

Mrs. Brodbeck and her companion waived extradition, and a few days after their apprehension they were handcuffed to police officers and flown back to Pennsylvania under heavy guard. Two female officers, including a Pennsylvania state trooper and a Centre County, Pennsylvania, deputy sheriff were included in the detail riding on the commercial flight from Spokane to University Park Airport in State College.

After landing at the airport, they were driven to the Rockview State Police Station, where they were fingerprinted and photographed. Yount was locked up once more at the Rockview State Correctional Institution, but this time he wasn't allowed outside the fence on any loosely supervised work details. And a few weeks later he was transferred to the maximum security State Correctional Institution at Huntingdon.

Mrs. Brodbeck was lodged in the Mifflin County Jail under two-hundred-fifty-thousand dollars bail.

Her husband of twenty-eight years loyally testified on her behalf at a bail reduction hearing. He said he had talked with her since her return to Pennsylvania, and they agreed she would live at their home if she was released on bail. And he stated that she could work at her old job at the beauty salon, where she was an employee for five years before dropping from sight.

But Chester Brodbeck also pointed out that she hadn't contacted him, their two daughters (both in their mid-twenties), or the couple's grandchild during the more than two years she was hiding out with Yount.

District Attorney Ray Gricar argued against a bail reduction, however, describing the defendant as unstable and unpredictable. She had already proven her skills at hiding out when she was the object of a nationwide manhunt, he said.

The plea for bail reduction was denied.

Testimony from State Trooper Madden during a preliminary court hearing seemed to shed some light on the quiet grandmother's motivations for taking off.

Madden said the couple's former landlady in Coeur d'Alene told him she telephoned Mrs. Brodbeck in jail and talked with her after the couple's arrest there. The police officer said the woman told him Mrs. Brodbeck said "she did it so she would be able to see the light of the outside world."

He said the landlady told him the defendant admitted

114

that she and Yount had arranged the escape, and that she was in love with him.

The criminal couple sat at the defense table on opposite sides of Diane's lawyer during the testimony, and did not look at each other. Her husband, mother, sister and both daughters quietly watched and listened from spectator seats in the courtroom during the proceedings.

On September 1, she was released from jail after family members posted a two-hundred-fifty-thousand-dollar property bond, and she returned to live with her husband in their home near Wellsville.

Several weeks later, minutes before jury selection was to begin for his trial, Yount pleaded guilty to a third-degree felony count of escape. As part of a plea bargain, the prosecution dropped a felony charge of conspiracy. He was returned to his cell in the prison at Huntingdon to await sentencing.

In late November, Centre County Court President Judge Charles C. Brown, Jr., ordered him to serve a three-to-seven-year term on the escape charge in addition to the life sentence.

Approximately a month later, as part of another plea bargain arrangement, Mrs. Brodbeck pleaded guilty to criminal conspiracy to commit escape.

The following February, Mrs. Brodbeck was sentenced by the same judge to a prison term of from twenty-seven months to five years for criminal conspiracy to commit escape. The minimum term was approximately the same amount of time she was on the run with her escaped convict companion.

In a presentence statement, the somber woman told the court that she was sorry for the pain and suffering she had caused her family and friends. "I didn't know it was possible to feel so much pain and go on living," she said.

As she was being led from the courtroom by sheriff's

deputies, she remarked that she thought the judge had been very fair. According to Pennsylvania state criminal codes, she could have been sentenced to a maximum of three-and-a-half to seven years in prison for the offense.

In the prison at Huntingdon, Yount was again busy with new court proceedings. More than twenty-three years after murdering and raping his student, he filed a new appeal to his murder conviction. He also filed an appeal of his guilty plea to the escape charge.

Inside Women

Chapter Eight

Mary Pentecost Evans
and
William Timothy Kirk

Mary Pentecost Evans had it all, or so it seemed.

She was beautiful, bright, and the educated daughter of a socially prominent and loving well-to-do family. On top of all that, she was a promising young lawyer with a prestigious Knoxville legal firm who was learning the business of criminal law from the ground up.

But sinister inner demons were at work that would lead her to commit an incredibly brash and dangerous act that shocked her family and friends, changed her life forever, and made international headlines.

She helped a convict she was assigned to represent to escape at gunpoint only four days before his scheduled trial for multiple murders. Then she ran off with him, sparking one of the most extensive and highly publicized manhunts in the history of the modern South.

The cultured twenty-seven-year-old lady lawyer from Tennessee and the hardened thirty-six-year-old stickup man from the streets of Chicago were an unlikely pair.

As Mary Pentecost, she grew up as the adored and

protected daughter of parents who lived in quiet gentility on a seventy-six-acre farm in South Knoxville. Her father, Bobby H. Pentecost, was vice-president of the University of Tennessee School of Agriculture. Her mother, Kaye, was a housewife. Mary also had a younger brother, Chris.

Contrary to her parents' conventional respectability, Mary was headstrong and willful, and she rebelled against the strict ways of other family members, and of the Mount Olive Baptist Church where her father was a deacon. She became a chain-smoker, drank wine and other alcoholic beverages, and often chose friends from the wrong side of town.

Nevertheless, during her childhood she was an excellent student, who brought A's home on her school report cards. Her excellent scholastic performance was continued throughout her college career.

She was baptized in her parents' church, and when she was twenty years old and in her second year of law school she married Thomas H. Evans, Jr. The groom was the handsome son of a wealthy businessman, and a fellow student at the university, although he was not attending the law school. The couple first met a few years earlier at a New Year's Eve party sponsored by a church group for high school girls.

Mary opted for a traditional wedding. She wore a dress sewn by her mother, and carried yellow roses. It may have seemed that she had at last outgrown her years of stubborn rebellion against the traditional lives of her parents, and the strict mores of the church which forbade dancing, drinking, and smoking.

However, the marriage that had begun with such high hopes, didn't even survive until she finished school. In September 1980, Mary was granted a divorce in Chancery Court of Knox County on grounds of irreconcilable differences. By that time she was in her senior year of law school and working as a clerk for a leading Knoxville law firm, Lockridge and Becker. Shortly after her divorce she began dating and taking out-of-town trips with one of her bosses, John Lockridge. He was one of the city's leading divorce lawyers, and a movie star handsome man.

Lockridge and his wife were divorced in March 1981, a few months before Evans graduated from law school. Soon after graduation, Mary went to work as an associate with the law firm, Tipton and Bell, in downtown Knoxville. After she had worked for the firm about a year, doing research, interviewing witnesses and generally learning the business from the ground up, she was given her first big criminal case. Her boss, James A. H. Bell, assigned her as associate counsel to represent a convict named William Timothy Kirk, who was accused of murdering two fellow inmates. Conviction could mean the death penalty.

The background of the young attorney's new client provided a study in sharp contrast to her own privileged life in the clean hill and mountain country around Knoxville. Kirk spent his formative years in Chicago where his hardworking father, William A. Kirk, held down two jobs, and his mother, Florence, a former schoolteacher, stayed home to care for their large brood. Tim, which was the name he preferred, was the baby of the family by eleven years, and he had five half brothers and half sisters.

Unlike Mary, whose career training was undertaken in the sheltered atmosphere of the university campus, Tim preferred the rowdy education of the streets.

And unlike his better behaved siblings, he was in trouble almost from the time he was old enough to venture from the house on his own. He was stubborn and scrappy, and he talked back to his teachers, skipped school, and got into fights. He made it plain that he believed rules were for other people.

121

When his desperate parents tried to straighten out his deplorable behavior by sending him to a military school in South Chicago, he bolted. His father tried to return him, but school authorities had their fill of the young troublemaker and wouldn't take him back.

The boy was a fast learner at the lessons he really cared about. He was barely in his teens before he learned to pass and write fake prescriptions for drugs. Then he busied himself learning the arts of burglary. By the time he was fifteen he moved on to armed robbery. Long before that the tough Chicago street kid, who strutted around in a black leather jacket, tight pants, and made his own rules, had learned to romance the local girls.

The handsome rusty-haired troublemaker was so good at romance, in fact, that when he was fourteen he became the steady boyfriend of a neighborhood girl named Junene. When they were sophomores, they dropped out of high school. At sixteen, they married. And they had their first baby before they were twenty. But the marriage didn't last.

Kirk didn't give the work-a-day world much of a chance, although he held jobs for a few weeks as a laborer, then as an apprentice bricklayer. From the beginning, he preferred to steal, supporting himself with everything from stickups of convenience and liquor stores to car theft. Either he wasn't all that good at his chosen profession, or he doomed himself by his own industry, because while other boys his age were establishing themselves in careers, going to college, or into the military, he was piling up a staggering number of arrests.

Sometimes he spent a few days in jail, and at others he was shipped off for a few weeks or months to a juvenile facility. Finally he got into serious trouble in Missouri, where his family had lived before moving to Chicago.

He was first convicted of robbing a bowling alley and sentenced to two years in the Missouri State Penitentiary. Free on parole a few months later, he robbed the home of a jeweler and drew another five-year term. He was arrested seventeen times before he was twenty-nine.

By the mid-1970s he was in trouble in Tennessee and served a year in the Shelby County Jail in Memphis, after strolling into a pharmacy and threatening to set off a bomb if he wasn't given drugs. The store operator wasn't easily cowed. He telephoned police.

Jerry Lucas, one of Kirk's former Memphis jailers, recalled years later that Kirk had an amazing ability to charm the ladies from behind bars. The former corrections officer said Kirk would simply get on the telephone and sweet-talk women into bringing him money. Once two women showed up to see Kirk at the same time, and one left in a huff. But the imprisoned thief sweet-talked her into coming back later, the former sheriff's deputy said.

By 1977 after being freed once more, Kirk got himself into serious trouble that he couldn't sweet-talk his way out of. Kirk, a woman, and a man whom local law enforcement officers knew as Robert "Bad Boy" Phillips, were convicted in the robbery of a Memphis area couple at gunpoint. They broke into the house, waited for the victims to return home, then tied them up, and stole jewelry, winning race track tickets, and a car.

This time authorities lowered the boom. Home invasion was a frightening crime, and Kirk drew a sixty-five-year prison term. He was thirty-one years old in 1978, and had already spent half his life as a professional criminal when he was first led through the gates of the Tennessee State Penitentiary at Nashville and locked up with some eight thousand other inmates.

Barely two years later he and Carl Crafton, a convict pal serving time for the stickup of a Chattanooga drug store, were nearly crushed to death during an abortive attempt to escape by jumping into the loader of a garbage truck. The compactor had begun to close on them when their terrified screams alerted the operator. Kirk wound up with broken ribs. Crafton, who was one of the most skillful jailhouse lawyers in the Tennessee State Prison system, survived with a fractured skull. The failed escape attempt also earned the convict buddies a transfer to the Brushy Mountain State Prison in Morgan county, a sparsely populated area of Tennessee some twenty-five miles west of Knoxville.

When Kirk and Crafton were processed into Brushy Mountain, it had a reputation as the most secure, and the toughest, most wretchedly dangerous lockup in the state prison system. And at that time, his cellblock was being virtually run by a tough black inmate gang known as the Memphis Mafia. The bosses of D block, which housed lifers and escape artists, were James Mitchell and James Nichols. Both were convicted murderers, serving life sentences.

Mitchell, Nichols, and their cronies used muscle and threats to extort weekly cash payments from white inmates who were unaffiliated with other prison gangs capable of providing protection. Even inmates who paid off were sometimes gang raped, and those who didn't were beaten or stabbed with prison shivs, fashioned by sharpening everything from metal scraps to screwdrivers.

Kirk and several other white prisoners banded together and refused to be bullied. So they were attacked, one by one. When the Memphis Mafia caught up with Kirk, he wasn't in very good condition to protect himself.

A few weeks earlier, he and two pals had wriggled

through the window of a schoolbus used to transfer them between Brushy Mountain and a hospital in Nashville, and leaped out. Kirk was already recovering from a kidney stone operation, and when he jumped from the fast-moving vehicle he broke his heel and ankle. He was returned to the prison on crutches, with his leg in a cast.

He was hobbling around in the exercise yard when two of the Memphis toughs stabbed him seven times with a sharpened screwdriver and stomped on him. One of his lungs was punctured and his good leg was broken before an inmate pal came to his rescue.

After Kirk was patched up at an outside hospital and returned to the prison in a wheelchair, he began working to build up his wasted muscles. He exercised in the yard where the enemy could see what was going on, and know he wasn't waving the white flag. He and his supporters continued to refuse to pay tribute. Both sides began preparing for a showdown. Then the Memphis gang obtained a gun, smuggled into the prison.

On Sunday morning, February 8, 1982, Kirk got one of his own, a contraband .25-caliber pistol. That evening, he and his cronies, who had armed themselves with shivs, took a couple of guards as hostages. One of the men used a walkie-talkie to warn other corrections officers to stay out of the cellblock for awhile. "We're just gonna kill some niggers," he explained. Then the convict vigilantes began their payback.

Stalking through D block, the tough street kid from Chicago unloaded the pistol at the Memphis toughs. Stalking past the cells of terrified black inmates who weren't part of the gang, he singled out his enemies and shot them down one by one. The victims knew what was coming, but they were trapped in their cells with nowhere to flee.

When the handgun clicked empty, Kirk reloaded and continued firing. After the shooting at last ended, Kirk's pals pulled one of the injured men close to the bars and worked on him with their prison knives. Then they jammed the locks to slow down medics they knew would be sent by prison authorities, and surrendered to the guards.

Authorities, tallying up the score after the night of slaughter, found the two ringleaders of the Memphis mob, Nichols and Mitchell, were dead. Two others were seriously injured. One man escaped by barricading himself in a corner of his cell behind his upended mattress. Corrections authorities later dug two bullets out of the stuffing.

Although the imprisoned members of the Memphis Mafia weren't completely wiped out, the leaders were dead, and their power at Brushy Mountain was broken. The white convicts had done what they had to do, according to the prison code. But there were different rules outside the grim yellow walls of the hundred-year-old penitentiary, and a few weeks later Kirk and six other members of the accused execution squad were indicted by a Morgan county grand jury for murder and several lesser offenses.

When Morgan County Judge Lee Asbury parcelled out the cases to defense attorneys in the area, Bell was named to represent Kirk. Bell and the other lawyers appointed by the judge were to be paid a pittance for defending the convicts, compared to their usual fees.

As her boss's associate counsel, it was up to Mary to do most of the interviewing and leg work. In late August, she drove to Brushy Mountain for her first conference with Kirk. It was the first of many visits to the ominous old maximum security penitentiary. During the visits she interviewed members of the corrections staff and other convicts. But most of her time was spent with her macho, tattooed, silver-tongued client.

The handsome, bearded convict with the handlebar mustache and the expressive brown eyes was already known to other prisoners for his ability to wheedle naive women into smuggling cash and contraband to him at the prison. Consequently, the inmates kept a close eye on Kirk as he and his pretty young lawyer spent increasingly more time together in the semi-privacy of small conference rooms set aside at the prison for interviews.

Efficient and professional, she took notes during the interviews, observing that he grew up in a bad neighborhood of Chicago and stole things since early in his life. She also wrote:

"Basically, his employment history is that he worked five and one half hours one time for a doughnut store, and he thought it was incredibly boring, and a stupid way to make money, and so he's never had another job since then.

"The defendant told me that he is very interested in escaping from prison, that he has always tried to escape on every occasion that he could find to do so."

In January, it was decided that Mary would leave the law firm she was with. Bell told her she could continue to help prepare the case, however, and when Judge Asbury was advised of the development he said she could sit at the defense table during the trial. Mary began mailing resumes. She wrote that she was willing to relocate anywhere in the United States.

Her job hunting began during an especially difficult and stressful period for the young lawyer, who was working on her first capital case. Even if she managed to help her client evade a first-degree murder conviction, he could still be in grave danger of losing his life to another revenge-seeking convict at Brushy Mountain. It appeared that he was a marked man, regardless of which way the jury decision went.

And there was a strong indication that the young lawyer's concern for her client's welfare was sparked by more than purely professional considerations.

Although Mary was still flying off for romantic mini-vacations with her older lawyer boyfriend, her meetings with Kirk were far from typical of normal attorney-client relationships. Most attorneys don't peck their clients on the cheek when they break off a prison interview.

Nor do they plot to break their client out of prison.

Early in the new year as the trial date rapidly approached, Mary stepped up her visits and became such a familiar face at the prison gate that trusting guards sometimes allowed her to pass by without the usual searches. Eventually, she would mark up twenty-one visits with her client at Brushy Mountain. A corrections employee, who later talked about the frequent and lengthy conferences with Kirk, described her as becoming defensive and snappy with officers. But as a member of Kirk's defense team, she had a legal right to meet with him.

Even though some of her conferences with Kirk extended for ten hours or more, she made time to obtain a court order and schedule an appointment with a psychologist for an evaluation of her client. She set up the meeting for the office of Dr. Gary Salk in Oak Ridge.

Mary had been offered a job to work as an assistant public defender in London, Kentucky, a small town of about four thousand people in the middle of the coal mining country about one hundred miles from Knoxville for fifteen thousand dollars per year. She accepted, even though it might have seemed to be a curious career move for a young lawyer who already had a foot in the door and important contacts within the legal establishment of the much larger eastern Tennessee community where she had cut her eyeteeth as a lawyer.

Mary paid a three-hundred-and-fifty-dollar deposit on a three-bedroom house in London, after advising her would-be employer that she couldn't report for work on her new job until the day after her client's appointment with the psychologist. It was also understood that she would be given a leave of absence so that she could help represent Kirk during his trial.

When she met with Salk prior to the evaluation, she suggested that the work would probably go better if the convict's manacles were removed. Some phases of the testing called on the subject to move objects around. Dr. Salk agreed. He was a sympathetic man, a lanky, bearded Quaker, and belonged to the Prison Aid Society of Tennessee. Among other things, the society provided inmates with free counseling services.

The young lawyer also confirmed that Salk had no receptionist, and she checked out the building exits.

Mary filed a request with prison authorities for permission to have her client's handcuffs and chains removed during the testing. The examination was scheduled for March 31, only four days before the trial of Kirk and other members of the accused execution team was scheduled to begin.

On the day of the test, Kirk was strip-searched at Brushy Mountain then dressed in a bright orange jumpsuit before three guards accompanied him on the approximate twenty-mile drive in a prison van to the two-story office building in Oak Ridge. Inside, the manacles and chains were removed. When a guard asked if the leg irons should be taken off as well, Dr. Salk said to remove them. The psychologist rejected Mary's request to be present during the testing. But he consented when she asked to meet privately with her client in another room for a few minutes before the testing was

129

started.

He filled in answers to test questions for about an hour before taking a break to use the bathroom. After chatting a few moments with his guards in the hall, he returned for more testing. Then he asked for another private meeting with his attorney. After huddling with Mary for a few minutes in the private office, he returned and completed his tests. Salk told him to wait in the hall, while the tests were evaluated.

This time when Kirk strolled into the hall, Mary didn't stay to join in the small talk with the men. She walked out the front door, and a few moments later Kirk pulled a .25-caliber pistol from his jumpsuit and levelled it at the three startled guards.

Kirk advised that he didn't want to hurt anyone, but said he was prepared to do what had to be done. "Put your hands on top of your heads, and march your asses into that office," he ordered.

The psychologist was still working on the papers when the guards walked in with their hands on top of their heads. Salk thought it was a stupid joke, until he saw the gun in Kirk's hand. Kirk ordered him to remain seated at the desk, then made the guards kneel on the floor while keeping their hands on their heads. He had already taken away their .38-caliber revolvers when his accomplice walked inside the office. Mary was carrying a brown paper bag.

Without asking for directions, she quietly took out a pair of heavy scissors and snipped the cord to the telephone on the stunned psychologist's desk. Acting unhurriedly but with cold efficiency, she went about the deadly serious business of carrying out the escape. She asked Salk if he had a radio. He replied there was one on the receptionist's desk. She dialed it to a rock station, and turned the volume up loud. She also clipped the cord on the receptionist's phone.

Returning to Salk's office, she handed Kirk a roll of strong packing tape. Kirk responded by passing the handgun to her. By that time the guards were stretched out facedown on the floor, and as her convict companion busied himself taping their wrists together, she held the gun on Salk. When Kirk completed taping the wrists of each of the guards together, he made them cross their ankles and taped them together as well.

After the guards were securely bound, Kirk ordered Salk to lie down on the floor with his hands behind his back. Then the psychologist was also bound and gagged. Throughout the process, Kirk was courteous to Salk and the guards, and careful not to cause needless discomfort. When one of the guards complained of shoulder pains from bursitis, the convict loosened the tape on his wrists a bit.

But there were no signs of friendly concern from Kirk's lawyer. She showed no visible evidence of either fear or nervousness. She was calm and thorough, and her every move appeared to be as carefully calculated as if she were working on a routine legal matter. Later, Salk would describe her as "cool as ice. He was rather cool, too," the psychologist added, "but he seemed more nervous than she did."

Salk said that at one point while he was bound and lying on the floor, the heel of Mary's boot was next to his face. She was tapping her foot in time with the music. "To me, that epitomized how calm and cool she was throughout the whole thing," he said.

Kirk asked a few final questions of his prisoners, including a query about possible heart ailments. After he was assured that no one was expected to have a heart attack, he directed Mary to tape the mouths of the men. Then he sent her outside for his change of clothes. Kirk helped himself to twenty-five dollars from the psychologist's billfold, but left the guards' money untouched.

It was almost exactly 4:00 P.M., when she drove her red Toyota Celica to the building entrance, picked up a bushy-haired, bearded man in civilian clothes, and steered the car into traffic.

It was nearly two hours before James Copeland, one of the guards, managed to free his hands and hopped outside, and down the hall to another office where he telephoned for help. A few moments later, a description of Kirk, his lawyer, and her car was being broadcast to police agencies throughout eastern Tennessee and the northwest portion of neighboring North Carolina.

At that time there appeared to be a possibility that Mary was a hostage or unwilling participant in the escape. But the chances seemed even better that she was a willing accomplice, and two lovers were on the run.

Early the next morning a host of law enforcement officers from various agencies, including Tennessee State Police investigators, accompanied by nearly as many lawyer acquaintances of the missing woman, searched the apartment she shared with another female attorney. Mary's jewelry, personal grooming items, and her birth control pills were missing.

Late that afternoon her Toyota was found abandoned in a subdivision between Oak Ridge and Knoxville about an hour's drive from the psychologist's office. A quick search of the car turned up a wrapping for a roll of tape, like that used to bind Salk and the guards, with a receipt dated the previous day; a road map of Kentucky; a map of Atlanta; a paper bag with a new pair of men's underwear and socks inside; Mary's new Kentucky bank book showing a recent six-hundred-dollar deposit; and several other items. There were no blood spots or other signs of violence in the vehicle.

Investigators no longer had much doubt that Mary was a willing accomplice, and the saga of the runaway lovers quickly became the big news in Knoxville. The carefully crafted escape and the massive manhunt it sparked rapidly became a national news story, then an international story. Less than a week after the dramatic escape, the FBI joined in the investigation after dozens of reported sightings of the couple indicated the fugitives had fled across the state line.

Reports were coming in to authorities that the couple had been seen in Tennessee, Georgia, North Carolina, Florida, Illinois, and several other states. Police agencies were keeping an especially close watch on the north suburban Chicago town of Palatine, Illinois, where a couple of Kirk's sons were living with a relative. He had written in letters that he wanted to see the boys. After talking with friends and acquaintances of the missing lawyer, federal authorities also listed various cities around the country she had visited and could be expected to have some familiarity with.

Mary was named in a federal warrant charging her with unlawful interstate flight to avoid prosecution for aiding and abetting the escape of a convict, and for aggravated assault. A wanted flyer warned that she and her companion were believed armed with the .25-caliber automatic and the three handguns taken from the guards. The flyer also cautioned that she reportedly had suicidal tendencies. She was described as being slender, five-foot, four-inches, to five-foot, five-inches tall, 103 to 118 pounds, with green eyes, and blond hair with brown roots.

The federal warrant for Kirk charged him with unlawful interstate flight to avoid prosecution for aggravated assault, armed robbery, and escape. Mug shots showing him both bearded and clean shaven were printed on the wanted flyer, and several possible aliases were listed. He was additionally described as of medium build, about five-foot, eleven-inches to six-foot tall, and 177 to 190 pounds, with brown eyes and brown shoulder-length hair.

As reporters tracked down acquaintances and colleagues of the fugitive lawyer and interviewed them one by one, a picture of a quixotic woman took form.

On one hand she was said to be intelligent, idealistic, methodical, and an apparently ambitious but exceptionally private woman who discouraged casual friendships and small talk. But uncomplimentary words such as "rebellious," "loner," "cold," "cynical," "aloof," and "abrasive" also kept cropping up in interviews with her former instructors and classmates at the university, and with other acquaintances in their descriptions of Evans.

On the other hand, she was seen to be mesmerized by the glib convict and fanatically determined not only to save him from the electric chair, but to win an outright acquittal on the murder charges. According to news and feature stories, she had given up on the system, however. Salk said he believed she fell in love with her client while working on his defense.

Steve O. Watson, assistant director of the Tennessee Bureau of Investigation, remarked, "Lawyers don't usually help their clients escape the law in quite this way." He said he didn't think anything like Kirk's escape had ever happened before in Tennessee.

"It's very simple," Bell told a journalist. "Mary is an impressionable lawyer. She's still a woman. She may think she's in love with him."

Mary's former boss said he believed she was brainwashed by Kirk's dominant personality and charm. He compared the event to Patty Hearst's behavior a few years earlier after she was kidnapped by a group of young terrorists who called themselves the Symbionese Liberation Army. After a period of captivity the young newspaper heiress wound up with an automatic weapon in her arms, helping the gang stage a bank robbery.

There was also talk about the Stockholm Syndrome, a phrase coined after two female bank clerks held hostage for five days during a bungled robbery in Sweden became engaged to a couple of their captors. Today the term is frequently used to describe people who react to extreme pressure or coercion by sympathizing with or allowing their abusers to control them psychologically.

And when a reporter talked with her former clergyman, who had moved to a pastorate in Florida, the minister recalled her as a free thinker who "could hurt you with her tongue."

Knoxville's shaken legal community found itself in the middle of a debate about how closely neophyte lawyers should be supervised when working closely with criminal clients. Jokes were bandied about at local watering holes about runaway lawyers with runaway hormones. And there was concerned talk that the case might somehow inhibit the work of female attorneys or destroy trust in their ability to handle criminal cases.

But the local legal establishment was also looking ahead to the time when Mary would be returned to the Tennessee Criminal Court system as a defendant, rather than as counsel for an accused client.

Meanwhile, as her family prayed and looked for spiritual guidance in their efforts to cope with the shock and worry, Mary and her renegade lover were making good their escape.

When the fugitives abandoned Mary's Toyota and its tattletale license tags, they switched to another car that was waiting for them. Within the next few days they stayed in an isolated East Tennessee farmhouse, then in a motel room in Statesville, North Carolina. While they were at the farmhouse, Mary cut her hair and dyed it back closer to its original brown. Kirk shaved his beard, and restyled his hair into an Afro.

In Statesville, they mingled with a crowd that was in town for a golf tournament, bought new clothes, and read newspapers and watched television broadcasts for stories about the fugitive lovers whose daring flight had captured the imagination of the country.

Ten days after the couple fled from the Oak Ridge office, Mary telephoned a woman friend she had attended law school with. Calling collect, she asked her friend to inform her father that she was safe and had never been happier in her life. The friend and her husband, who listened in on the call, notified the FBI.

A few hours later, federal officers were hurrying to Columbia, South Carolina. The call had been made from the Trailways Bus terminal there. But there was no trace of Mary Pentecost Evans or William Timothy Kirk.

The day after the call, the Anderson County Grand Jury returned criminal indictments charging each of them with four counts of robbery, four counts of aggravated kidnapping, and escape.

As increasing numbers of FBI agents and other law enforcement officers became involved in the burgeoning manhunt, new sightings of the couple were reported at the rate of three or four every week. Agents and local police investigated reports of sightings in Pennsylvania, Massachusetts, Nebraska, and in Nashville.

Investigators checked out the corpse of a blond girl dressed in blue jeans who was found in a quarry in Cleveland, Tennessee. There was no I. D. on the body and her face was virtually destroyed. The remains of another girl found in Anderson county, a short distance from where Mary's Toyota was abandoned, was also checked out. Neither body was that of the missing lawyer.

There was concern among some of the investigators and others that if the pressure of the manhunt became too great for Kirk, he might murder his companion to help hide his trail.

Three weeks after the couple fled, Tennessee's Governor Lamar Alexander posted a five-thousand-dollar reward for information leading to the capture of the fugitives. Approximately a week after that, Mary's family issued a formal statement to the press, expressing their love and confidence in her, and their concern for her safety. In the statement, they accused the press of inaccuracies. They wrote that they expected her to be vindicated, and remarked, "We abhor the reports which appear to assume Mary's guilt in this matter."

By the time the statement was issued, Mary and her convict charmer had ridden buses to Florida and were hopping about the Sunshine State, living in motels. When they checked into the Econo-Line Motel in Sarasota, they registered as Robert Farmer, Jr., and Sharon Farmer, from Tennessee. Kirk told most people who inquired about his job that he was a salesman. Then the couple rented an old Mercury from a used car rental agency, and applied themselves to the task of obtaining new I. D.

Drawing on some of the lessons he learned on the streets and in prisons, Kirk spent an afternoon with Mary in a local cemetery. There they copied down the names and birthdates of four children from headstones, a nine-year-old boy, and three little girls, one two-year-old and two others who died within a week after birth. Each had died when they were too young to have obtained a social security number, or a driver's license that could be used to help trace them. But their birth records would be on file with the county, and copies could be obtained and used by the fugitives to acquire false identification in the form of driver's licenses and social security cards.

As Kirk watched, Mary picked up cards listing birth information about the four children at the Sarasota County Health Department. She explained she wanted the information for a genealogy class at the University of South Florida.

A short time later driver's licenses were issued at the Department of Motor Vehicles office in Sarasota in the names of Lisa Jo-Ann Richard and Robert Allen Allred. Lisa Jo-Ann was the two year old, and Robert was the nine year old whose names were copied from the tombstones.

For a time the lovers stayed in a bungalow on Siesta Key, an island barely bigger than a sand spit just off Sarasota, and made a few side trips in the rented car to North Carolina. But they always returned to Florida, and after a few weeks when Kirk decided they had pushed their luck by staying too long in one place they drove across the state to the Atlantic Coast. During two months in Florida, including the trips back-and-forth to North Carolina, the couple would put five thousand miles on their rental car.

Shortly before they left the Gulf coast, however, Kirk quit making the rental payments on the car. When the payments stopped and the vehicle wasn't returned, the manager of the rental agency reported it stolen. But the fugitives weren't driving the rental car anymore, anyway. Kirk had laid out two thousand three hundred dollars in one-hundred-dollar bills for a 1977 Thunderbird. The former owner of the car recalled that the buyer's pockets were stuffed with cash.

While the couple remained on the lam, Judge Asbury was going ahead with plans to put Kirk and his accused convict confederates on trial for the terrible Sunday night of bloodletting at Brushy Mountain. The judge severed the fugitive's trial from those of the others, and early in April the proceeding began at the old Morgan County Courthouse in Wartburg. Attorney Creed Daniel, of Knoxville, had been appointed to replace Mary as cocounsel with Bell. An empty chair was set at the defense table for the defendant.

Neil Cohen, a professor from the University of Tennessee Law School where both Mary and her father graduated, was also permitted by the court to join the defense team as a cocounsel. Cohen pointed out that the trial was the first capital case in America to be tried while the defendant was absent.

Kirk's old prison pal, Crafton, was a key defense witness and clearly made a good impression on at least some members of the jury of seven women and five men. He had taken psychology courses, and was comfortable and smooth on the witness stand. He provided the jury with a vivid description of prison life, and of the pressures from the Memphis gang that led to the shootings on D block.

According to his testimony, it was a simple case of self-defense: kill or be killed. It seemed clear from the colorful testimony that Kirk and his cronies were at the top of the Memphis gang's hit list.

The jury deliberated a little more than eight hours before returning a verdict of guilty on two counts of voluntary manslaughter; three counts of intent to commit voluntary manslaughter; and one count of aggravated kidnapping.

Most court observers considered the verdicts to be a victory for the defense. By avoiding conviction for first-degree murder, Kirk had sidestepped the death penalty. One juror told reporters off the record that the panel believed the defense contention that Kirk and his codefendants were motivated by fear for their own lives.

The jury recommended a life sentence, plus seven to twenty-five years on the convictions. But Judge Asbury delayed formal sentencing until after Kirk's recapture.

After arriving on Florida's Atlantic Coast, the fugitives had settled in at a Best Western motel in Daytona Beach. On July 14, they registered as Robert Allen Allred and Lisa Jo-Ann Richard, and paid cash for a small fourteen dollar-a-day room with a kingsize bed. Then they applied themselves to the job of enjoying the sun and the sand, and visiting the Daytona Beach Kennel Club to bet on the dogs. They watched the races in afternoons and evenings, and usually played two-dollar bets. And usually they lost.

Evenings after the races they drank rosé wine in their room and in the motel lounge; played card games; or leafed through magazines.

After nearly two months on the run, their financial resources were rapidly dwindling, and their opportunities to replenish their cash were sharply limited. They were afraid to get jobs that would plug them into the taxing and social security systems and risk exposure through their phony I. D.; and the search for them was already intense enough without Kirk heating it up by pulling a robbery.

Kirk introduced his girlfriend to the seedy world of pawnshops. On one occasion, they hocked a gun and a gold necklace for one hundred and forty dollars at Joe's Pawn Shop in suburban Orlando. A few days later, Kirk redeemed the weapon, but left the jewelry.

* * *

When they began telephoning from the motel and asking friends to telegraph cash to them, their time and luck started to run out as well as their money. Mary made one cash pickup at the Western Union Office in Daytona that was sent in the name of Lisa Richard. Kirk made two pickups of money wired to Richard Allred. The clerk was suspicious of Kirk and tipped off the FBI that a man who looked a lot like the face on one of their wanted posters had been there to pick up money.

The FBI and other law enforcement officers at last had the break they had been looking for. But they were already closing in. By the time they were tipped off by the Western Union clerk, they had already talked with the operator of the pawn shop where the gun was hocked and confirmed that the customer fit Kirk's description.

On a stiflingly hot late summer afternoon on August 17, Mary walked into the Western Union Office in Daytona. Kirk waited a few yards away in a battered white station wagon parked alongside the street.

Mary had put on weight and her hair was long again, styled as it had been during her lawyering days. She was wearing a pair of blue jeans and a black T-shirt when she slid her purse onto the counter and prepared to sign for the three hundred and fifty dollars. Suddenly six FBI agents, with guns drawn, materialized as if from nowhere and yelled, "Freeze, Mary. FBI!" In moments an agent was snapping cuffs on her hands, while another was dumping the contents of her purse on the floor.

Outside, another team of federal lawmen had dragged Kirk from the car and had him cuffed and spread-eagled facedown on the pavement. He had eighty-seven cents in his pocket when the agents jumped him. The fifteen-year-old Ford was registered in the name, Lisa Jo-Ann Richard.

The couple had been on the run for 139 days. They

were tired, broke, and scruffy.

When arresting officers took a good, close look at Kirk they noticed that he had altered a couple of his old tattoos. The rose and arrow previously decorating his left forearm were now covered by a drawing of the Grim Reaper. Another new tattoo on his right arm had eliminated his initials, "T. K."

Later as one team of agents searched the motel room, others drove the prisoners in separate cars to Orlando where they were jailed overnight. The search of the motel love nest turned up an intriguing collection of possessions. Among property confiscated by the agents were: pawnshop receipts; a copy of the *Anarchist's Cookbook;* several instant photos of the couple; birth certificates for three females and a male, including Robert Allen Allred and Lisa Jo-Ann Richard; a pair of driver's licenses with headstone aliases used by each of the fugitives; a bullet-proof vest; birth control pills; a bottle of hydrogen peroxide; a platoon of bottled nail polish and polish remover; designer clothes; magazines carrying their horoscopes, Sagittarius for her, Aquarius for him; and various other items.

The day after the arrests, Knoxville lawyers attended a hastily arranged hearing in Orlando where the couple waived their extradition rights. A U. S. Magistrate released them from federal custody and turned them over to state authorities from Tennessee. The prisoners were shackled and driven back to Knoxville in a caravan of cars, each riding in a different vehicle. During the trip however, they stopped briefly in Henderson, South Carolina, and the couple was allowed to brush their cuffed hands together as the sun set. One of the guards later recalled the tender scene.

"She was acting like a woman in love," he was quoted in the *Washington Post.* "You could see it in her eyes every time she looked at (Kirk). She seemed relieved to be caught, but scared that she was about to face the music."

They were returned to Clinton on Friday night, amid a glare of television and still cameras. Mary's eyes were red-rimmed, and her hair was dirty and stringy, but her long fingernails were perfectly polished. She was locked up in the women's section of the three-story Anderson County Jail for the weekend. Her muscular companion of the last four-and-a-half months remained in Clinton just long enough for the couple to say a few hurried words of goodbye, and for him to kiss her on the cheek before he was whisked away and driven back to prison in Nashville.

"They just stood and looked at each other in a daze like they hated to leave each other," a sheriff's department officer who witnessed the star-crossed couple's last moments together later recalled.

Mary had changed from her T-shirt and scruffy blue jeans into a neat pale blue business suit, blouse and platform shoes for her Monday morning bond hearing before Circuit Judge James L. "Buddy" Scott at the Anderson County Courthouse a few miles west of Knoxville in Clinton, Tennessee. She had spent her first nights at the jail, held on one hundred thousand dollars bail.

Less than a year earlier, she had applied for a job in Anderson county as an assistant district attorney. Now, instead of appearing as an officer of the court, she was a defendant in what promised to become one of the most notorious and bizarre criminal cases in county history.

It was a curious and poignant gathering of lawyers preparing to witness the criminal justice system in action at the beginning of the ponderous process that would ultimately determine the fate of one of their own. Most of Mary's close friends and many of her acquaintances had gathered protectively around her. Her former roommate was there to assist in her defense with attorney Robert W. Ritchie. Other attorney friends

143

were in spectator seats.

District Attorney General James Ramsey, who was representing the state, had sat next to her father in a property class during law school, and the hearing marked the first time in ten years he had seen Pentecost. Ramsey argued for raising Mary's bond to five hundred thousand dollars. Her attorney asked that her bond be lowered to $79,999.

"She was a willing participant before, during and after the event," Ramsey declared in his argument for the high bond. "She's violated a public and professional trust already. There has been speculation that she has forfeited her law career. If she has evinced a willingness to forfeit that, then she would be willing to forfeit quite a lot."

During testimony by character witnesses for the defendant, Knoxville lawyer Jerry Becker, whose firm had employed her as a law clerk while she was still a student, described her as a self-starter who was principled, committed, and did high quality work. "I believe that Mary Evans is a person who cares very deeply about the principle of equal justice under the law," he declared.

A woman, whose daughter grew up with the defendant, recalled a childhood filled with Sunday afternoon visits to the Mount Olive Baptist Church. "I know her almost as well as I know my own daughter," the witness assured the court. "If Mary Evans says she'll be here for the trial, she'll be here."

The defendant sat in stony silence while her parents and others in the packed courtroom intently followed the proceedings. As the hearing neared conclusion, Judge Scott set bail at fifty thousand dollars on each of the charges, a total of four hundred and fifty thousand dollars. The bond was only fifty thousand dollars short of the amount asked by Ramsey, but Mary's father testified that he was ready to stake everything he had on her honoring the pact to show up for trial.

When Mary's attorney asked him if he had any qualms about putting up his home, Pentecost emotionally replied, "As God is my witness, I have none."

Mary waited behind bars at the county jail until her father posted an $802,000 property bond, that included pledging the family's $176,000 home and nearly seven hundred thousand dollars worth of subdivision property in nearby Monroe county owned by close relatives. Less than a week after her arrest, Mary walked out of the County Jail with her parents and climbed in their car for the short drive to her childhood home. Her codefendant, who was being portrayed by some friends and the press as a prison-wise Svengali who had seduced a naive young girl, remained behind bars.

A few weeks later, Mary's attorneys arranged for her to begin seeing a Knoxville psychiatrist. The lawyers had already notified prosecutors they would contend her mental condition was impaired when Kirk's dramatic escape was pulled off at the psychologist's office.

Near the end of November the court ordered her admitted to the Middle Tennessee Mental Health Institute in Nashville for determination of her mental condition at the time of the escape, and to evaluate her ability to assist in her own defense.

Kirk was only a few miles away, back once again in the old penitentiary at Nashville. He was held on Death Row, for his own safety as much as to prevent another possible escape.

Early in March, 1984, nearly a year after Mary Evans ran off with her client, she pleaded guilty before Judge Scott to aiding and abetting Kirk's escape. The

145

prosecutor joined Mary's lawyer in recommending she be given a suspended sentence and placed on three years' probation. According to the plea bargain arrangement she would voluntarily enter a mental hospital for extensive psychiatric treatment. All other charges of armed robbery and kidnapping would be dismissed.

The agreement called for Mary to repay the twenty-five dollars stolen from the psychologist, to pay for the three guns taken from the guards, and for a damaged telephone.

If Mary had been convicted on all the charges previously filed against her and given the maximum penalties, she could have been ordered to serve eight life sentences.

As part of the pact, Kirk also pleaded guilty to armed robbery and escape. The prosecutor recommended tacking another forty years onto his sentence for the shootings at Brushy Mountain. Kirk's attorney said his client agreed to what he described as a package deal because he thought it was in Mary's best interest. Although the convicted killer peered at Mary frequently during the hearing, she didn't return his glances.

Ramsey explained that he didn't believe he could obtain a conviction against Mary because psychiatrists had agreed she was insane when she helped Kirk make his escape. Even the state's psychiatrist had decided she was insane. Consequently, the prosecutor agreed to the deal.

Judge Scott wasn't bound by the agreement, and he announced that he would decide if he would accept the plea bargain deal, after hearing testimony from psychiatrists. "Probation is a privilege, and they've got to convince me she's deserving of probation," he explained.

The development sparked a flurry of anger and disgust among some professionals in Knoxville's criminal justice system. Many law enforcement officers who had

146

spent hundreds of hours on the case were outraged. Feathers were already ruffled over the district attorney's decision to forego prosecution of an old childhood friend of Mary for wiring money to her in Florida. Ramsey agreed not to press the case in court in return for the woman's cooperation.

It appeared to some elements in the community that the stage was set to give a wrist slap penalty to the woman who had betrayed her trust as an attorney, betrayed the legal community, and betrayed her family and friends, while cavalierly tossing away her good name and career to become the gun moll of a dangerous lifetime criminal. In coffee shops and local lounges and taverns, residents of Knox and Anderson counties grumbled about two separate sets of rules: one for members of the legal profession; another for everyone else.

In an angry editorial, the *Knoxville Journal* described Mary as a woman who threw away her "career by springing a convict who said he loved her," and was on the lam for months in "an adventure whose high points seemed to have been betting on dog racing, taking care of her fingernails and avoiding pregnancy."

Ramsey also came in for fierce criticism in the editorial for bargaining away the jury's responsibility to make determinations in the case. The action was taken in the interests of a fellow lawyer who committed a felony and would now never be prosecuted for it, the newspaper trumpeted. In what was almost a sidelight, it was pointed out that Mary still had her license to practice law. She voluntarily surrendered the document a few days later, and in a letter to the state Supreme Court's Board of Professional Responsibility, admitted the charges against her were true.

The prosecutor said that if he had gone ahead with the trial, it was a sure thing Mary would have been acquitted as temporarily insane. Despite his strong defense of the decision, however, Ramsey conceded that even his mother gave him a tongue-lashing over the affair.

* * *

At the hearing several days later, psychiatrists testified that it wasn't love that drove the pretty young attorney to run away with the bushy-haired convict, but
madness.

In documents filed with the court, the doctors wrote
that she told them, "the escape was not a Romeo and Ju-
liet thing like the newspapers reported and that the
point was not sex. The point was I would not be me anymore."

On the witness stand they described her as living in a
terrifying hallucinatory world of disembodied voices,
brightly colored balls of light, sneering demons, pounc-
ing tigers, and flying carpets. When she was seventeen
she repeatedly dreamed over a two-week period of stabbing a boyfriend until there was nothing left of him but
holes; during her marriage she chased her husband out
of their home with a kitchen knife because she wanted to
be alone; and about six months before meeting Kirk she
tried to commit suicide with an overdose of prescription
medicine, the psychiatrists said.

"She's clearly a paranoid schizophrenic," Dr. Robert
Sadoff testified. He said he didn't believe she was capable of love.

According to the Philadelphia psychiatrist, she was
terrorized by inner demons that tormented her since
childhood, and she fantasized that she could draw
strength from the persuasive and domineering convict.

"I had no choice . . . I was mentally ill, and Tim Kirk
was my only salvation. He would teach me to control
myself. I had to go with Tim because I had to save my
soul," the witness quoted her as telling him.

Dr. Sadoff contended the troubled attorney depended
on the convict as her last chance of sanity, and the only
alternative was suicide. And he warned that he feared
she would still try suicide "when she realizes that there
are no Tim Kirks around, no magic that will make her

148

strong and in control."

Dr. Jerry Embry testified that she was tormented by voices that used to tell her not to let people know she was sick because they wouldn't like her. Sometimes she would curl up in a fetal position in a cubbyhole under the kitchen sink and scream for the voices to stop, he said.

The psychiatrist, who spent nearly sixty hours examining Mary, said Mary believed Kirk could protect her from the alien beings that were tormenting her. He explained that she felt her head had been invaded by alien beings who wanted to torment and control her. She felt she had to do something to save her convict client and herself, he explained.

He said she began idolizing Kirk after she was assigned to help represent him, and came to believe he could remake her into a different person and save her from psychological disaster.

Judge Scott asked if Mary's feelings for Kirk could be considered to be love. "It really only could be considered love . . . in the sense that an infant perceives a parent. It was a sense of need," Dr. Embry replied.

Describing her as a loner who had difficulty controlling her urges, the witness said she once drove to Atlanta where she ate at a McDonald's, then made the long return trip home. When she was younger, she once burned a hole in the head of her Barbie doll and slashed open a favorite teddy bear with a knife, Dr. Embry recalled.

Interrupting the testimony to question the witness himself, the judge observed that law libraries have publications dealing with the insanity defense that describe various hallucinations similar to some of those Embry had been describing. Judge Scott also pointed out that those same publications were available to Mary, and that she had the education and intelligence to understand them.

Dr. Embry said he didn't believe she was faking mental illness. "She would have to know an awful lot of theory to pull this thing off," he declared. He also testified that he didn't believe Mary posed a danger to others, as long as she submitted to regular mental treatment.

Dressed neatly in a dark dress and brown jacket, Mary watched and listened to the testimony without visible emotion. But her father, seated in the spectator section, brushed at tears as her sobbing voice was heard on seven minutes of a tape-recorded interview with one of the psychiatrists that was played for the court.

"They are so bad sometimes," her voice was heard saying of the hallucinations. "It's like a bunch of them talking all at once, and I can't understand what they're saying."

Earlier in the hearing Gary Tullock, who interviewed Mary for six hours while preparing a presentencing report, suggested that if she was put on probation she should be assigned to community service and put in some of that time cleaning out cages at the local zoo. The probation officer said in his report that Mary told him she obtained the pistol used in the escape from Kirk during one of their meetings at Brushy Mountain.

He also said she told him she was never in love with the macho convict. "She cared for him as a friend and at the time she knew she was thinking about him in a different way," Tullock wrote.

Judge Scott delayed sentencing until the next day, and recommended that Mary testify before he announced his decision. "If she has a repentant spirit, I would like to hear about it. I want to do justice and I can't do it based on what I have heard here," he said.

"I'm concerned because frankly, I do not feel she has a

repentant spirit. She didn't think it was wrong then and she doesn't today."

Mary's lawyer, however, contended that it would be dangerous to her mental health for her to testify. Ritchie assured the stern jurist that his client was, nevertheless, repentant and remorseful.

Before beginning Mary's hearing, the judge had sentenced Kirk to another forty-year term to be tacked onto the sixty-five-year prison term he was already serving for armed robbery. Sentence was still to be pronounced in Morgan county for the shootings at Brushy Mountain.

Judge Scott followed the prosecution's recommendation in regard to the offenses committed by the killer convict during the escape. However, when the courtroom was cleared at the end of the day, speculation was divided about the possibility the judge would do the same when it was time to sentence Kirk's former fellow fugitive.

Ritchie still refused to allow Mary to take the witness stand when court reconvened the next morning. Before announcing the sentence, the judge said he didn't believe she had cooperated fully with authorities in identifying people who had helped them while they were on the run.

Then he tossed aside the probated sentence the defense and state had agreed on, and ordered a three-year prison term without probation for the renegade lawyer. It was the maximum penalty allowable for the offense. Judge Scott revoked her bond and ordered her taken to Brushy Mountain, which had been converted to a classification center for men and women.

Mary whispered to her lawyer, and Ritchie asked the judge to amend his order and send her somewhere else. He claimed the staff at Brushy Mountain was hostile to his client. After some discussion it was agreed that Mary would be temporarily housed in the Knox County Jail.

A few days later, exactly a year after she and Kirk began their near five month odyssey on the run, the disbarred attorney was handcuffed and loaded aboard a prison van. Then she was driven to the Tennessee State Penitentiary for Women in Nashville.

Several weeks later she broke her self-imposed silence with the media, and gave a far-ranging interview to Nashville's largest newspaper, *The Tennessean*. Chain-smoking cigarettes and with her blond hair pulled back in a braid, she talked about her anger over the frenzied press coverage of her case and speculation about her mental state. She was also angry at a news report she had been denied a job as a paralegal at the prison. She said she never applied.

Mary said she read and watched soap operas while awaiting her release. And she revealed that a man in Malaysia had written, asking to marry her. Another would-be suitor from the West Indies also wrote. She refused to comment when she was asked if she had heard from Kirk, who was locked up a few miles away.

In May, 1984, Judge Asbury sentenced Kirk to four to ten years on each of the counts of manslaughter, and from one to five years on each count of assault with intent to commit voluntary manslaughter. The jurist stipulated the term was not to begin until Kirk completed serving the armed robbery sentence. Based on all the sentences ordered since he first walked through the doors of the penitentiary in Nashville, Kirk would not become eligible for parole until 2038, when he was ninety-one-years-old.

Six months after Mary was locked up in the women's prison, she appeared before the Tennessee Board of Parole for her first hearing. Polite, several pounds slimmer,

Danielle Steel

Ted Bundy

Carole Boone Bundy

Kristen Joan Svege Watson
(COURTESY OF SAN LUIS OBISPO *TELEGRAM-TRIBUNE*)

Charles "Tex" Watson
(AUTHOR'S COLLECTION)

CERTIFICATION OF VITAL RECORD

COUNTY OF SAN LUIS OBISPO

SAN LUIS OBISPO, CALIFORNIA

CERTIFICATE OF REGISTRY OF MARRIAGE

PERSONAL DATA. LICENSE TO MARRY. CERTIFICATION OF MARRIAGE

9715

GROOM PERSONAL DATA

NAME OF GROOM — FIRST NAME: **CHARLES**	MIDDLE NAME: **DENTON**	LAST NAME: **WATSON**	DATE OF BIRTH: **12-2-45**

AGE: **33** YEARS — NUMBER OF THIS MARRIAGE: **First**

RESIDENCE OF GROOM — STREET ADDRESS: **Box A-E Room 7206, CMC** — CITY OR TOWN: **San Luis Obispo** — COUNTY: **San Luis Obispo**

PRESENT OR LAST OCCUPATION: **Minister** — KIND OF INDUSTRY OR BUSINESS: **Prison Chapel** — HIGHEST SCHOOL GRADE COMPLETED: **15**

NAME OF FATHER OF GROOM: **Clarence Denton Watson** — BIRTHPLACE OF FATHER: **Texas** — MAIDEN NAME OF MOTHER OF GROOM: **Mary Elizabeth Montgomery** — BIRTHPLACE OF MOTHER: **Texas**

BRIDE PERSONAL DATA

NAME OF BRIDE — FIRST NAME: **KRISTIN** — MIDDLE NAME: **JOAN** — LAST NAME: **SVEGE** — DATE OF BIRTH: **7-22-59**

AGE: **20** YEARS — NUMBER OF THIS MARRIAGE: **First** — BIRTHPLACE: **New Jersey**

RESIDENCE OF BRIDE — STREET ADDRESS: **435 Cuesta Dr.** — CITY OR TOWN: **San Luis Obispo** — COUNTY: **San Luis Obispo**

PRESENT OR LAST OCCUPATION: **Casa De Vida** — KIND OF INDUSTRY OR BUSINESS: **Home for Handicapped** — HIGHEST SCHOOL GRADE COMPLETED: **12** — MAIDEN NAME OF BRIDE:

NAME OF FATHER OF BRIDE: **Tommy Olav Svege** — BIRTHPLACE OF FATHER: **Norway** — MAIDEN NAME OF MOTHER OF BRIDE: **Joan Bronson** — BIRTHPLACE OF MOTHER: **New York**

AFFIDAVIT OF BRIDE AND GROOM

WE THE BRIDE AND GROOM NAMED IN THIS CERTIFICATE EACH FOR HIMSELF STATE THAT THE FOREGOING INFORMATION IS CORRECT TO THE BEST OF OUR KNOWLEDGE AND BELIEF AND THAT NO LEGAL OBJECTION TO THE MARRIAGE NOR TO THE ISSUANCE OF A LICENSE TO AUTHORIZE THE SAME IS KNOWN TO US AND HEREBY APPLY FOR LICENSE TO MARRY

BRIDE (SIGNATURE): *Kristen Joan Svege* — GROOM (SIGNATURE): *Charles Denton Watson*

LICENSE TO MARRY

AUTHORIZATION AND LICENSE IS HEREBY GIVEN TO ANY PERSON DULY AUTHORIZED BY THE LAWS OF THE STATE OF CALIFORNIA TO PERFORM A MARRIAGE CEREMONY WITHIN THE STATE OF CALIFORNIA TO SOLEMNIZE THE MARRIAGE OF THE ABOVE NAMED PERSONS REQUIRED CONSENTS FOR THE ISSUANCE OF THIS LICENSE ARE ON FILE

SUBSCRIBED AND SWORN TO BEFORE ME ON **8-15-79** — DATE LICENSE ISSUED **8-15-79** — LICENSE NO. **25316** — COUNTY CLERK: **Nisbeth Wollam**

EXPIRATION DATE **Nov. 13, 1979** — COUNTY OF ISSUE OF LICENSE **San Luis Obispo**

WITNESSES

SIGNATURE OF WITNESS: *Norman Ezell* — ADDRESS OF WITNESS — STREET ADDRESS: **Gloryland Ministries P.O. Box 542** — CITY OR TOWN AND STATE: **Modesto, CA 95353**

SIGNATURE OF WITNESS: *____ Platt* — ADDRESS OF WITNESS — STREET ADDRESS: **500 Nelson** — CITY OR TOWN AND STATE: **Arroyo Grande, CA 93420**

CERTIFICATION OF PERSON PERFORMING CEREMONY

I HEREBY CERTIFY THAT THE ABOVE NAMED BRIDE AND GROOM WERE JOINED BY ME IN MARRIAGE IN ACCORDANCE WITH THE LAWS OF THE STATE OF CALIFORNIA

DATE: **September 7** **19 79** — AT: **San Luis Obispo**, CALIFORNIA

SIGNATURE OF PERSON PERFORMING CEREMONY AND OFFICIAL TITLE: *J. A. Milton* **Ordained Minister**

NAME OF PERSON PERFORMING CEREMONY: **Rev. John S. Milton** — OFFICIAL TITLE: **Assemblies of God**

ADDRESS — STREET ADDRESS OR TOWN AND STATE: **207 Pilgrim Way, Arroyo Grande, CA 93420**

LOCAL REGISTRAR OF MARRIAGES (COUNTY MARRIAGES)

DATE ACCEPTED FOR REGISTRATION: **SEP 19 1979** — LOCAL REGISTRAR — SIGNATURE: *Wm. C. Ziearih* Recorder

STATE OF CALIFORNIA. DEPARTMENT OF HEALTH. OFFICE OF THE STATE REGISTRAR OF VITAL STATISTICS

CERTIFIED COPY OF VITAL RECORDS

19262

STATE OF CALIFORNIA } ss
COUNTY OF SAN LUIS OBISPO

DATE ISSUED: **AUG 27 1992**

This is a true and exact reproduction of the document officially registered and placed on file in the office of the SAN LUIS OBISPO COUNTY RECORDER.

Jim Cooney

FRANCIS M. COONEY
COUNTY CLERK - RECORDER

This copy not valid unless prepared on engraved border displaying seal and signature of the County Registrar.

ANY ALTERATION OR ERASURE VOIDS THIS CERTIFICATE

Marriage license of Charles and Kristen Joan Watson
(AUTHOR'S COLLECTION)

Sue Lyon

Garry "Cotton" Adamson

Sue Lyon submitting to a routine search before her prison wedding.

Garrett Brock Trapnell

Joyce Bailey Mattox

Jon E. Yount

Diane Brenda Brodbeck

William T. Kirk

Mary P. Evans

Eugene Kerns

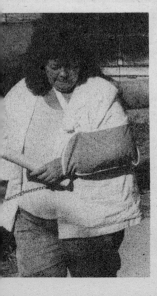

Sandra Kay Beeman

Frank Gable
(COURTESY OF DOUG BEAGTEL
THE OREGONIAN)

Karen Steele
(COURTESY OF
SHAN GORDON)

Doris Irene Oliphant Frost

 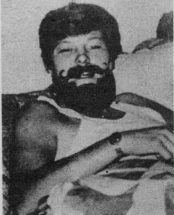

Dana Sue Jones

James Earl Ray

Anna Sandhu Ray holding her marriage license

Richard Ramirez

Kelly Marquez
(COURTESY OF KELLY MARQUEZ)

Allan Legere
(COURTESY OF CANAPRESS PHOTO SERVICE)

Caroline Norwood Allan
(COURTESY OF CANAPRESS PHOTO SERVICE)

Lemuel Smith

Dawn Langley Simmons

Ken Bianchi

John Wayne Gacy, Jr.

and with her blond hair again pulled back in a single French braid, she admitted she had made a serious mistake, and said she was sorry for her disastrous fling with the convict conman.

She was dressed in an attractive beige sweater jacket, white skirt, rust blouse and boots, and flanked by her parents as she replied to questions from board members. "I regret it very much," she said of the escapade. "There's no doubt in my mind that it was a serious mistake."

"I had gotten the impression ever since I started practicing law . . . that justice is something that's hard to find," she explained. "I did feel a tremendous pressure to do something. I knew that there was nothing legally I could do."

Members of the board voted by a slim 3-2 margin for her release after serving the minimum amount of time on the sentence. Chairman Neville Trammell joined with the two female members of the board to recommend parole, but attached a proviso that she submit to treatment from a mental health specialist.

Shortly after that she was transferred to the Community Services Center, a work-release facility in Chattanooga. She went to work as a clerical worker with a local law firm, earning the minimum wage of $3.35-an-hour filing, typing, and doing research. She remained there only a few days, however, before she had to leave because other attorneys complained it wasn't proper for a disbarred lawyer to be working for the firm.

Finally, a little less than eleven months after she was sentenced to prison, she left the work-release center on parole and climbed into a car for the ride home with her parents. This time she went to work at a Knoxville factory helping to assemble stereo speakers on a regular 7:30 A.M. to 4 P.M. shift.

She didn't stick with the factory work long, however,

and soon moved to South Florida to live with her younger brother and accepted a job as a data processor for a construction company in Boca Raton.

In May, 1985, she remarried. But she didn't change her name. The groom was thirty-five-year-old William S. Evans, Jr., the first cousin of her former husband. It was her ex-spouse, in fact, who introduced the two. According to documents filed at the Palm Beach County Courthouse in West Palm Beach, the couple planned to live a few miles south of there in Pompano Beach. Her ex-husband had also settled in Pompano Beach.

If Kirk's heart was broken by the news, he soon got over it. The following August, officials with the Tennessee Department of Corrections gave him permission to marry a pretty brunette from Nashville whom he had met during an earlier escape. By that time, Kirk had been transferred to the Southeastern Tennessee Regional Correctional Facility near Pikeville. The convict Casanova was one of only twenty-five maximum security prisoners kept in a special cellblock away from eight hundred minimum security prisoners there.

A month later in a ceremony held behind the prison walls, Kirk exchanged vows with thirty-one-year-old Mary K. Paris. The bride wore a knee-length dress, with white shoes and carried a bouquet. The couple's honeymoon was a two-hour visitation, held under the watchful eyes of guards.

The new Mrs. Kirk first met her husband while he was free following an escape before his escapade with Mary Evans. She didn't know at that time he was an escaped convict.

Within two years, Kirk had filed a suit in U. S. District Court against state corrections officials, seeking release from maximum security and two hundred

154

thousand dollars in damages. He claimed his constitutional protections against cruel and unusual punishment were being violated by his prolonged status as a maximum security prisoner.

In an interview with a Knoxville radio station, he explained that he wanted to spend more time with his family. "I've been married for two years and have a one-year-old son," he said. "My priorities are them, getting out to where I can have visits with them for a longer duration."

Corrections department authorities transferred him back to the penitentiary in Nashville, where he could be closer to his family. There was no public explanation from Kirk or anyone else of how a prisoner held in maximum security had become the father of a baby boy, William Michael Kirk.

Chapter Nine

**Sandra Kay Beeman,
Edgar Eugene Kerns, Jr.,
and Thomas E. Bowman**

As a guard at the Allegany County Detention Center in Cumberland, Maryland, Sandra Kay Beeman found herself facing a classic conundrum. She was surrounded by so many young men, and there was so little time.

But the plump divorced mother of two grown children made the best of the time she had available to her during her busy graveyard shift at the jail in the bustling mountain town.

Her attraction to the troubled men who streamed in and out of the county lockup was so obvious that one of her fellow employees and closest friends there warned her about her unseemly dalliances with inmates.

The forty-six-year-old guard's concerned pal simply couldn't understand why she didn't look outside the jail for men if she wanted romance in her life. Unfortunately, Sandra ignored the friendly words of caution.

In fact she became so closely involved with an accused burglar, who was temporarily locked up at the jail late in 1989, that the couple eventually decided to unite in a prison wedding.

During the dreary months after thirty-three-year-old Thomas E. Bowman was convicted on the breaking and entering charge and transferred to the Maryland Correctional Institution in nearby Hagerstown, she wrote regularly and visited him faithfully twice-a-week.

Finally, they set a wedding date, and Bowman arranged for a clergyman to perform the ceremony on August 25, 1990. Sandra helped him get a copy of his birth certificate for the marriage license, and the rings.

But, the bride never showed up for the Saturday wedding.

The jilted convict was crushed. Much later he recounted how he tried telephoning her to find out what was wrong. After making several calls, he at last reached her only to be coldly informed that she wanted nothing else to do with him.

Bowman said she was the first woman who had stuck by him, and he loved her.

Then, four days after she left the disappointed convict waiting at the altar, she made national news.

At 2:30 A.M., Wednesday morning, August 29, an inmate appeared suddenly at the control room of the Allegany County Detention Center. Edgar Eugene Kerns had the crook of his arm in a choke hold around Sandra's neck and was pushing her ahead of him. Fellow inmate James Vernon Barnes followed close behind. They were armed with a crude but classic prison weapon fashioned from a heavy object jammed into a sock.

Michelle Puderbaugh was the only other guard at the jail when he showed up at the command center. The prisoner tried to force her into the visitors' area where she could be locked inside, but she broke away and sprinted down the hall into a toilet. The guard, a five-year veteran at the jail, locked herself inside to prevent being taken hostage. She stayed there until an inmate trustee told her it was safe to come out.

The escapees fled into the night, taking Sandra with them as an apparent hostage. They took her car keys, but left her purse behind.

The escape was precisely timed during an approximate twenty-minute period when the shift supervisor Cpl. Gary Huffman was away from the jail to pick up a carryout dinner for himself and his two fellow guards.

Sandra usually made the post midnight run to a nearby convenience store to pick up the meal for herself and her colleagues. That night, however, she asked her supervisor to make the pickup. Earlier in the shift she also volunteered to make most of the checks of the cellblocks.

Somehow the inmates managed to pass through six locked doors to carry out their daring escape, the first at the detention center in seventeen years.

The next morning, the news media in Maryland and surrounding states headlined stories about the jail break and the apparent abduction of the unarmed guard. Guards and other law enforcement officers were not permitted to carry guns inside the jail.

Police said it appeared the men made their escape in Mrs. Beeman's 1983 Plymouth Reliant, which was described as a white car with a maroon top.

According to descriptions of the fugitives in police wanted bulletins, the dark-haired, heavily bearded Kerns was thirty years old, and of average height and build. He was from Martinsburg, West Virginia, and he and his fellow fugitive were identified as the only two of the approximately one hundred inmates at the jail locked in the maximum security area.

Although Kerns was serving a 180-day sentence for grand larceny and writing bad checks, he was also facing more serious charges at the time of his escape. Authorities disclosed that he had sparked a two-state manhunt, after being accused of the attempted murder and kidnapping of his girlfriend and her daughter.

Kerns's fellow escapee was identified as thirty-five-year-old James Vernon Barnes, a dangerous bandit and sex criminal who had been transferred to the jail in Allegany county from a state prison in Virginia to await trial on charges of rape, kidnapping, and possession of a deadly weapon. He was already serving a fifty-year sentence in Virginia after convictions for kidnapping, robbery, and rape.

Sandra's friends and family were horrified and fearful for her safety when they heard the shocking news about the escape.

Her twenty-four-year-old son told a reporter for Baltimore's *Sun* that he didn't believe his mother, a ten-year veteran jail guard, would have willingly opened the doors. "I'd like to get my hands on both of them," he said of the escapees.

The young man and his twenty-one-year-old sister had lived with their mother in her trailer home until a few days earlier when he moved into his own home in nearby Cresaptown. He said he last saw his mother when she brought some cooking utensils and other items to the house.

Friends indicated that despite the company of her children, the jail guard was unhappy and had been lonely since her divorce four years earlier from her truck driver husband, Lester Beeman.

Like Kerns, she also traced her roots to nearby Martinsburg. She was a teenager when she left West Virginia to study cosmetology in Cumberland. Then she worked as a beautician until her marriage, when she left that job to raise a family and take care of her homemaking duties.

After her divorce, she bought the house trailer in Frostburg, and she and her children moved in.

Like the missing guard's son, Allegany county sheriff's department authorities were also worried about her safety, but puzzled about the escape.

Kerns and Barnes were in adjoining cells on the second floor of the detention center, where all the male prisoners were housed. To make their escape, the inmates had to negotiate two locked doors in the maximum security block, go through a third door to a stairwell, and yet another door at the bottom of the stairs to reach the control room.

Finally they passed through two more locked doors, including one that is electronically locked, to reach the outside.

A sheriff's department spokesman said it appeared Mrs. Beeman was making a routine check of the hallways between cells in the central cellblock area of the second floor when Kerns and Barnes put their escape plan into motion.

But the spokesman was admittedly puzzled over Mrs. Beeman's reasons for opening the cell doors of the two men held in the maximum security block. Jail policy stipulated that two guards had to be present whenever any cells were opened. And even though there was evidence that an unsuccessful attempt had been made to file through bars with hacksaw blades, there was no question that the guard's keys had been used to open security doors in the jail.

Undersheriff Gary W. Simpson said authorities

wanted to know if she opened the doors under threat. The sheriff's department major described the missing guard as "a dependable corrections officer." He said there had never been any problems with her.

Cumberland's location near the northwestern tip of Maryland, about a half-hour drive from both Pennsylvania and West Virginia, made it a strong possibility the fugitives had fled across state lines, and the FBI quickly entered the manhunt. Six agents hurried to the city and began contacting relatives and other acquaintances of the escapees in efforts to pick up leads on their whereabouts.

Police in Maryland, Pennsylvania, West Virginia, and Virginia were notified to be on the lookout for the trio, and for the white and maroon Plymouth Reliant.

Maryland state police and local officers meanwhile had set up roadblocks in the Cumberland area. About fifty police officers searched the immediate area around the jail, while a state police helicopter helped in the search from the air. But there was no trace of the escapees, or their perceived hostage.

Police were already investigating the possibility the missing guard hadn't been abducted but may have gone with the escapees willingly, when their suspicions were confirmed.

Mrs. Beeman telephoned her daughter to tell her she was safe. "I'm fine. I'm with him," she was quoted as saying.

Four days after the dramatic jailbreak, Barnes was captured near his home in Hampshire county, West Virginia. The escapees had split up soon after fleeing the jail, and there was no trace of Kerns and Beeman. Investigators said however that Barnes led them to the

161

prison keys, hacksaw blades, and Kerns's institutional uniform, which had been ditched by the fugitive lovers.

About six weeks later, the comanager of the Beach Motor Inn on the shores of Lake Ontario in Hamilton, Ontario, Canada, was idly flipping television channels when he caught the tail end of a segment of *"Unsolved Mysteries."*

Joe Mitchell first watched a sobbing woman pleading for another woman to surrender to authorities. Then the photo of a middle-aged, moon-faced woman appeared on the screen.

Mitchell yelled for his wife. Moments later, Nancy Mitchell confirmed her husband's split-second observation. The woman on the screen looked so much like one of the occupants of Room 12 at the motel that she could have been a twin. Seconds later a picture of a man flashed on the screen. The photo was a dead ringer for the woman's companion. When the quiet, nondescript couple registered three weeks earlier they had signed in as Mr. and Mrs. Fred Smith.

The Mitchells telephoned the Hamilton-Wentworth Regional Police Department, and reported they believed a pair of criminal fugitives from the United States were checked into their motel. An officer was immediately sent to the motor inn to keep an eye on the couple in Room 12, while a colleague began attempting to obtain more information about the fugitives. Before moving in, police had to know more about whom they were dealing with.

But the toll-free 800 number provided for viewers of the popular true crime show couldn't be used in Canada to contact authorities in the United States. Finally the regional police got in touch with an off-duty constable whose wife had made a video-tape of the show.

Detectives and members of a tactical squad watched

the segment, and a few minutes before 1:00 A.M., they moved in to make the arrest. But the couple registered as Mr. and Mrs. Fred Smith had already fled, without bothering to check out or pay the bill for the last few days' rental of their $39.90 per-night room. They had been tuned into the same crime show.

Police tracked them to the nearby Dynes tavern, but again missed them by minutes. The couple had left in a taxi. But cab company records showed they were dropped off at the Red Rose Motel, some five miles from the site of their previous room.

Before dawn that morning police surrounded the Red Rose Motel and called out for the couple to surrender. When officers heard scuffling inside, they forced open the door. The occupants surrendered without a struggle.

Despite their use of assumed names when they registered at the motels, they were quickly identified as the missing jail guard and her escaped lover from Maryland. They were almost out of money, and had only a little clothing and a few personal grooming items with them.

Car trouble and their fear of being recognized if they tried to replenish their rapidly dwindling funds by obtaining jobs had eaten up most of the nest egg they had counted on to finance their escape and resettlement.

Mrs. Beeman eventually disclosed that only three hours after the escape they ran their car into a guardrail, and she broke her arm. She said Kerns wanted to take her to a hospital, but she refused because she was afraid they would be caught if she sought treatment.

Consequently, throughout their first few days together, he took care of her, assisting her in and out of bed, helping her to wash, and to dress herself.

Eventually they sold her car, and continued their

163

flight by bus and on foot. She said they stayed in motels and at campsites, and eventually bought another car, which they sold in Canada. Kerns thought he would be safe there from extradition to the United States. He was wrong.

After their arrest in Canada, the couple was jailed in Hamilton on local charges of accommodation fraud and impersonation, while authorities awaited the arrival of fugitive warrants from the United States.

Curiously, two other fugitives from the United States were arrested in Ontario the same day by police following up tips by television viewers to their presence in Canada.

A few days after Mrs. Beeman and Kerns were apprehended, the local charges against them were dismissed, and they were deported from Canada and returned in handcuffs to Maryland. News reporters and photographers were present to record the tender moments when the runaway guard and her lover hugged and kissed in front of the Allegany County Sheriff's Office.

At the conclusion of a brief court hearing they were ordered to be held temporarily without bail.

Charges against Kerns included escape, assault and battery, and other counts. His companion was named on two counts of aiding and assisting to escape, delivering contraband (a pair of hacksaw blades) for use in an escape, and on other charges. Conviction on the charges carried a maximum term of thirty years in prison.

Sandra told a reporter she hoped she wouldn't be sentenced to serve that much time in prison, but if she did, her brief idyll with Kerns would make it worthwhile.

She said she was in love with him, and she had made her choice. The only thing she admitted regretting was bad feelings she said her escapade with her lover had created between her and her children.

Once more Kerns was locked in the maximum security section at the jail. Later he was transferred to the Roxbury Correctional Institution near Hagerstown.

After spending one night at the detention center in Cumberland, his companion was moved to the Garrett County Jail. Selection of the jail in neighboring Oakland was a decision made to avoid any potential problems with Mrs. Beeman's former colleagues. Bail was later set for her at five hundred thousand dollars. No one posted the money, and neither her children nor the disgraced former jail guard's two sisters living in Maryland attended the bail hearing.

In 1991 she was sentenced to a five-year prison term for assisting an escape, and was locked up at the Women's Correctional Institute in Jessup. Kerns was also ordered to serve additional time for the escape, and remained behind bars at Hagerstown.

A few months before that, however, Sandra talked with a reporter for the *Cumberland Times-News,* and said she hoped someday to marry Kerns and to bear his son. She claimed they had known each other in Westernport before meeting again at the detention center.

Kerns asked her for dates when they first knew each other but she declined because she was going with someone else, she said.

Sandra confirmed she had planned to marry Bowman. According to her account, she felt sorry for the lonely prisoner because he didn't have any visitors, and she wanted to help him. But Kerns talked her out of her

165

wedding plans at the last minute, after convincing her that it would be foolish to marry someone she didn't love.

The former guard also talked of dating two former inmates from the detention center after their release.

"I never had sex in the jail with anybody," she insisted however. "Never. Never. I have never done that in the jail."

Chapter Ten

Karen Steele Gable
and
Frank E. Gable

Frank E. Gable has a personality disorder that causes him to be attracted to women who are his intellectual and social superiors, according to a psychologist.

So it might appear that Gable's chances of developing a new romantic relationship with a good-looking woman with brains and background were almost nil, because he was a career criminal expected to spend the rest of his life behind bars.

But that was before Karen A. Steele fell in love and proved that sometimes one should expect the unexpected.

A thirty-one-year-old redheaded beauty, she was one of those fortunate women who appeared to have it all, including a husband. The daughter of a prominent doctor and a busy socialite mother active in charity work, she grew up in the sheltered academic environment of the University of Wisconsin at Madison, where

167

her father was known for his accomplishments in the field of kidney research.

Karen met her husband while they were attending college, and she completed law school after their marriage. After college, the young couple moved across the country to Oregon. They settled in a comfortable home in a suburb of Portland. The house was set off with a picket fence and flowers, and there was a small garden to putter in. The couple even had a dog.

Soon after arriving in Oregon, Karen accepted her first fulltime job as a lawyer. She went to work for the public defender's office in Portland. It was a good job for a young lawyer to cut her legal eyeteeth on. The cultured young woman from the mid-west was soon appearing in courtrooms alongside clients who were among some of the most sordid members of society. They were accused drug dealers, junkies, rapists, thieves, and at least one individual charged with attempted murder.

But she didn't stay in public service for very long and moved to a job with a private Portland law firm. Then she was assigned to help with research and interviews in a federal weapons case against Frank E. Gable, a longtime troublemaker, wife beater, and violent criminal who was in the Marion County Jail in Salem.

With several months credit for good behavior, Gable had been only a few days away from early release from a one-year jail term in downstate Coos County for assaulting his wife, when he was charged in one of Oregon's most notorious and baffling murder cases.

He was removed from the Coos County Jail in Coquille and driven nearly 150 miles northwest to Salem, where he was arraigned in the Marion County Circuit Court on six counts of aggravated murder and one count of murder. He was charged with the savage knife slaying of the director of the Oregon State Corrections Department. The indictment accused him of murdering Michael Francke while robbing him, or while stealing something from the victim's car. In one count of the indictment, authorities indicated the murder had something to do with Francke's job as the state's prison chief.

Gable was first questioned about the murder in May, 1989, after he was arrested on federal charges of being an ex-convict in illegal possession of a weapon. But he was released after submitting to a polygraph test. Investigators began taking another, closer look at his possible involvement in the slaying, after his arrest four months later following the fight with his wife.

Then a thief who was in the Marion county jail with the suspect told authorities Gable had admitted murdering Francke during a car burglary.

Gable insisted that he had nothing to do with the murder and blamed rumormongering by Salem speed freaks who were maneuvering for deals with authorities on various criminal charges tied to their methamphetamine abuse and other drug activities. Before being locked up in Coquille, he had helped the police department of Salem's twin city, Keizer, as an informant, providing tips on his drug-dealing cronies.

Gable was already known to police in Oregon as a violent career criminal, who abused his wife, used and sold drugs, and stole anything that wasn't nailed down. He was a brutal and vicious man, whose background and character were about as different from Karen's as it could be.

His long police and prison record included: less than a year served on a two-year sentence in 1979 to the Oregon State Correctional Institution in Salem for forgery and for second-degree robbery in a gas station stickup in Coos Bay; more than two years served at the Oregon State Penitentiary after convictions for burglary and failure to appear; and approximately four years served at the penitentiary from 1984 to 1988 on a second-degree robbery conviction for manhandling a woman clerk at a grocery store and taking $125 in cash and food stamps from the till.

Nearly two years younger than Karen, Gable complained about a miserable childhood. He said he and his mother found his alcoholic father dead in the family car. And he claimed that after his father's death he was sexually abused by another adult male relative.

As a teenager and young adult he abused amphetamines and other drugs, sold drugs, and worked as a debt collector for other dealers. While other young men were enlisting in the military, establishing themselves in legitimate civilian careers, or hitting the books at college, he was in and out of jails and drug rehabilitation programs.

If it was true that he had been dealt a rotten hand as a child, he wasn't doing anything to turn his luck around. He was married to his wife, Janyne Vierra Gable, less than two years when she filed divorce proceedings against him on May 30, 1990. Mrs. Gable cited irreconcilable differences, and was quoted in the press as saying it was ridiculous to stay married to a man she didn't love.

Earlier she told reporters, "When he wasn't in the bag, his thought processes were clear and precise. He was in touch with reality, he was good with Jessica," she said of her daughter from a previous marriage.

But Gable was apparently "in the bag" a lot during the short, tempestuous marriage. Even before he attacked his wife with a broken plate, he had broken her arm, blackened her eyes, and threatened to kill her, according to press reports.

170

By the time Mrs. Gable filed for divorce, her bad-boy husband had already been blamed for Francke's murder, although he hadn't yet met Karen.

Steele first made the 120-mile round-trip drive and walked into the jail in Salem to meet the smooth-talking, dark-haired criminal on August 1, 1990. It was the first of many trips, and almost daily telephone calls between the two.

Gable had a gift for gab, yet he was pleasingly attentive when Karen talked. And for a man who had spent much of his adult life behind bars, and was facing the strong possibility of more months or years in prison, his conversation could be surprisingly provocative and amusing. He was also slim, handsome, and his dark horn-rimmed glasses helped give him an outward appearance that was more intelligent than menacing.

The gloss had begun to rub off Karen's marriage, and her conferences with Gable provided a refreshing respite from her personal troubles. She would later tell a reporter that she and her husband were already drifting apart, when she fell and cut her knee one day as she was jogging. She recalled that Gable sympathized with her and told her how sorry he was after she described the mishap to him.

On November 1, 1990, during one of her jailhouse visits, he handed her a letter and asked her not to read it until she got home. In the letter he said he was in love with her.

In an affidavit Karen later filed in federal court, she described her contacts with her client as "wholly professional" until he gave her the letter. The letter "expressed feelings beyond those attendant an attorney-client relationship," she wrote.

"Following that visit with Mr. Gable, our relationship developed into one involving deep personal commitment." Continuing her story in the court document, she said that her visits with the prisoner were professional, but that on some occasions she also communicated with him on a purely personal basis.

By the end of November she told her husband she was emotionally involved with a client and wanted a divorce. After that, she and Gable began to hold hands and snatch an occasional surreptitious hug during their visits, Karen was quoted in the press as saying.

Gable's legal affairs weren't progressing as well as his love life, however. He drew an eight-year prison term for the weapons offense.

After learning of Karen's personal involvement with the suspect, her law firm had withdrawn from the case, and she left her job. Former colleagues of the love-struck lawyer stated in another federal court affidavit that a plea agreement negotiated between Gable and federal prosecutors was dumped because of the couple's controversial relationship. The lawyers wrote that the relationship might have damaged her ability to "exercise independent professional judgment on behalf of the defendant."

But the sentence on the weapons offense was peanuts compared to the penalty Gable faced if he was convicted on the murder charges. Oregon legislators had restored the state's death penalty in 1985, providing for the possibility of execution by lethal injection for killers convicted of aggravated murder.

Michael Francke's murder on January 17, 1989, in Salem, was especially vicious. The hardworking prison chief was stabbed in the heart at about 7:00 P.M., as he was walking to his parked Pontiac Bonneville after leaving his office in the Dome Building. The murder wasn't discovered until about five hours later by a security guard.

Somehow the fatally injured man had managed to stumble from the scene of the attack, back to a south porch of the building, and break a windowpane in a French door before he collapsed. The autopsy on his body indicated that he was stabbed by someone using a knife with a blade that may have been as much as seven inches long.

The victim also had several other cuts on his arms and hands, that were either defensive wounds or were inflicted when the window was broken. A former district court judge in Santa Fe, New Mexico, who later became head of the state prison system before being picked for the job in Oregon, Francke was a solidly built 215-pound, six-foot, three-inch man who wasn't afraid of a good scrap. But investigators uncovered evidence that shortly before his murder he had been frightened of something, and when he was home stayed close to a shotgun and a loaded .45-caliber pistol.

Police were faced with a mind-boggling array of possible motives for the slaying. Because of Francke's job as the state's corrections chief, there seemed to be a good possibility that his murder was a revenge or hate slaying by a disgruntled convict who blamed the victim in some way for personal or prison problems. Leads indicating that he was about to blow the lid off corruption in the prison system were also given serious consideration.

But it seemed also that the killer might be an employee with a grudge, a professional rival — or a stranger who had struck out in a random attack. And there was the possibility, as well, that a hate-filled former defendant, who appeared before him when he was a judge, might have followed him to Oregon for revenge.

Authorities eventually settled on the probability, however, that Francke was killed by someone who was after documents or computer disks naming police snitches from Salem's drug underworld. The killer may have been after Francke's briefcase, or have been surprised while burglarizing the victim's car in a search for the documents, according to speculation.

Whatever the motive might have been, it was clear that the slaying was savage and frightening. It was a despicably nasty act that was viewed as a direct challenge to the power of society to make laws and to protect the people charged with enforcing them.

The long-bladed knife was plunged into Francke's chest with such force that it sliced through his raincoat, suit jacket, several business cards he carried in a shirt pocket, and his lung before burying itself in his heart.

But the slaying was also the beginning of a perplexing mystery that challenged teams of crack homicide investigators from the city and state and the FBI for fifteen months. The case ultimately became the most expensive homicide investigation in the state's history; and ripped open a Pandora's box of rumors and accusations about widespread corruption in the Oregon State Prison system.

The suggestion that Francke may have been killed because he was investigating prison corruption provided investigators with another possible motive to check out. And before the case was finally laid to rest, authorities conducted thirteen different audits and investigations of the Corrections Department. However, although the probes turned up the presence of illegal activities by some employees of the prison system, authorities determined there was no evidence of a widespread conspiracy or link to Francke's murder.

* * *

Investigators, in fact, had focused their suspicions on several other suspects, before turning their attentions toward Gable. At that time he was already in the Coos County Jail for assaulting his wife with a broken dinner plate. But at the time of the murder, he and his wife were living in Salem, where she worked as a licensed practical nurse at the Oregon State Hospital. The corrections department headquarters was located in the Dome Building on the hospital grounds.

And Mrs. Gable later stated that her husband was away from home on the night of the slaying, but returned in time the next morning to drive her to work. He became terribly upset when he saw police lines as they approached the hospital and wouldn't go back onto the grounds, she said.

While preparations were underway for Gable's murder trial, Steele was having troubles of her own. The romantic relationship between the accused killer and the lawyer had become a matter of public interest. Karen divorced her husband and used a big portion of her divorce settlement to pay a defense lawyer to help her hang onto her license. And she devoted every ounce of additional energy she could to helping out with Gable's legal defense.

Gable wasn't an easy client for his court appointed attorneys to work with. He was arrogant and cocky, and bickered with them over strategy and other aspects of his defense. He petulantly boycotted the trial one day, after a state police detective testified that during an interview at the jail in Coquille, the defendant had sobbed uncontrollably and curled up in a fetal position on the floor. In the taped statement, Gable told detectives that God had instructed him to help track down the prison chief's killer.

Gable returned to court in a better mood after taking the day off, and apologized for his childish behavior.

Karen was a loyal spectator throughout the exhausting proceeding. Each morning of the trial she would find a seat for herself near the front of the courtroom, where the defendant could easily turn in his seat at the defense table and see her. As soon as Gable was escorted into the courtroom, he would glance into the spectator section to see if she was there. He frequently turned and exchanged smiles with her, between the testimonies of witnesses.

Two months after the trial began, and after eighteen hours of deliberation, the jury of nine women and three men returned unanimous verdicts of guilty on all counts. Four prosecution witnesses had testified Gable admitted the slaying to them.

The defendant refused to enter the courtroom to hear the verdicts. But as he was being returned from the courthouse to the jail he shouted to news photographers and television camera operators that his lawyers had "dump-trucked" him. He was locked up under a suicide watch, and Karen was his only visitor.

The day after his conviction, Gable refused to talk with his attorneys about defense strategy during the penalty phase of the trial. His failure to cooperate delayed the proceeding for a day.

In Oregon, as in several other states, possible death penalty cases are bifurcated, heard in two parts. During the first part of the trial the jury is expected to decide guilt or innocence. Then, if they return a verdict of guilty to a crime that carries the death penalty, another short trial is held after which they retire once more to debate the severity of the penalty. The choice at that stage was a recommendation of a sentence of from thirty years to life in prison—or death by lethal injection.

Tom C. Bostwick, Marion County deputy district attorney, told the jurors in his opening statement during the penalty phase of the trial that Gable had demonstrated a pattern of violence and disrespect for the law. "The facts will demonstrate to you that he really is a dangerous man," the attorney declared.

As the jury was hearing new testimony four days after Gable's conviction, he and Karen were issued a marriage license at the Marion County Courthouse. The next day, two radio reporters were ejected from the courthouse coffee shop after they tried to interview Karen and she refused to talk with them.

A few hours later they were married in the same courtroom where he was on trial. The Rev. Bob Biggs, who met Gable through a volunteer prison ministry, performed the wedding in a two-minute ceremony after the judge called a brief recess. The only other people in the courtroom at the time were a woman who acted as a witness, and police officers guarding the bridegroom.

After the trial resumed, Gable's defense submitted a motion asking the judge to permit introduction of evidence about two alternate suspects in the case. One of the men had confessed the murder to police, then retracted the admission. The other bragged to a girlfriend that he was involved in the slaying, but later committed suicide while he was locked in the Marion County Jail. Gable's guilt had already been determined, however, and the motion was denied.

In what appeared to be almost a sidelight to the proceeding, testimony by a defense psychologist shed some light on the motivation behind the curious pairing of the killer and the lady lawyer he married. Stephen Scherr testified that Gable had a glitch in his personality that caused him to be attracted to women he believed were smarter and socially superior to him. But that didn't explain why the new Mrs. Gable was attracted to the desperado she had just married.

Gable had urged his lawyers to call his new wife as the final defense witness. On the last morning of testimony, however, he advised the judge he had decided against calling her as a witness and was ready to rest the defense case.

The convicted killer was still upset with his lead defense attorney, and insisted he didn't want the lawyer arguing his case. So John Storkel, another member of the defense team, presented the closing summation. He pleaded with the jury to spare his client. The lawyer said that as a child Gable had endured years of sexual abuse from his foster father, and was neglected and mistreated by an alcoholic mother.

"You've got to look behind the easy smile to see that this is a scared human being," he pleaded.

Arguing for the death penalty, Bostwick reminded the jury that Gable was a dangerous man. He declared that prison employees and guards deserved to be protected from attacks by people such as the defendant.

The jury voted to spare Gable from the death penalty, and he was sentenced to life in prison without the possibility of parole. Gable turned toward his new bride who was watching from the spectator seats, smiled, winked, and blew her a kiss. Then he was led away.

The man who had murdered Oregon's top corrections official was sent to the Idaho State Prison to serve his sentence. Oregon corrections authorities utilized an interstate program that permits swaps of certain inmates, in determining Gable's prison assignment.

Conjugal visits are not permitted in the maximum security prison in Idaho. Only a brief kiss and embrace are allowed for well behaved convicts at the beginning and end of visits in the prison day room. If a prisoner creates discipline problems, visits are conducted by telephone as the convict and his guest sit on opposite sides of a thick plate of reinforced glass.

As the new groom settled back into the prison routine he knew so well, his bride was working as a waitress on the graveyard shift at an all-night cafe. According to news reports, the once promising young lawyer was earning about two hundred dollars, including tips, for a forty-eight-hour week slinging hash and pouring coffee.

Chapter Eleven

**Doris Irene Oliphant Frost
and
Dana Sue Jones**

Nurses, physicians and police officers are taught and counselled to avoid emotional involvement with patients and criminals they come in contact with on the job.

Violation of that precept can lead to serious trouble — as it did for Doris Frost.

The slender nurse was married to a locally prominent physician only a few months, when she helped a younger woman escape from the Colorado State Hospital for the criminally insane where she was a patient, and they ran off together.

The ten-day trip ended in tragedy when twenty-five-year-old Dana Sue Jones shot herself to death in a rented New Mexico apartment with a gun provided by Mrs. Frost.

The sordid episode had begun several months earlier while the nurse was working at the state psychiatric

180

hospital in Pueblo and met Dana Sue. Mrs. Frost hadn't yet married her doctor husband at the time of her first meeting with the dangerous patient, and worked at the hospital for about two years.

Dana Sue was committed to the hospital after being found innocent, by reason of insanity, in the grisly knife slaying of a man in Denver.

Twenty-nine-year-old Raymond Wayne Terry was found by authorities tied to a bed, and ripped to pieces with a long-bladed butcher knife. He was stabbed 117 times, and a large, bloody letter "D" was carved in the mutilated flesh of his chest.

The mother of a baby daughter, and a husky woman who sometimes wore a black beard and handlebar mustache while posing as a man, Dana was arrested after police found her in the house covered with blood. She was accused of slaying the victim on February 4, 1986, after picking him up at a Denver bar.

After she was declared criminally insane and committed to the hospital, the former Tennessee woman told psychiatrists that she had undergone a horrible childhood filled with emotional, sexual, and other physical abuse. She blamed her parents and other members of her family, and claimed she was deliberately burned and had been held at gunpoint. She confessed she also had a history of killing small animals.

The hospital had no maximum security facilities for women, so Dana was housed in a general adult psychiatric services ward with more than thirty-five other patients while undergoing treatment for her mental ailments. Her fellow patients did not know the details of the ghastly crime she was accused of committing.

Somehow during the treatment process the relationship between the nurse and the dangerous mental patient turned from professional to intensely personal. One of the nurse's concerned supervisors finally questioned her about the disturbing relationship, and in February, 1988 Oliphant resigned.

Hospital spokesmen never revealed publicly if they demanded the resignation, citing state policy that prohibits release of information about employees.

She found a new job as a surgical room nurse at the St. Mary-Corwin Hospital. The same month she left the psychiatric hospital, she married Dr. Harold Frost.

However, even though the job change now prevented the two women from seeing each other on a regular basis, and Doris had married, the two women continued to pursue their romance by telephone and through the mail.

Dana telephoned the nurse at her home and the love-smitten couple carried on long talks together. As the summer approached, the telephone calls became a daily occurrence, and the conversations routinely continued for an hour or more. Some of the talks lasted for three hours.

The women also exchanged a blizzard of letters while carrying out a torrid and bizarre correspondence. Dana eventually wrote more than one hundred letters to the new Mrs. Frost, sometimes churning out three-a-day, and mailed them to the nurse at her home. Some were dotted with explicit sexual fantasies of lesbian love. Others made dark references to Satanism.

Mrs. Frost replied with dreamily romantic letters of her own. The women shared sugary lovers' confidences in the letters about their affection for each other and their desire to make new lives together. Finally, they began to lay plans to make their ardent fantasies come true.

182

Portions of two of Mrs. Frost's love letters, later revealed in legal documents, provide insight into the depth of her passionate attachment for her homicidal heartthrob. In both letters, she addressed Dana as "Sam."

"I am pretty confused at this point," the infatuated nurse wrote. "I know life without you would hardly be life at all and I don't really want to think of that," she continued. "Life without you would require giving up almost everything I've accomplished at this point. Can I do this? Can I not do this?"

Another time she wrote about difficult decisions she was facing. She pointed out she had built a comfortable life for herself after returning to school, marrying, and buying a house and car.

"I have a job that is interesting and does good for mankind. I work with people that like and respect me. I have two kids that are self-sufficient and responsible citizens. And I plant flowers," she told her lover.

She went on to describe her life as enviable, although it could be better, and it could be worse. "So along comes Sam," she wrote.

"Sam offers me the golden carrot—what everyone wants in their lives." She gushed that Sam offered her love, excitement, ecstasy, adventure, dedication, and devotion. And there was no comparing that with what she had at that time, she mused. "It's like apples and oranges. They are the fruits of life but one is as essential as the other. I want it all!"

At the hospital, Dana began giving away some of her favorite possessions to other patients. She presented one surprised friend with a birthday card, two weeks early. It was curious behavior for the menacing woman, who had earned a reputation among some of her fellow patients as a bully.

Then during a late Friday night shift change, the lovesick women reached out for the "golden carrot."

As a hospital employee opened the locked door of the ward a few minutes before midnight to report for the new shift, the burly patient brushed her aside and darted through. Although staff members briefly pursued her, she bulled her way through a second unlocked door, plunged outside, and moments later leaped into a car that was waiting with the engine running. With Mrs. Frost at the wheel, the vehicle speeded away from the hospital grounds.

Employees immediately notified police and mental health authorities. Despite a county-wide alert and roadblocks that were quickly set up, however, the two women eluded the police dragnet.

The escaped patient was described in the police alert as five-feet, seven-and-a-half-inches tall, about 160 pounds, with blond hair and hazel eyes, and three earrings in her right ear. She was wearing a white top and white pants when she fled from the hospital.

Photographs of Dana in a normal pose as a female and in her male disguise were distributed to police agencies and to the media.

Her presumed companion was described as five-foot, two-inches tall, about 115 pounds, with brown hair and brown eyes.

Pueblo police said the women were believed to be travelling in Mrs. Frost's grey 1986 four-door Volkswagen Jetta.

In an appeal for help from the public in locating the couple, Captain Ruben Archuleta, chief of the police department's investigative division, cautioned private citizens not to attempt to apprehend them. He asked instead that anyone who sighted them or knew their whereabouts immediately contact police, and if possible provide a description of the clothing the women were wearing as well as their location.

Mrs. Frost was believed to have been carrying a .38-caliber pistol in her car, Archuleta warned.

Even at that early stage of the search for the missing pair, Archuleta told news reporters that it was possible the fifty-six-year-old nurse had willingly accompanied the fugitive patient. But he added that police were concerned about the married woman's safety because of Dana's violent background.

Investigators quickly determined that Mrs. Frost had withdrawn money from a savings account, and taken out a loan shortly before the escape. Her nest egg reportedly amounted to approximately three thousand dollars. But she was apparently dressed in a soiled gardening outfit when she left her home, and didn't even take along a change of clothes.

Mrs. Frost's loyal husband and other family members were also worried, and they shared their concern with police and the news media. Contacted at his home on Pueblo's south side, the doctor said he believed his wife was lured across town to the psychiatric hospital by a telephoned plea for help from Dana, then abducted.

The mental patient likely climbed into his wife's car at the hospital, then took her along on the escape against her will, he theorized. Dr. Frost added that he believed Dana had quickly taken control of the pistol that his wife normally kept locked in the glovebox of her car.

Mrs. Frost left the house without his knowledge, and he first suspected she had been kidnapped when police showed up at the home at about 2:30 A.M., looking for the escaped mental patient, the doctor said. He described his wife as a very trusting and warm person with many friends. "People need help and Doris is the one to jump in," he told *The Pueblo Chieftain*.

By contrast, the worried husband described Dana as a patient who was notorious among the hospital staff as a manipulator. People were afraid of her, he remarked.

The chief of the state hospital medical staff appeared to be in at least partial agreement with Dr. Frost's assessment of the runaway patient. He told reporters that she was extremely dangerous and clearly had the ability to manipulate others. But he observed that it was difficult to pin down exactly what kind of relationship existed between the two women.

The hospital executive added that security measures on the ward would be studied and reassessed as a result of the escape.

According to the talk in local coffee shops and tap rooms, most residents of the Arkansas River city, about one hundred miles south of Denver, were less puzzled about the kind of relationship the women were involved in. It appeared obvious from the cautious statements of police and from news reports that the two women were lovers.

But there was less unanimity of opinion about the personal safety of the runaway nurse. There seemed to be no question that Dana was a chillingly dangerous maniac, who had killed at least once and was fully capable of killing again. Police and other people were alarmed and fearful that Mrs. Frost, or someone else, could become the next murder victim.

Pointedly avoiding use of the word "lesbian," Archuleta even complained to the press about the media emphasis on the "relationship" between the two women. "It takes away from the fact that we're trying to bring her back safely," he said.

• As the search for the women was expanded and became nationwide, the FBI joined local and state police in the effort. Pueblo was only a few hours drive from New Mexico, Oklahoma, or Kansas, and there appeared to be a good chance the fugitive patient and her companion may have crossed a state line.

Pueblo police also checked out a tip that the women were seen in the mountains near the city, but determined that the report was false.

In Denver, police beginning new work shifts were alerted to be on the lookout for the pair, because of Dana's former connection there. Authorities in Tennessee, Dana's home state, were also contacted and given descriptions of the two women.

Then on June 15, five days after the escape, Dr. Frost called a news conference at his office, and revealed that he had received a chilling telephone call from his wife the previous night.

The shaken husband said he answered a telephone call at about 7:00 P.M., and was greeted with the sound of sobbing. Then the frightened voice of his wife pleaded, "Honey, help me?"

Moments later he heard a terrified scream, and the telephone connection was broken, he said.

"I'm positive it was Doris, and Doris is in trouble," Dr. Frost told reporters. "The first part of that call was terror, and the second part was pain."

Dr. Frost also complained that he didn't believe police were showing sufficient concern for his wife, and criticized what he described as hints of a lesbian relationship between Doris and Dana.

187

Police had shown him some of the letters Dana wrote to his wife, which she dropped off at her son's home the previous Wednesday, he said. The physician described them as, "sick, sick, sick."

He conceded that Dana might have convinced his wife to experiment with lesbianism, and consequently the nurse's curiosity could have led her to help in the escape. But he insisted that he believed any involvement his wife may have had with lesbianism was no more than an experiment.

"My wife is not a lesbian," he declared. "She's a grand lady!"

Dr. Frost explained that he called the news conference to announce what he termed, "Operation Doris." Operation Doris was his way of informing the public about the danger his wife was in, and encouraging private citizens to help police, he added.

His wife was in great danger and terrible trouble that she couldn't get out of, and others had to help if she was to survive, the worried husband told reporters. "If we can't, she'll die."

Police cautioned the press that the telephone call may have been made by a crank. But they said they were also worried about the missing nurse's safety.

Mrs. Frost's children shared their stepfather's dread. And in an interview the day after Dr. Frost talked with the press, David Tekavec, her son, said he also didn't believe his mother had intended to help Dana escape.

He said he believed she drove to the hospital planning to talk Dana out of some outrageous scheme outlined by the mental patient during a telephone call earlier in the evening. Then, he surmised, his mother lost control of the situation.

Tekavec said both he and his sister were doing their best to prepare themselves for bad news. "At this point, it's unlikely that she's alive," he said of his mother. "We can only hope she is."

Tekavec's sister, Barbara Hart, had worked as a nurse on the same ward with her mother at the psychiatric hospital.

Like his stepfather, Tekavec also bristled at the talk that was going around about a scandalous lesbian love affair between the missing married woman and the runaway mental patient.

"At the very worst, even if my mom was considering a relationship like this, it wouldn't be with a psychotic from the state hospital," he declared.

Tekavec described his mother as a caring person who sincerely wanted to help the troubled young woman at the state hospital, and explained that she left some of Dana's letters at his home in Colorado Springs because she thought they might be useful some day as therapy tools.

She worried that if her husband read the letters he would misunderstand what was going on and force her to sever her counselor-patient relationship with Dana, Tekavec explained. Dana didn't trust doctors and nurses at the hospital, and his mother was taken in by her desire to be helpful, he said.

Although other nurses and some doctors at the psychiatric hospital were admittedly frightened of their dangerous patient, Mrs. Frost was not. Her son described her as never being afraid of anything in her life.

The same day Mrs. Frost's son talked with the press about his fears for her safety, police issued a warrant for her arrest on charges of assisting in an escape.

* * *

As police were initiating the search in the first hours after Dana fled from the hospital, she and her companion were checking into a motel in Taos, New Mexico. Two days later they continued driving south until they arrived in Albuquerque, New Mexico, and checked into another motel.

On June 14, four days after the escape, a couple rented a studio apartment in Albuquerque. One of the renters appeared to be a solidly built young man, who signed the seven-month Sun Pueblo Apartments lease as Sam Spitzer Smith. The renter's slender companion signed as Sandra Evans.

Six days later at 1:30 A.M., on Monday morning, June 20, the petite woman who had checked into the apartment as Sandra Evans told security guards there had been a shooting. Inside the apartment, authorities found her roommate dead of a gunshot wound to the head.

The victim was quickly identified as the fugitive patient from the Colorado State Hospital, and her distraught companion as the runaway nurse. Mrs. Frost told Albuquerque police that Dana had committed suicide by shooting herself. The death weapon was Mrs. Frost's .38-caliber pistol.

While Dana's body was transported to the local medical examiner's office for autopsy, Mrs. Frost was taken to the Bernalillo County Detention Center in Albuquerque and held without bail.

The autopsy report disclosed that Dana died instantly after a single gunshot was fired into her head. A spokeswoman for the Albuquerque Police Department reported that the wound was "consistent with suicide." But the investigation was continuing, she said.

In Pueblo, Mrs. Frost's husband greeted the news that his wife was safe with relief. And he loyally continued his public support for her. A couple of days after the shooting in Albuquerque, a spokesman for the doctor said he was hiring a lawyer, as well as a physician and a psychiatrist to evaluate her.

Later, in a prepared statement Dr. Frost once again publicly confirmed his support and love for his troubled wife. She was "courageous, honorable and gallant," according to his glowing description. But he claimed she had been "brainwashed by a cunning and accomplished manipulator, sociopathic personality/psychotic killer."

Tekavec told the press he was sorry Dana was dead, but he was overjoyed that his mother was alive and safe. Mrs. Hart described herself and other family members as relieved, but concerned over her mother's emotional well-being.

Dana's mother flew to Colorado from Tennessee, and was horrified when she learned news stories had cited court records detailing psychiatric treatment in which the young woman claimed to have suffered incest and other childhood abuse.

The Tennessee mother said her four children were well treated and that Dana was so pretty she was pampered when she was a little girl. They were a churchgoing family, she said. But after Dana slashed her wrist with a fork at school when she was fourteen and told a girlfriend that she was trying to commit suicide, it was learned that she had been sexually abused by a family member.

The anguished woman, whose name was not used in news reports, said Dana seemed to respond well to two years of therapy, and there were no more serious problems with her until she enlisted in the military and left home. It was through Dana's service in the military that she wound up in Denver.

Dana's mother said that making up stories was one facet of her daughter's mental illness.

191

One of the three psychiatrists who had examined the dangerous mental patient told reporters he had confirmed much of what she told him with other sources. And he firmly stood by his report.

In Albuquerque, meanwhile, Mrs. Frost had confirmed to authorities in a lengthy statement that she was a willing collaborator in her companion's escape from the hospital. She wasn't a kidnap victim.

Police revealed she also told them that after her lover decided to commit suicide, she advised her where to point the pistol in order to inflict the fatal shot. And she said Dana took her hand and placed it on the pistol before the weapon was fired. But Doris said she couldn't remember if her hand was actually on the weapon when it discharged.

Mrs. Frost was formally charged in District Court in Albuquerque with assisting in a suicide and with harboring or aiding a felon. Both counts were felonies, and each carried maximum terms of eighteen months in prison, or up to two years behind bars if aggravation was proved. Bail was set at ten thousand dollars.

Several days after the charges were filed, however, a grand jury in Albuquerque decided there was insufficient evidence to support the accusations of assisting in a suicide. The charge of harboring or aiding a felon was also eventually dismissed by the prosecution.

But despite the developments in New Mexico, Mrs. Frost still faced serious criminal charges in Pueblo. She was charged there with a single count of aiding in an escape, a felony that on conviction carried possible sentences of one to eight years in prison, a fine of from one thousand dollars to one hundred thousand dollars, or a combination of both.

* * *

And near the end of July the Colorado Board of Nursing ordered temporary suspension of her license, pending resolution of the charges against her. She had become a licensed practical nurse in 1959, and in 1985 became a registered nurse. A few days after the license suspension, she was admitted to St. Mary-Corwin Hospital for treatment of an ulcer, which her lawyer said was apparently tied to stress.

Mrs. Frost ultimately entered into a plea bargain agreement, that held out the promise of eliminating the last remaining possibility she would be sentenced to prison for her role in the tragic escapade with Dana.

Early in April, 1989, nearly ten months after the ill-fated escape plan was put in motion, she pleaded guilty in Pueblo District Court to a felony charge for aiding in the patient's escape and to a new misdemeanor count of reckless endangerment of the public. The felony charge carried a possible maximum sentence of up to eight years' imprisonment in the Colorado State Women's Correctional Facility. The misdemeanor charge carried a sentence of up to six months in the Pueblo County Jail.

According to the plea agreement proposal, pending approval by the court, she was asking for a deferred sentence on the more serious felony charge of aiding in the escape and two years' probation on the misdemeanor. The pact also called for her to continue therapy, which she had already begun.

District Judge Dennis Maes scheduled sentencing for approximately six weeks later.

After the hearing, however, a deputy district attorney told reporters that he considered Mrs. Frost's escapade to have been an isolated incident she would be unlikely to repeat, and said he didn't consider her to be dangerous. He said that even if she was convicted during a

193

trial, it was unlikely she would be sentenced to jail.

Defense Attorney Randall Jorgensen told a reporter that the agreement would give his client an opportunity to get on with her life. He said her desire to nurture had made her an easy victim and claimed she wasn't the only employee who had been taken advantage of by the skillfully manipulative mental patient.

Jorgensen added that Mrs. Frost also planned to ask the nursing board to return her license so she could return to work.

On May 15, 1989, Judge Maes ordered a two-year deferred sentence for the nurse, and placed her on probation for one year. He also ordered her to pay a fine of $526 to the court and stipulated that she was not to work with psychiatric patients.

Almost everyone in the courtroom appeared to be satisfied with the sentence. The only immediate complaints came from a man who identified himself as Jack Wilson, and said he had custody of Dana's five-year-old daughter.

The dismayed Denver man complained that the nurse deserved more severe punishment for providing Dana with the gun used in the suicide. "Why would anyone ever furnish anyone with a gun in that situation?" he demanded.

The judge explained that he did not have jurisdiction in facets of the case involving the suicide, which occurred in New Mexico.

Wilson stalked out of the courtroom making angry accusations that there was a cover-up and justice had been denied.

Chapter Twelve

Anna Christine Sallings Sandhu Ray
and
James Earl Ray

When she announced plans to marry James Earl Ray, freelance courtroom artist Anna Christine Sallings Sandhu expected it to be difficult.

But it's doubtful if the attractive blonde Knoxville divorcee anticipated just how rocky the next few years would be during her turbulent marriage to the man imprisoned for the murder of civil rights leader, Martin Luther King, Jr.

According to her accounts, she had to endure humiliating searches during prison visits, received anonymous death threats, was menaced by another motorist while driving, and was viciously attacked by another convict.

Ray had already been behind bars for nine years after the April 4, 1968 sniper slaying in Memphis, when the couple first saw each other in a Morgan county courtroom near Knoxville.

Soon after King was killed with a single shot in the

neck as he stood on a balcony at the Loraine Motel, Ray was linked to the assassination through finger-prints found on the sniper rifle used in the slaying. He managed to flee the country, but was apprehended several weeks later in London by officers with Britain's famous Scotland Yard.

By the time he met his future bride, the career criminal, who had tried his hand at everything from bootlegging, car theft, armed robbery, and murder, was on trial for carrying off an ingenious escape.

The previous June, Ray had leaped from a window he pried loose in the jerry-rigged bathroom of a prison bus, while he was being transported between a hospi-tal and the Brushy Mountain State Penitentiary in the isolated rural community of Petros, Tennessee. He was finally recaptured in the hilly, snake-infested woods a few miles from the prison three days later after one of the most intensive manhunts in that state's history.

Ray's brief hiatus from Brushy Mountain wasn't his first escape. He was on the run after a previous prison breakout from the penitentiary at Jefferson City, Mis-souri, when King was assassinated.

Sentenced to twenty years behind bars after he and a confederate stuck up two grocery stores, Ray twice attempted to break out of the maximum security prison before he was successful. On his third try on April 23, 1967, he hid in the false bottom of a huge breadbox and rode out of the gates in a truck. He re-mained free until his arrest in London more than a year later.

Mrs. Sandhu met Ray after accepting an assignment from a Knoxville television station, WBIR, to sketch the short fifty-year-old convict at a preliminary hearing on the latest escape charge. Tennessee state statutes did not permit use of television or still cameras in courtrooms.

A slender, attractive blonde, she was an excellent artist with the ability to execute lifelike sketches that captured the personality of her subjects quickly.

Like Ray, she came from a big family. She was the oldest of six children, and had lived in the Knoxville area since she was six years old when her parents moved there from Virginia. She had been divorced since 1974, following a five-year marriage to a former exchange student from India.

Mrs. Sandhu and Ray didn't speak to each other until she attended a second court hearing on the escape charge. Ray was ultimately ordered to serve a one-to-two-year sentence for the escape.

He talked with the courtroom artist again when she accompanied a television reporter during an interview.

By that time she had checked out as many books at her local library as she could find that dealt with the King assassination and Ray's arrest and involvement in the crime. The stories told in the books were contradictory, she decided.

Mrs. Sandhu later recalled that they shared the same sense of humor and joked about some of the ridiculous questions Ray was asked by television reporters.

They also chatted about his legal situation, the Bible, and about art and her career. He asked her why Pablo Picasso's paintings were so expensive when they were so bad. Later, as the year-end holidays approached, she sent him some books for Christmas. He responded with a thank-you note and invited her to visit him at the prison.

After she was put on his visitors' list, they had a long talk in a private meeting. That chat was followed by many others.

The talks began a friendship that quickly bloomed into an unlikely romance between the thirty-two-year-old former wife of a college professor and the lifelong bachelor with the pasty-faced pallor of a long-term prisoner. In the summer of 1978 when Ray was summoned to Washington, D.C., to testify before the House Assassinations Committee, she went along.

In Washington, she threw herself wholeheartedly into the campaign to prove his innocence, talking to Congressmen about his case and doing everything else she could to enlist support for Ray. She later complained that the committee was spending four million dollars on the probe and hadn't even considered all the evidence.

A few months after the Washington trip rumors swept the local news media that she and Tennessee's most internationally infamous convict were planning to marry.

Some of the first efforts by the press to confirm the story were directed at Warden Stonney Lane at Brushy Mountain. He replied that he had heard rumors about a marriage, but Ray hadn't applied for permission.

"I've had about five calls from reporters," he grumbled during one telephone interview. "I'm not his agent."

Lane also said, however, that he expected to approve the marriage if Ray applied, just as he would do for any other inmate. The warden said his part in the process was primarily determining that both parties were single.

The story about the impending wedding was true, and in fact, Anna was the one who proposed getting married. She was convinced that Ray was innocent and believed that he might win an earlier release if he were married.

She confirmed the story of the wedding plans and gave an exclusive copyrighted interview to a reporter with her hometown newspaper, the *Knoxville Journal.* Within a few days she was talking with reporters from other newspapers and media outlets, including the *Nashville Banner,* despite what she said were her fiance's instructions not to give an interview to the afternoon daily.

It was a stressful period in the bride-to-be's life. A few days before her plans to marry Ray were revealed, her father died. Then her mother moved from Knoxville to Oregon. But Mrs. Sandhu was determined to go ahead with the wedding and she seemed to welcome the publicity that was building up.

Early in October, shortly before the planned nuptials, she flew from the McGhee Tyson airport just outside Knoxville to New York for a guest appearance on NBC's "Today Show."

Her message during the interviews with the print and electronic media was consistent: James Earl Ray was not a racist or mad man-killer. He was a nice person with a refreshing sense of humor, who was innocent of the terrible crime he had pleaded guilty to.

199

"First of all, I know that James is innocent," she told a reporter for the *Banner*. "If I thought that he was a murderer or would be capable of such a thing, I wouldn't be able to love him."

Mrs. Sandhu said she expected Ray to be released someday from his ninety-nine-year prison sentence for the King slaying, that she was looking forward to living with him, and hoped to bear his children.

She described her fiancé as a man who was religious, sensitive, strong and unprejudiced. He didn't hate blacks, she insisted.

By that time Ray was claiming that his guilty plea in the Shelby County Criminal Court in Memphis was coerced by his court-appointed attorney, Percy Foreman, who represented him during the King proceedings.

According to Ray's story, he was tricked into buying the 30.06 pump-action sniper rifle used in the slaying by a mystery man named Raoul, whom he met in Montreal. But he insists that he didn't fire the weapon and didn't even know that there was a plot to assassinate the civil rights leader.

Ray and his defenders have repeatedly pointed out that his background prior to the King slaying was always nonpolitical.

He was one of seven children of George Ellis Ray, who had also broken out of prison after being sentenced to a long term for robbery. A year later the elder Ray fled from the Fort Madison Prison in Iowa, settled in Alton, Illinois, got himself a factory job, and stayed out of trouble.

* * *

James Earl Ray was born in the southern Illinois Mississippi River town on March 10, 1928. He didn't care much for school, and quit when he was sixteen. In March 1946, a couple of years later, he enlisted in the Army for a three-year term. He didn't complete his enlistment, however, and was given an honorable discharge two days before Christmas in 1948 after serving three months in the stockade.

With his brief military career behind him, he launched a career as a small-time criminal. He bootlegged liquor, committed some burglaries, and became a stickup man.

He was a crook and a thief, but he never belonged to any white power groups such as the Ku Klux Klan.

During her appearance on the "Today Show" Anna announced that the marriage ceremony would be performed at the prison by the Rev. James Lawson. He agreed to officiate after being contacted by Ray's latest lawyer, Mark Lane. Lane was the tenth lawyer to represent Ray since the King slaying.

Anna said that she admired Lawson and considered him to be a true Christian. She quoted him as saying he would be honored to say the vows.

The announcement of Lawson's role in the planned nuptials was a startling disclosure, and drew even more press attention to the story. The black clergyman was a close supporter of King. In fact, it was Lawson who had invited King to Memphis to support striking garbagemen just before the civil rights leader was slain.

Lawson left Memphis after King's assassination, and became pastor of the Holman United Methodist Church in Los Angeles. After it was revealed that he had agreed to perform the wedding ceremony, he told reporters he had doubts about Ray's guilt. He added that he would marry the couple even if he was convinced that Ray was the assassin, however.

On October 13, 1978, the couple was married in a thirty-minute ceremony attended by a few friends, relatives, and Ray's attorney, Lane, inside the maximum security prison's second-floor visitors' lounge.

"This signifies that the best of your lives is yet to be, the past is behind you," the minister told the wedding couple. "The reason I am here is because I see it as a sign of grace."

The couple exchanged simple gold wedding bands.

The bride wore an off-white pleated skirt and matching crocheted blouse for the nuptials. The shaky groom was dressed in grey trousers, a dark jacket, blue shirt, and a dark blue tie.

After the ceremony, the wedding party shared a cake baked by Ray's cellmate. Later, the bride and groom were permitted to spend ten minutes of semi-private conversation while seated at a table in the prison chapel without the guests present, but watched over by four guards.

Corrections authorities did not permit photographs to be taken at the wedding. In a bitter letter to Corrections Commissioner C. Murray Henderson, Ray later complained that the bride was told she could film the wedding, "until your office found out about it through some grub-street reporter," and issued a special order barring pictures.

He charged that corrections officials had joined with the press to claim falsely there were plans to sell the photos for millions of dollars. He asserted that prison regulations governing marriages permitted photographs, and complained that he was being unfairly treated. By the time the letter was written, however, the wedding was long past.

No one from the press was allowed to attend the ceremony, but Lawson later played a tape of the proceedings for the media. And the bride talked with reporters waiting in a cold drizzle of rain outside the grim monolith of the prison, confessing that both she and the groom were nervous during the ceremony.

"I didn't know my right hand from my left hand," she said. "I could feel him trembling with my arm."

A coat was draped over the bride's shoulders to protect her from the rain and chill as she talked. And tears welled in her eyes when she said she knew that the marriage wouldn't be easy, but they were prepared for whatever they had to endure. She added that it was the happiest day of her life. Then the bride left for the lonely drive back to Knoxville. The groom had already been returned to his cell.

Tennessee prison regulations prohibited conjugal visits, and Ray was not scheduled to become eligible for parole until 1998 when he would be seventy years old. According to prison rules, the couple was allowed four-hour-long visits twice weekly, under the watchful eyes of guards.

Convicts and their wives or girlfriends were permitted to sit at a table during the closely monitored visits and to hold hands.

The day before the wedding Mrs. Sandhu said in an interview that she thought it was terrible that conjugal visits weren't allowed. However, emotional support was the main thing that two people could bring to a marriage, she said she believed.

Ray's attorney also talked with reporters outside the maximum security prison after the ceremony, and announced that he had new evidence believed to show conclusively who was really responsible for the King assassination. The high-profile lawyer was attempting to obtain a new trial for his client, and Ray had already conferred with Jesse Jackson in an effort to enlist his support.

Jackson later wrote a foreword for Ray's book, *Who Killed Martin Luther King?: The True Story of a Convicted Assassin* (National Press Books, 1991), charging that the Tennessee convict hadn't acted alone, and that there was a cover-up in the assassination. Jackson said he suspected a government conspiracy, and called for the opening of FBI files on the case that were ordered sealed until the year 2027.

During the first year of the couple's marriage, the new Mrs. Ray regularly drove the roughly forty-five miles between Knoxville and the stark prison to visit her husband. Between visits, they exchanged long letters. Anna also kept busy with newspaper interviews and appearances on television talk shows, spreading the word that her husband was unfairly pressured into pleading guilty to the King assassination, and should be awarded a new trial.

While his bride busied herself publicizing his new trial efforts, Ray spent much of his time in the prison law library, poring over legal decisions and looking for anything he could find that might be helpful. When he wasn't in the library, in his cell, or working in the prison laundry, he spent much of his time lifting weights or jogging.

* * *

A few months after the wedding the former state Corrections Commissioner publicly accused Anna of posing as a Knoxville television journalist in order to obtain two interviews with him at his home in Sparta, Tennessee.

Harry Avery said she claimed she was working for Channel 10 (the CBS affiliate in Knoxville), when she showed up shortly before her wedding with a companion she introduced as a cameraman. The bogus cameraman didn't have a camera. She explained that the camera was being used for another story, the former corrections official declared.

Avery said that when she returned a second time after claiming her tape recorder malfunctioned during the first interview, he learned that she was really there to obtain information for Attorney Lane.

Governor Buford Ellington had fired Avery from his job as chief of the Corrections Department in 1969, after reports circulated that the prison official had interviewed Ray as a prelude for writing a book.

Anna later told reporters that at her husband's request she interviewed several people who had links to the King case. Others, including Ray's attorney, were working hard to maintain interest in the assassination and the new trial efforts. But Anna had emerged as one of her husband's busiest and most determined advocates.

On the first anniversary of her marriage to Ray, she said she was in love with him more than ever. She insisted she wouldn't trade places with anyone.

"Some women must think I'm crazy to be married to a man who has a ninety-nine-year jail sentence," she was quoted in an Associated Press story. "But we are very close. I see him twice a week and our relationship is solid. I've had no problems being Mrs. Ray."

She said she planned to give her husband an antique gold cross as an anniversary present. Although he wasn't especially fond of jewelry, she said she wanted him to have the cross to symbolize her love for him.

"You know, I thought I'd be doing most of the comforting, but he's the one who has had to give me a lot of emotional support."

She wasn't exaggerating. Her prison marriage to the man whose act of murder sparked destructive race riots throughout the nation was marked by difficulty and danger. She admitted she was troubled because the marriage was unconsummated. And as Mrs. Ray, she was treated by some people as a racist who hated blacks.

Her assignments as a courtroom artist abruptly dried up. Although she said she suspected she may have made a few art sales because of who her husband was, some galleries refused to hang her paintings. Owners reportedly were afraid of attracting demonstrations.

Anna eventually found a low paying job in a pizza parlor, but was fired after management learned who she was married to.

Her car was vandalized more than once while it was parked at the prison.

She was awakened at various times at night and cursed or called filthy names by anonymous telephone callers.

Someone killed her two housecats with poison while she was away.

Perhaps her most frightening experiences occurred during visiting days at the prison, however. She complained that female corrections officers at the prison subjected her to humiliating searches, and badgered her with nasty remarks.

Once when she was driving home from the prison, another car approached with two men inside who attempted to force her off the road, she claims.

And her arm was broken when she and her husband were attacked by another convict one day in a prison visiting room.

In 1981 Ray was hospitalized after two black inmates jumped him in the institution's law library. As one convict held him from behind, the other began repeatedly plunging a foot-long prison "shank," or sharpened piece of metal, repeatedly into his flesh. By the time the men finally broke off the attack and fled, Ray had been stabbed twenty-two times in the face, arm, and chest.

Ray was rushed to a hospital in Oak Ridge and patched up with seventy-seven stitches. Two days later he was returned to the prison and checked into the infirmary. When his wife visited him following the attack, she brought along her watercolors, and after he pulled off his bandages, she sketched the injuries.

News stories about the attack indicated that it was carried out by members of an organization for black convicts known as the Alke-Bulan Society, that was chartered by the state. But when investigators from the Tennessee Bureau of Investigation asked Ray who the knifemen were, he said he was unable to identify them. He had spent enough of his life in prisons to know that men who break the convict code of silence often die violently.

Several days after the attack, Ray was transferred from Brushy Mountain to the Tennessee State Penitentiary at Nashville. He was locked in the segregation building for his own protection. His cell was only a few feet from the convicts on Death Row, and within yelling distance of the electric chair.

His transfer to Nashville was a grim homecoming. He had been locked up there after he was arrested for a robbery in Tennessee, years before the King slaying.

The Music City was a four-hour drive from Knoxville. So Anna followed her husband, and moved to Nashville where she could be closer to him. However as a convict in segregation, his visits with her were trimmed to two one-hour meetings weekly.

It was during one of those visits that Anna was injured in another attack by a prisoner who was said to be connected to the Alke-Bulans. Ray and his wife were talking in the visitors' room when a black convict rushed in and smashed her on the arm. Moments later guards broke up the melee.

The strain was beginning to tell on Ray's loyal wife, and she gradually began cutting back on her visits. But she continued to write to her husband and to stay in touch with telephone calls.

On October 13, 1988, their tenth wedding anniversary, she announced that she had enough of the marriage and had told her husband she was going to seek a divorce on grounds of irreconcilable differences. She explained that she made the decision after he told her she wouldn't share in the profits of the book he was writing blaming the King murder on an FBI conspiracy.

By that time, he had been returned to Brushy Mountain. She had settled in the tiny community of White House in rural Robertson county about midway between Nashville and the Kentucky border. Mrs. Ray said her husband agreed that filing for divorce might be the best thing for her to do.

Despite the disagreement over the book profits and the talk of divorce, she continued to describe him as "too wonderful" to carry out an act as terrible as the King assassination. She said, however, that they didn't agree about who was really behind the murder conspiracy.

She suspected the Soviet government. He continued to claim the FBI was behind the reputed plot.

Although Anna talked with a lawyer, she didn't follow through with the divorce proceeding. Instead, on February 5, 1990, more than a year after the surprise announcement, her husband filed for divorce.

In a two-page petition filed in the Morgan County Clerk's Office at Wartburg, Tennessee, the sixty-two-year-old convict cited irreconcilable differences between him and his wife. Although he didn't indicate specific problems in the petition, relatives said he was disturbed because she hadn't visited him at the grim prison in East Tennessee for several years.

Barely three weeks before Ray filed for divorce, his wife telephoned the *Banner* to criticize plans by the Ku Klux Klan to mount a "James Earl Ray Support March," in Pulaski, Tennessee. The event was planned as a counter demonstration to a Brotherhood Weekend

March, previously scheduled for the south central Tennessee town a few miles north of the Alabama border.

Anna was upset when she heard of the KKK proposal, and responded by criticizing the racist group for making white people look bad and calling on them to get rid of what she described as "silly costumes."

She said she was sick of hearing that her husband should be given a medal. She pointed out that a medal wouldn't replace the lost years he had spent behind bars since the slaying, and said he wasn't proud of his reputation as King's assassin.

She didn't say anything during the telephone interview about new trouble in her marriage or the possibility of divorce.

Somehow the troubled marriage continued to drag on until mid-November, when Anna filed a divorce petition in Davidson County Circuit Court in Nashville. In the petition, she accused her husband of inappropriate marital conduct, although she didn't specify exactly what the objectional behavior was.

She also asked for a share of the profits from Ray's book that was scheduled for publication later that month.

Contacted at his Bethesda, Maryland office, the publisher told a reporter that he didn't believe Mrs. Ray was entitled to share in the profits from the book. Royalties would be used for the James Earl Ray Legal Defense Fund, he said.

This time Anna had called on big time divorce lawyer Marvin Mitchellson to represent her along with Dulin Kelly, a local attorney from nearby Hendersonville. Mitchellson was nationally known for his Hollywood and other celebrity clients.

Ray responded to Anna's latest move by claiming in court documents that he should be awarded the divorce because of what he claimed was her desertion and adultery. He also asked for a share of her home in White House, and a portion of the income from sales of her paintings. Her paintings were only salable because of her relationship to him, he contended.

Ray was struggling to return public attention to his claims of an FBI assassination plot in the King murder, and to win another chance at a trial. Locked behind prison walls, however, he was at a disadvantage and couldn't keep up with his wife in the media war.

Anna continued to make herself available to the press, and labelled her marriage to Ray as interesting, but a nightmare. She explained that she stopped going to see him in December, 1987, because of unpleasant experiences, such as the attack by the other inmate, that usually accompanied the visits or closely followed them.

Ironically, after she began to break off her relationship with her husband, she attracted a new set of enemies. Once hated for her ties to the man many people considered to be America's most dangerous white racist, now some of Ray's sympathizers were harassing her because of her disloyalty to him, she complained. The windows of her car were smashed as it was parked outside her home. Dulin Kelly told the press that she was afraid the KKK was after her.

It was true that she had turned from being one of Ray's strongest advocates to one of his most outspoken critics. She said she no longer believed that he was innocent of the King murder. And she accused him of

211

being an expert manipulator, and claimed that he "sort of staged" his stabbing for attention.

Anna also continued to make herself available to the news media, and she and her husband were interviewed for national television shows hosted by Geraldo Rivera. She was flown to New York for the media event. Her husband was still being periodically shuttled from prison-to-prison interviewed at the Riverbend Maximum Security Institution in West Nashville.

After concluding with Rivera's show, Anna revealed that she planned to appear on "Donahue" and would have some shocking things to say. She didn't wait for a "Donahue" appearance, however, before publicly claiming that she and her husband had skirted Corrections Department regulations and engaged in sexual relations several times.

She said it was about two and a half years after the wedding before she and her husband finally consummated the marriage while he was in the prison hospital at Brushy Mountain. After that, they engaged in many other sexual trysts at the Tennessee State Penitentiary at Nashville — including the Death Row visiting room, she claimed. Anna said she didn't enjoy the furtive love romps but went along with the idea to accommodate him. At Nashville, the lovemaking occurred in a corner of the visiting room hidden from any guards who might be walking by the door, she said.

Mrs. Ray claimed a great deal of sexual activity occurred at the prison visiting gallery between convicts and their female guests. She added that she thought guards were cooperating as well. Prison spokesmen firmly denied the accusations.

Anna also provided reporters with what was apparently an example of the "inappropriate marital conduct" she accused her husband of in the divorce papers. After she learned she couldn't have children, she began gaining weight, and put on about sixty pounds, she said.

She accused her husband of hurting her feelings one day when they were talking by telephone, and she said she was planning to visit. Anna said he responded by asking if she thought the waiting room would be large enough for her to get inside.

Ray had tried to head off his wife's titillating tell-all confession by obtaining a restraining order from the courts to prevent her from discussing their marital relationship or making other public derogatory statements about him. He claimed she was earning substantial amounts of money from television talk shows, magazines, and newspapers for interviews. But the petition for the order was denied.

The latest accusations from Ray's estranged wife were diverting him from his goal of focusing public attention on his efforts to blame the King assassination on an FBI plot and gaining a new trial. In a telephone interview from the prison in Nashville, he issued a firm denial to the press of any sexual activity between him and his wife during their near thirteen years of marriage.

In another court action, Ray was ordered to give Anna three thousand dollars in earnings from the book. In her petition to share in the proceeds, it was stated that a mortgage company had already begun foreclosure proceedings on her house. She claimed she wasn't able to support herself through sales of her paintings.

At the time of this writing, final resolution of the divorce was still pending.

Fatal Affairs

Chapter Thirteen

Olivia Shell Jackson
and
Maurice Jackson

Falling in love with a convict can be fatal — especially if the romance continues after he is released from prison.

But that was probably the furthest thing from Olivia Shell's mind when the lonely guard at the Southern Michigan State Prison in Jackson met inmate Maurice Jackson. A stickup man, who had been serving a ten-to-twenty-year prison sentence since February, 1981, he served the early years of his armed robbery term elsewhere, and was transferred to Southern Michigan in May, 1989. Olivia Shell had already been working there for two years as a corrections officer.

At the time there was no special man in the life of the thirty-one-year-old guard, and she was impressed by the hardened convict's masculinity. And it wasn't long before their relationship turned from purely professional to intensely personal.

217

The corrections officer realized that despite the prison sentence Jackson was serving, and his long criminal history, she was hopelessly in love with him.

When Jackson's parole was approved and he was freed from prison in October, 1989, it seemed that Olivia's dream of building a life with him outside the walls could be realized at last. She quit her job and married the handsome ex-convict.

With the approval of parole authorities, the couple moved to Birmingham, Alabama.

But the old, easy relationship they had shared in prison had changed drastically. Although Olivia had somehow managed to block out thoughts of the handsome convict's violent past while he was in prison, once he was free and they were married she was forced to confront it.

In the spring of 1990, Birmingham police began to log calls from the frightened, tearful woman complaining that her husband was beating her. The honeymoon had lasted less than six months.

They quarrelled over money, and just about every other aspect of their lives together. Neighbors soon got used to their noisy, violent fights.

By late summer Olivia had taken all the fighting she could stand. She left her husband and moved into an apartment in the East Avondale area of the city. A sociable, normally cheerful woman, she quickly made friends with her new neighbors. And she confided to some of them that her husband had beaten her, and she was deathly afraid that he was going to kill her.

During quiet evening chats while relaxing in a front porch swing and in other talks, the troubled woman told a next-door neighbor that she was planning to file for divorce and resume using her maiden name. And she talked repeatedly about her fears for her safety.

At last Olivia and her husband agreed to get together and talk with a lawyer. On Wednesday, October 17, 1990, the feuding couple met at a gas station near the Birmingham Police Department's South Precinct headquarters.

They got into such a violent argument that the manager of the gas station called police. Patrol officers dispatched to the station separated the couple and ordered Olivia's husband to leave.

It was nearly 8:00 P.M., and already dark, before the dejected and fearful woman arrived home. She told a friendly neighbor that her husband had threatened to kill her, and she was scared to death. The sympathetic neighbor agreed to watch her car and turn on the lights, while Olivia walked upstairs to her apartment.

Moments later the neighbor heard Olivia screaming for her to call police. Patrolmen speeded to the apartment, but they were too late. When officers walked inside Olivia's modest upstairs apartment with the neighbor, they found the former prison guard lying on the floor in a pool of blood. She had been repeatedly stabbed in the chest.

A few minutes after police made the grisly discovery, an officer ran down and captured Olivia's husband following a desperate foot race. He was taken to the Jefferson County Jail in Birmingham, and charged with the murder of his estranged wife. Bond was set at one hundred thousand dollars.

* * *

At the conclusion of a brief trial early the next year, a Jefferson County District Court jury returned a guilty verdict against him. A few weeks later the morose wife-killer was sentenced to serve a life prison term, without the possibility of parole.

Shortly after the slaying, Sgt. Fred Clanton, a homicide officer with the Birmingham Police Department, told a journalist the former prison guard should have known better than to become involved with someone like Jackson. The onetime stickup man had a long criminal history, the veteran lawman pointed out.

"You read about this type of thing happening all the time, people marrying people in prison," Clanton told the *Birmingham News*. "This is sometimes the result."

Chapter Fourteen

**Carol Menon Montecalvo
and
Daniel John Montecalvo**

When Carol Menon left the Roman Catholicism of her childhood to become a Protestant, she plunged into her new life with all her heart and spirit.

She had been lonely and depressed much of the time after struggling through a painful divorce from her husband, a native of India whom she had met when they were students at the Buffalo campus of the State University of New York.

Although she had grown up in a strict but loving family in Buffalo that included an older sister and a younger brother, she was working as a teacher and living alone in Madison, Wisconsin, when she became convinced it was time to develop a new relationship with Christ.

In her apartment a few blocks from the sprawling campus of the University of Wisconsin, she poured over the Scriptures, communed with the Lord privately and as a member of prayer groups, and at every opportunity talked with friends and acquaintances about her love for Jesus.

She became involved in a prison ministry program, sharing the Gospel with the inmates of area jails and penitentiaries. So there was nothing surprising about her response when a religious friend who worked with convicts suggested that she contact an inmate in the Federal Correctional Institution at Oxford, Wisconsin, and try her luck at leading him to Christ.

The convict's name was Daniel John Montecalvo. And he was serving a long sentence for bank robbery.

A short, dark-haired, dark-eyed man, Montecalvo was everything that Carol wasn't. He was street smart and prison-wise. She was naive and trusting.

Carol had grown up in a family that stressed honesty, hard work, and education. And she responded to their expectations for her by earning a bachelor of science degree in psychology. Then she decided she didn't want to be a psychologist after all, returned to school, and earned a master's degree in education.

Montecalvo soaked up most of his education on the streets and in prisons and jails. He grew up as the oldest of two sons in a miserable home in the suburban Boston town of Chelsea. His father made a living as a burglar and petty thief, and was in-and-out of jails and prisons during Daniel's early childhood.

The boy was nine years old in 1950, when his father was shot to death during a frigid winter night in a gunfight with police. The elder Montecalvo was busy doing what he did best, committing a burglary, when he was interrupted and killed.

Daniel appeared to be a chip off the old block. He was small, but scrappy, and more than held his own in fights with other boys in the neighborhood and at school. He also soon demonstrated that he shared his late father's penchant for taking other people's property as his own. By the time he was ten, he had already started revolving-door travels through local juvenile detention facilities.

He was barely out of his teens when he began sticking up banks. He robbed banks in Boston, Cleveland, and Baltimore. But he was arrested after hitting his second bank in Baltimore. He subsequently pleaded guilty to bank robbery, and was sentenced to twenty-five years in prison.

Bank robbery is a federal offense, and Montecalvo was shipped west to the federal prison at Leavenworth, Kansas. But he had been transferred to a federal prison in Springfield, when a group of liberal lawyers became interested in his case.

These attorneys were convinced Montecalvo was a victim of the system and should be freed. It was true, as the lawyers contended, that he had endured a horrible childhood. A judge was sufficiently impressed by the argument so that Montecalvo was freed on parole, only four years after being sentenced.

223

But he couldn't stay out of trouble, and after a bout with alcoholism and a minor brush with the law, he robbed another bank. A few months later he was locked up at the federal penitentiary at Marion, Illinois, with some of the most escape-prone and dangerous convicts in the United States. He had been ordered to serve a thirty-year term.

Throughout his life, Montecalvo seemed to veer unerringly into bad habits. One of the worst, and one which would repeatedly get him in hot water, was gambling. From appearances, it seems that he wasn't very good at it. And when he ran up some gambling debts at Marion that he couldn't, or wouldn't, pay, authorities decided to transfer him to another prison for his own safety.

In January, 1978, he was sent to the federal prison at Oxford, a few miles from Madison. Carol wrote her first letter to him the following October. She was thirty-three. He was thirty-seven.

She wrote every day for two months, before they agreed to meet. She drove to the prison shortly before the end of the year to talk personally with him about Jesus. It was the beginning of a series of regular visits. Carol drove to see and talk with him as often as she was permitted to by prison regulations.

They read the Bible together, discussed the Scriptures, and gradually began to share confidences and personal information about each other. It seemed that her efforts to save the soul of the troubled convict had borne sweet fruit when he was baptized.

* * *

The relationship had borne other fruit as well. The idealistic schoolteacher and the seemingly repentant bank robber realized they were in love, and wanted to be married. But prison authorities turned down their request. Prison marriages were not permitted at the maximum security federal penitentiary, and Montecalvo still had eight years of his sentence to serve before he could even be considered for parole.

Carol prayed about the problem. Then, her convict sweetheart was transferred to the federal prison at Terre Haute, Indiana. Regulations were more relaxed there, and when Montecalvo once more asked for permission to marry, his request was granted.

On a bright and clear Monday, July 14, 1980, the beaming couple was united during a ceremony in the prison's exercise yard, as two of Carol's friends from church, bemused guards, and a handful of convicts watched. Carol wore an ankle-length, light-colored cotton dress and carried a bright bouquet of fresh cut flowers. Her groom wore a snappy new blue suit she had bought for him.

The new Mrs. Montecalvo probably considered it to be just that much more proof of the power of prayer when, less than a month after the wedding, authorities announced a surprise recommendation approving her husband's early parole. With the permission of his parole board, Montecalvo moved back to Wisconsin to live with his wife.

* * *

Although Carol had left teaching, she was earning a good salary working in sales with the local telephone company. She became the couple's major breadwinner, while her husband struggled to adjust with his new status as a married man and law-abiding citizen outside prison walls. It wasn't easy, and again he had a couple of minor brushes with the law. He also began slipping away to spend private moments away from his wife at local taverns.

When Carol was transferred to California a few months after their marriage, her husband went along.

In California, they settled in suburban Los Angeles, and quickly developed new ties with the active Christian community there. They began attending the nondenominational Overcomers' Faith Center Church. Carol joined a women's service group, and Dan became associated with a men's fellowship. He also found a job through their Christian friends as manager of a hotel. A couple of years after the move West, they put a down payment on a house in Glendale.

Then the troubles started again. Carol left her job with the phone company, and wound up working for about half what she had been earning. Then Dan was hospitalized with an ulcer, and had to take time off from his job at the hotel. Suddenly the couple was having serious financial troubles.

Carol prayed; Dan gambled and drank.

His luck at the blackjack tables was good for awhile, but it eventually soured, and he soon found himself in debt to Las Vegas casinos for thousands of dollars.

Then he and Carol began taking out a series of expensive life insurance policies on her. Despite all his difficulties, Carol was deeply in love with her husband, and she wanted to be sure he would be provided for if she died before he did.

Carol had a whopping six hundred thousand dollars worth of insurance on her life when she was shot to death on March 31, 1988.

Police called to the couple's home a few minutes after 11:00 P.M., found Dan walking unsteadily out of the front door and clutching his side with one hand. He had been shot in the back, but remained on his feet until he was loaded into an ambulance for the ride to the nearby St. Joseph's Medical Center in Burbank. A few hours later surgeons removed a single .25-caliber slug from his midsection where it had lodged after plowing through his back a few inches above the hipbone.

Inside the Montecalvo house, police found Carol on the floor of the hallway with two gunshot wounds in her neck. Emergency efforts to start her heart beating again were unsuccessful. She was dead.

The distraught husband told police that he and his wife were doing some last-minute packing for a vacation trip the next day to Hawaii, when they decided to take a late evening stroll together. As they returned home, she walked inside the house ahead of him. Moments later he heard a shout and a gun being fired.

Montecalvo said that as he ran inside someone

grabbed him from behind, and fired a shot into his back. It appeared the couple had returned home just in time to surprise burglars inside the house.

"I worshipped that woman. She didn't deserve to die like that, and I want her murderers caught," the victim's husband told investigators.

Police officers also wanted the killers, or killer, caught. But it was a baffling case and during the early stages of the investigation they didn't have much evidence to work with.

Ballistics and other forensic tests disclosed that Carol and Dan were shot with different guns: she with a .38-caliber revolver, and he with a less powerful .25-caliber pistol. But neither of the handguns was recovered.

Nevertheless, investigators had leads on several people as possible suspects. But it was months after the murder before they narrowed their list down to a single leading suspect: the husband of the victim.

Dan had been a strong suspect since early in the investigation. Police interest in the new widower was especially piqued when they pulled up and printed a copy of his criminal record on their computers. And he began to look even more like the possible killer when they learned about the staggering amount of insurance on his wife's life.

Montecalvo didn't help any when he collected more than half the insurance settlement and began blowing hundreds of thousands of dollars at casinos in Las Vegas.

There were other aspects of the case, as well,

that didn't fit in with the early theory and Monte-calvo's claim that Carol was shot to death by a surprised burglar or burglars. Forensic tests indicated that the first shot was fired into the left side of her neck while she was standing in the hallway. Then the killer had stepped up to her as she was lying on the floor, pointed the barrel of the gun a few inches from her neck, and fired the second shot.

Startled burglars don't usually kill people execution-style. A frightened thief might shoot someone who has surprised them, but they don't stick around and fire a second shot into the head or neck to make sure the victim is dead. Executioners do that. And Carol's death had the disturbing appearance of a deliberate execution.

In the middle of March, 1990, almost two years after Carol's death, her husband was arrested and charged with her murder.

Early the following September at the conclusion of a near three-month trial, which included tearful testimony from the defendant about his innocence and his love for his wife, a jury returned a verdict against Montecalvo of guilty of first-degree murder.

The victory was especially sweet for the prosecution because it was won entirely on circumstantial evidence — an incredibly difficult feat. Montecalvo hadn't helped his case any by insisting on sharing the role of defense attorney with his lawyer, and questioning witnesses. Defendants do not make good defense attorneys.

On December 3, 1991 Judge Jack Tso gave

Montecalvo a tongue-lashing, telling him that murdering his wife for money was the ultimate act of cowardice and evil. Then he sentenced the former bank robber to a term of from twenty-seven years to life in prison.

A few days before Christmas that same year, Montecalvo married one of his late wife's best friends, the mother of two grown sons. This time, the ceremony was conducted in a judge's chambers.

Pen Pals and Cheerleaders

Chapter Fifteen

**Christine Lee, Cindy Haden,
Kelly Marquez, Others,
and
Richard Ramirez**

Although it's true that California is home to handsome surfers and Hollywood hunks, one of the most ardently pursued bachelors in the Golden State is a gaunt sadist expected to end his miserable life on Death Row.

Richard Ramirez earned his chilling nickname, the Night Stalker, for a grisly string of Satanic mutilation and sex slayings that terrorized the Los Angeles area for nearly two years in 1984 and 1985.

Yet, the menacing, gap-toothed Ramirez with an appetite for heavy metal music, cocaine, rape, and murder was barely behind bars before he was acquiring a perplexing harem of beautiful women and girls who were outspokenly devoted to him.

During Ramirez's gruelling fifteen-month marathon trial in Los Angeles for thirteen murders and

233

a host of other felonies, a bevy of pretty cheerleaders quickly formed and scrambled for seats as near to the front of the courtroom as they could get.

Several dressed totally in black in grandstanding efforts to get the bony defendant's attention, and earn one of his appreciative smirks.

Some claimed to be college students conducting research. Others, like Bernadette Brazelle, were more honest. The dark-haired college student admitted she was in love with the accused killer. One day in court she wore a sticker with the words, "I Love Your Smile."

Bernadette described the curly-haired killer as movie star handsome, and talked of his need for someone caring to steer him on the right path.

A young woman who identified herself as Diana Harrell agreed with the infatuated media art student's assessment of the defendant's appearance. She told columnist Dennis McCarthy of the suburban Los Angeles *Daily News* that women were crazy about Ramirez, and after he was freed he should become a rock star or actor.

Diana had barely left after being turned away by a security guard outside the packed courtroom, before another young woman dressed all in black showed up.

The woman, identified by the columnist only as "Patty," reportedly assured him that the thin defendant loved her, instead of Diana. Patty said she knew that, because Ramirez told her so during her visits with him at the jail.

But Bernadette's remarks about salvaging Ramirez were especially revealing: Experts who have studied the phenomena of women obsessed with men on Death Row or others accused of especially notorious sex slayings and serial murder, say that some of them may see themselves in the role of mother or savior.

At least one woman began writing to Ramirez and visiting him because she wanted to turn the boastful Satanist to Christianity. A fundamentalist clergyman from Los Angeles, who later attempted to peddle her letters from the serial killer, confessed that she lost the spiritual struggle for Ramirez's soul.

One woman infatuated with Ramirez met him through her brother who was an inmate at the San Francisco Jail where the accused Night Stalker was locked up on charges of murdering a sixty-nine-year-old Bay Area man, Peter Pan, and the brutal beating of the victim's wife, Barbara.

And a member of the Los Angeles county jury reportedly brought a Valentine to the courtroom for Ramirez during his fifteen-month trial there. According to a story in Los Angeles's now defunct, *Herald-Examiner,* a member of the defense team had the Valentine in his briefcase in a red envelope with "Mr. Ramirez" written on it.

The same week the Valentine was reportedly picked out for the defendant, the jury listened to lurid testimony about one of his victims whose eyes were gouged out. In other testimony the panel heard about Satanic graffiti scrawled in blood on the bodies of victims, or on walls in their homes.

Other victims, who survived ghastly ordeals of beatings and rape, testified that the Night Stalker forced them to swear allegiance to Satan. Several of the women Ramirez had selected as prey were about the same age as those who were pursuing him in prison.

Long after Ramirez was sentenced to death following his conviction on twelve counts of first-degree murder, one count of second-degree murder, and several lesser charges, he was still receiving mash notes and love letters from attractive young women.

They continued to write to him and to clamor for visits while he was held at the San Francisco jail. A Sheriff's Department spokesman said there were so many requests from people, most of them women in their twenties, that several had to be turned away. Authorities simply couldn't handle the traffic.

The Sheriff's deputy said he believed the primary attraction was Ramirez's celebrity status. He had seen similar behavior with other especially notorious prisoners, he added. Women school around notorious serial sex slayers like pilot fish chasing a shark, feeding greedily on the scraps of his notoriety.

Ramirez and his guests used telephones to talk with as they faced each other through a protective barrier of heavy glass. The police spokesman added that the visitors were apparently women who hadn't previously known the defendant, because there were too many of them to be merely family or friends.

One of the women who visited him several times at the Los Angeles County Jail reportedly shared his worship of Satan. Identified in a *San Francisco Examiner* news feature as "Page" and a Satan worshiper, she was quoted as saying that meeting the Night Stalker was "the ultimate high."

She kept a picture of the Night Stalker on her bedroom wall. Like the convicted serial killer, the receptionist and occasional model said she listened to the bone-jarring music of the same heavy metal bands that he favored: AC/DC and Black Sabbath.

She also recalled that he wore a medallion of a pentagram under his T-shirt, and said she once painted the occult symbol on her hand to show it off to him as she arrived for one of her visits. The circled and inverted five-pointed star is believed by some people to be a symbol of Satan.

Most of the other women who sought access to Ramirez in jails and in prison talked about less esoteric subjects during their visits and in their letters. Some of them discussed love, marriage, and having his babies. Others indicated they simply wanted to be his friend.

In return, he sometimes wrote back from his seven-by-ten-foot Death Row cell at San Quentin a few feet from the state's notorious gas chamber, or called them collect by telephone. Often he asked for cash gifts and sexy photographs. He liked pictures that showed their feet.

Some of the Night Stalker's letters were illustrated with crudely sketched hearts or more erotic doodles of thick smacking lips and protruding tongues.

Most of his correspondents wanted to visit, and his schedule became so hectic that he had to ration audiences with him. He not only had to juggle visits from his female correspondents, but he had to make time for members of a large and loving family who made the trip to San Quentin as often as they could.

Inevitably, perhaps deliberately, the rough schedule the imprisoned killer set up occasionally resulted in more than one of his female admirers showing up at San Quentin's waiting room or one of the jails at the same time. Those meetings were seldom friendly.

Kelly Marquez, an attractive friend of Ramirez, who lived in the San Francisco Bay Area was harassed. A former nude model who later turned to real-estate sales, Marquez claimed she first wrote to Ramirez and began visiting him because of her opposition to the death penalty.

During Kelly's pregnancy, a female admirer of Ramirez tracked her down and attempted to kick her in the stomach. She was also hounded with telephone calls and threatening notes. Once, a dead cat was left in front of the trailer park near her mobile home.

Incredibly, since Ramirez's multiple convictions, one of his most outspoken defenders is one of the jurors who voted for his conviction and recommended the death penalty.

When she appeared on television's popular "Donahue" show in May, 1992, Cindy Haden objected to being referred to as a girlfriend of the convicted serial killer. She asserted that she was merely a close friend.

During an earlier appearance on "Geraldo" however, she referred to herself as Ramirez's best friend.

The former juror's fellow guest on "Donahue," Christine Lee, was less coy about her relationship with Ramirez. Only a few weeks earlier, the former New Jersey woman, who had moved to the Bay area near San Quentin, had publicly boasted of accepting a proposal of marriage from the condemned thrill killer.

The attractive blond divorcee claimed in an interview with the supermarket tabloid *The Globe* that corrections authorities at California's San Quentin prison were even going to provide the lovers with a private trailer where they could share conjugal visits two weekends per month.

The *Globe* story quoted heavily from love letters she received from her prison sweetheart. He asked her for revealing photographs, inquired about her two little boys, and talked about his love for her, her beauty, and his desire to suck on her toes. Ramirez once sent her a ribbon, that he said was a first place award for the most luscious body.

* * *

Despite Christine's boast of honeymooning some day in a trailer at San Quentin, the statement was no more than her own fantasy. It's true that California is one of eight states that permits conjugal visits, but that privilege is not extended to Ramirez and his companions on Death Row.

But there were other glaring holes in the would-be bride's version of fairytale love with the nightmare killer and rapist, as well. During the few weeks between publication of the interview and her appearance on "Donahue" together with Cindy the love match between Christine and her reputed one-time fiancé had badly deteriorated.

In his introduction at the beginning of the television show, Donahue identified Cindy as the woman who got in the way of the engagement.

Christine conceded to the talk show host that her relationship with Ramirez was in trouble, and complained that other women in addition to the one-time juror were also visiting him at the prison.

According to Christine, he told various women that he was in love with them. But it was all part of a scheme to weasel money out of older women, and she was the one he was really in love with, she claimed. Christine was then in her mid-twenties.

Ramirez telephoned her as she was preparing to leave home for her appearance on the show, cursed and accused her of costing him money, she said. She claimed he told her he was a businessman and she was ruining his business.

* * *

At one point when Donahue began to read from some of the Night Stalker's correspondence, the show host asked who a woman named "Lana" was. She was another woman in love with Ramirez, Christine replied.

In one of the letters Donahue read, Ramirez's admirer told him that she had already given him most of her life savings, but would do anything to get him money if only he "wouldn't marry that bitch Christine." Donahue didn't identify the author of the letter.

Later in the show, Christine charged that Ramirez told Cindy he was in love with her in order to get gifts of money from her. Christine knew it was true, she said, because the former juror once sent money to her by mistake. Cindy denied he ever asked her for money, and insisted she never gave him any.

Although Christine claimed Ramirez had given her a half-carat engagement ring after sending her a catalogue and telling her to pick the jewelry out, she wasn't wearing it on the show.

She repeatedly betrayed her jealousy of her fellow guest on the show, scowling and muttering objections and accusations. When Donahue referred to Cindy as a "young woman," Christine's reaction was immediate. "Young?" she snorted in feigned disbelief.

As their white-haired host worked to control the interview, the women bickered over their relationships with Ramirez like a pair of junior high schoolgirls tangling over the class jock. Christine

241

took the offensive, while Cindy sought to defend herself.

Christine accused Cindy of "hanging all over" Ramirez. Cindy denied it.

Christine said Ramirez called Cindy "Grandma" behind her back. Cindy conceded that she was older, but wasn't specific about her age.

Cindy had moved north from Los Angeles to be closer to Ramirez, Christine asserted. That wasn't true, Cindy said, she moved because of her job.

Christine said Cindy accused her during an earlier television show of being "delusional." Cindy agreed she had described Christine as delusional.

"You're the one that's delusional," Christine snapped back.

When Donahue showed a videotape of Ramirez in the courtroom, Christine squeezed off another verbal shot at her perceived rival.

"There he is," Donahue said, as Ramirez was shown in the picture.

"And there's Cindy, drooling," Christine quickly interjected. Despite Christine's observation, Cindy couldn't be seen on the tape.

Prompted by the host, Christine petulantly accused Cindy of being in love with Ramirez. Cindy had already said she was only a friend, and although she voted for his conviction that she later became troubled by doubts because she didn't believe he was properly defended.

Cindy said she visited about twice a week with

the man she had helped convict and condemn to the gas chamber. She was attracted to him because he was a victim of injustice in the courtroom, and needed a friend, she explained.

Chapter Sixteen

Sue Terry
and
John Wayne Gacy, Jr.

If it's true that opposites attract, that may explain the bizarre love affair between Sue Terry and John Wayne Gacy, Jr. They were about as different as they could be.

As a twice-divorced homemaker from Centralia, Illinois, who was the mother of eight children and grandmother-caretaker for two others, she created and nurtured life.

As the sadistic homosexual thrill-killer of at least thirty-three young men and boys, Gacy brutally extinguished life.

He was the most notorious convict on Death Row at the fortress-like Menard Correctional Center at downstate Chester, Illinois, when Sue read a newspaper story about him.

Then and there the lonely, plump grandmother decided that the condemned sex-strangler was someone she would like to write to. Three days after she wrote to him, he wrote her back.

The exchange of letters was the beginning of a curious pen pal relationship that Sue would later tell the world quickly blossomed into love and a proposal of marriage from the imprisoned serial slayer.

She disregarded a warning from him against talking about their relationship with the news media. Gacy later explained that he cautioned her to avoid publicity because he was concerned that there were "a lot of kooks," who might want to injure her or her children if they knew of her friendship with him.

Nevertheless, Sue quickly found herself thrust into the limelight, and she eagerly told her story of prison love to newspapers, magazines, and on television talk shows. She revealed that she was surprised to find out for herself he wasn't the monster he had been depicted as in the press.

Instead, although he was initially wary that she might be trying to pump him for information for the news media, she said that he quickly warmed up, and she found him to be a kind and caring man.

Defending him as best she could, she insisted he was too nice to have committed the gruesome crimes he was convicted of. And she suggested that the only reason he had appeared so guilty was because of the bodies found on his property. The case was poorly investigated, she claimed.

No man had ever been as considerate toward her and her children, she told one reporter. "Just a few hours spent with him when I visit him in prison makes life seem so much brighter and hopeful."

She loved him and would marry him, she said.

Although Gacy publicly denied that he proposed marriage to her, there is no question that he seriously romanced his pen pal by mail and during a series of personal visits at the prison.

In 1988 the forty-three-year old Terry turned over a package of forty-one letters to the *Chicago Sun-Times*. Gacy had typed them in his Death Row cell, and mailed them to her.

Sue said they represented her correspondence from the convicted killer during a three-month period, but she had received many more than that between early October 1986 and mid-February 1988. The Chicago tabloid published a six-day, Page One series of copyrighted articles based on interviews and excerpts from the letters.

Sue had barely disclosed her purported marriage proposal before three other women publicly claimed Gacy had also asked them to tie the knot.

Gacy responded by announcing that he was corresponding with about forty pen pals, most of them female. In a telephone interview with *The Chicago Tribune,* he described his role with his female correspondents as being like providing "advice to the love-lorn from Death Row."

Sue said he received a dozen or more letters at the prison daily. Some of his correspondents were from other countries, including such far-flung geographical locations as Canada, Australia, and Sweden. One fan predicted that some day Gacy might be considered a hero.

Ironically, despite his own chilling predicament —
the criminal courts ordered twelve separate death
sentences and twenty-one life terms for the thirty-
three murders he was convicted of — many of his
correspondents wrote seeking advice for solving their
own problems.

Norman Grimstad, Jr., an East Moline, Illinois
man that Gacy was corresponding with, reported
that the serial killer had complained of having multiple sclerosis. Grimstad, who said he initially wrote
Gacy seeking an autograph, told a reporter that
Gacy claimed he was so ill with the incurable nerve
and muscle disease that he was bedridden much of
the time.

Prison officials refused to confirm the report, re-
marking that the medical condition of inmates was
confidential.

During Sue's long relationship with Gacy, he advised and told her how to handle her personal affairs and her family. Once he even told her who she
should or shouldn't permit to drive her car, she said.
She also claimed that he also gave wholesome advice
to her children, that was helpful in dealing with the
normal problems of growing up.

Sometimes he gave her more advice than she
wanted and that led to quarrels, she said. In some
of his earliest letters to her, he revealed his need to
control her as well as their relationship.

After she complained that she was too heavy, he
said his own bulky five-foot, eight-inch frame had
ballooned to 205 pounds, and told her she needed
self-discipline. If she would lose weight, he promised, he would continue his battle to win his freedom for her.

* * *

Although in his letters he sometimes called her "Pieface," one of her old childhood nicknames, she quickly learned to be careful about the pet names she used for him. Gacy vehemently objected to any name that might suggest femininity or weakness.

She learned about that when he told her he didn't want her to call him "Babe." He also turned thumbs-down on "Honey Bunny," and grumped that "Sweetie Pie" was unmanly. Both of his former wives had referred to him simply, as "John," he said.

Psychologists expert at delving into the darker corners of the human mind, who were familiar with Gacy's crimes and his background, weren't surprised by Sue's disclosure of his aversion to certain pet names. He had a history of denying his homosexuality, and worked hard to prove his manliness. He was known for making a point of his affection for such macho sports as football and hockey.

His letters—like the outward behavior that he showed to neighbors, work associates, and other acquaintances unfamiliar with his most closely guarded secrets—betrayed his efforts to appear tough and knowledgeable. He liked being John Wayne Gacy, a take charge guy.

Before police began unearthing bodies from under his house in December, 1978, he operated his own small construction contracting business. And during his free time when he wasn't trolling the streets for victims, he often hung out at a working man's bar a few miles from his home in Norwood Park township just outside the northwest city limits of Chicago.

During his first marriage to a woman he met when he was working in Springfield, Illinois, he fathered two children: a boy and a girl. His second marriage was to a girlhood chum of his sisters. She was recently divorced and the mother of two little girls when they married.

Gacy grew up in an immaculately kept home in Chicago with a loving mother and two sisters, but his machinist father was a brutal alcoholic who abused him both emotionally and physically.

Sue also grew up in an unhappy home, and was pregnant for the first time when she was fourteen. Instead of attending high school like most other girls her age, she quickly found herself saddled to the job of raising a houseful of babies and coping with unhappy marriages.

Although she worked for a short while as a cocktail waitress, most of the time she was kept busy with her homemaking and mothering chores. According to her account, her second marriage was especially violent, and her husband once smashed her in the head with a baseball bat. Another time he tried to cut off her fingers, she said.

During the heady days when Sue was conducting newspaper interviews and making television appearances, she wore her dark hair in bangs. It was a style, she said, she chose to cover the scars from the attack with the baseball bat.

When Gacy showed what appeared to be genuine

concern for the welfare of her and her children, she welcomed the attention with open arms. Life as a single mother supporting a large brood on social security disability payments was lonely and difficult.

She lived in a modest house in Centralia with her children and two children of an older daughter. She was soon making the 140-mile, round-trip drive to the ominous prison in Chester almost every week.

Once when she suggested changing her visits from Thursday to Friday, Gacy rejected the idea. He explained he didn't want to miss Catholic Mass on Friday afternoons. It even angered him when his lawyers, whom he referred to as his legal staff, came to see him on Fridays, he wrote.

Often Sue took one of her children with her on the visits, and they liked the trips so well that they sometimes quarrelled over who was going to get to see "Uncle John."

The visits were conducted in a small white room a few feet off Death Row, spartanly furnished with a table and a chair. Prison guards cuffed Gacy's hands for the visits. But he was allowed to be alone with his guests, although he was monitored by an overhead television camera.

Sometimes they reached across the table, and he joined his beefy cuffed hands with hers. The couple was allowed one kiss when saying goodbye.

Their conversation often focused on Sue's activities, her children, and Gacy's dreams of being paroled from prison and the life they would build together. Already behind bars at that time for eight years after the slayings, he estimated that it might be another ten years before he was finally released, Sue later recalled.

But he also talked frequently about his parents, his love for them, and his inability to please his father. The elder Gacy died on Christmas Day, 1969, while John was serving a prison sentence after a sodomy conviction for sexually molesting a teen-age boy in Waterloo, Iowa.

During a period when Gacy was writing Sue almost daily, he tackled dozens of other subjects, however. He criticized the British royal family, mentioned his dislike of reporters, talked of lawsuits filed against him and on his behalf, discussed the Olympics and his fondness for professional football, and told her what television shows he liked best.

Gacy enjoyed true crime stories on television, and once mentioned that he thought a television drama based on the book, *The Billionaire Boys Club* was his kind of movie. He added that he liked Charles Bronson, and had watched the first three movies of the hard-boiled actor's *Death Wish* series that week.

In another letter he asked Sue to pass a copy of *The Man Who Killed Boys,* a book about his serial killings, on to him after she was through reading it. And he conceded it was true that he got along well with his second wife, adding that she had been to Menard to visit with him.

In a reply to a query from Sue, he assured her that he was no longer writing to another woman he had corresponded with. He said she was threatening him, and made an ominous reference to mysterious associates in "the East," whom he had turned the problem over to.

Occasionally he talked about the grim prospect of his life being ended by poisons being injected into his veins in the silent and foreboding death chamber that was located only a few feet from his cell. Admitting the odds were against him, he vowed however to make the state of Illinois spend millions of dollars before the death sentence was carried out.

Gacy also discussed his emergence as a prison artist, and explained that he couldn't give paintings to her children because he was a businessman and had bills to pay for supplies. He sold his work to friends at reduced prices, but insisted that he needed to be paid for his costs and labor.

Eventually, Sue wound up with several of his paintings, however, including a clown portrait. Gacy loves clowns, and used to dress in a clown costume and entertain at parties when he was living in his house on the outskirts of Chicago.

Hundreds of the serial killer's amateurish paintings of such subjects as clowns, Indian chiefs, landscapes, folk art, dwarves, monsters, and skulls have been sold. Although many of the buyers are people who are little known outside their own circle of acquaintances, Gacy has also sold to a few celebrities. Offbeat film director John Waters and actor Johnny Depp are two of his clients.

In late spring of 1988, an exhibition of his paintings was opened in Los Angeles with a party that included champagne and a clown cake. Music was provided by a recording of "The Chair," a work composed by a Death Row inmate several years earlier.

Gacy also exhibited his paintings at the Menard Correctional Center's annual art show, and with the work of other prison artists at the Illinois State Fair in Springfield.

While Gacy busied himself painting however, his romance with Sue was beginning to fall apart.

The special friendship between the serial killer and the southern Illinois grandmother ended less than five years after it began. Sue was sick in body and spirit. And she was no longer describing the burly Death Row convict she once defended with such zeal as "kind" or "sensitive." He had admitted to her that he murdered the thirty-three boys and young men he was convicted of slaying, the disillusioned woman told the press.

Sue described the Death Row convict she had once talked of marrying as an evil, manipulative con man who had taken advantage of her trust.

Forty-seven years old by that time, she had moved with her family to a ranch-style house near Carbondale, Illinois, and said her health was failing. She was sick with diabetes and heart trouble. While there was still time, she wanted to set the record straight and tell the world that he was a sadistic killer who deserved to die, she said.

She claimed that Gacy told her he was the "president of the club" when multiple murders were involved.

253

* * *

Still awaiting execution after more than a decade on Death Row, and denying that he knew anything about the thirty-three slayings, Gacy also denied that he admitted his guilt to his former sweetheart. In his final letter to her, he accused her of lying, and ordered her to leave him alone.

Chapter Seventeen

Caroline Norwood
and
Allan Legere

Caroline Norwood was married with an ailing husband and six children, most of them grown up, when she decided that one of Canada's most notorious criminals needed her.

So she quit her job as editor of the *Courier*, a weekly newspaper in Digby, Nova Scotia, and became one of the serial mutilation and torture killer's most outspoken and ardent supporters.

Barely six months after writing her first letter to the handsome, curly-haired bodybuilder imprisoned at the Atlantic Institution in New Brunswick, she announced to the press that they were planning to marry.

"I just got through talking with him," Mrs. Norwood told a reporter while discussing her telephone conversation with Allan Legere. "He's really good. He's really happy."

* * *

She indicated they planned to tie the knot sometime after obtaining divorces from their current spouses. Legere had already started divorce proceedings, and Mrs. Norwood estimated that it would take her about two months to formally dissolve her marriage.

"People fall in love with people all the time in and out of jail," she was quoted as saying. "I'm not questioning it. I'm not asking why. I'm just accepting it for what it is."

Curiously, Legere, who had another girlfriend as well as a wife, wrote to a newspaper in Moncton after the wedding announcement, denying that he planned to marry the Nova Scotia housewife.

But he later wrote to a television station, claiming he was still the smitten woman's "ace of hearts."

Few people, if any, shared the strange couple's interest over the possibility of an impending wedding.

Only a few months earlier, Legere had spread terror through the province after carrying off a daring escape from prison guards while shackled in a body chain, leg irons, and handcuffs.

At the time of his escape, he was already serving a life sentence for his part with two companions in the torture and murder of the elderly co-owner of a mom-and-pop store during a brutal home invasion robbery in the rural New Brunswick hamlet of Black River Bridge. The victim's wife was also horribly beaten, but survived.

In May, 1989, Legere developed an ear infection

and was transported from the Atlantic Institution—the maximum security federal prison is more commonly known as Renous after the village where it is located—to a hospital in Moncton for treatment. He made the two-hour trip in the back of a prison van.

But he was a prison-wise convict who had been in-and-out of local jails and penitentiaries since he was sixteen, compiling a long record for cat burglaries and other more violent crimes.

A former barroom bouncer, he had developed a fearsome reputation as a hell-raising drinker and brawler. He was respected, or feared, for holding his own in fierce face-offs with the tough loggers, papermill workers, and hunters in the rugged backwoods country of New Brunswick, or in the midst of the habitual violence of prison life. He wasn't a man other convicts were anxious to pick a fight with, and he knew his way around.

Before leaving his cell for Moncton, he apparently hid a weapon, or sham weapon, in his rectum. The anus is a favorite hiding place for convict contraband, and strip searches that include inspection of body cavities are routine in most maximum security prisons.

Legere was given a strip search, and sullenly complied with the anticipated command to "spread his cheeks" so a guard could peer into his anus and check for contraband. But the guards did not use a hand scanner for the search, and the object was apparently inserted so deeply that it was missed.

The cunning convict also smuggled out a key for the shackles which he had managed to construct from solder. It was apparently hidden inside a cigar he was permitted to take with him, even though he was a nonsmoker.

As soon as he arrived at Dumont Hospital, Legere asked his guards for permission to use a restroom. Moments later he slammed out the door, brushed past a startled guard, and scampered down the hallway. When the driver of the prison van moved to stop him, he took a vicious swing at the guard with the metallic object, snarled at him to stay back, and continued running.

According to some later reports, the object was believed to be a collapsed metal television antenna, or a sharpened screwdriver. But Legere would eventually claim that it was merely a piece of rolled up tinfoil. His guards were armed only with Mace.

Despite police roadblocks that were quickly set up, scores of lawmen, tracker dogs, and a helicopter that was sent into the air to help in the manhunt, Legere managed to hijack a car and complete his escape.

He headed north, back toward the prison, and faded into the thick forests and bogland of the Miramichi. A rugged region in northern New Brunswick, the area gets its name from the Miramichi River that runs through it. Legere had grown up there.

Months later the desperado publicly scoffed that the guards who escorted him to the hospital were too old, too fat, and too stupid to catch him.

Legere was young, healthy, and had built up his

powerful body as many convicts do by working out with weights and through the prison-enforced discipline of regular meals and regular sleep. He was also an accomplished woodsman, who knew how to survive off the land, and off people weaker than he.

Soon after his escape, Royal Canadian Mounted Police and local law enforcement agencies began logging reports of a series of savage beatings, robberies, and murders. Most of the crimes were centered in the Miramichi.

During the next seven months, a seventy-five-year-old woman, two middle-aged sisters, and a Roman Catholic priest were murdered in the Miramichi region. Each of the female victims were raped. The older woman's sister-in-law was also raped, as well as beaten, and horribly burned, but survived. Many police, most of the local press, and frightened residents blamed the crime wave on Allan Legere.

Shortly after Legere fled from his guards, police put the Crown prosecutor, who convicted him in the Black River Bridge storekeeper's murder, under twenty-four-hour protection.

At last in late November after one of the most extensive manhunts in Canada's history, the fugitive was recaptured at a police roadblock during one of the worst blizzards of the season. He was making a desperate dash along a slippery logging track in the stolen detached tractor of a semitrailer truck when he was stopped by two members of a police tactical squad and a dog.

The heavily armed lawmen seized a knife and a

loaded .308 lever-action Browning rifle while making the arrest. Legere reportedly told a witness he was headed for the airport in Chatham and planned to hijack an airplane and fly to Iran.

Instead he wound up back at Renous, locked in an isolation cell. Several months later, following a painstaking investigation of the Miramichi murders, authorities lodged a series of new criminal charges against him that could keep him in prison for the rest of his life. Canada does not have the death penalty.

Legere was still being held under close watch the following April when Mrs. Norwood wrote her first letter to him. He wrote back, inviting her to continue the correspondence. They met for the first time during one of his court appearances on charges stemming from his escape.

Outside the courthouse, angry men and women had jeered and screamed at Legere as he was led into the courtroom. "Hope you die soon," one man yelled. Others simply chanted, "Hang him." Legere was ultimately convicted on charges of escape, kidnap, and assault stemming from his flight from the hospital and his activities during his half-year on the run.

He was a violent, desperate man. But if the old adage that opposites attract is true, Caroline Norwood seemed to be living proof.

Ten years older than the renegade killer, she was a native of Maine, where she worked for awhile as a reporter for a newspaper in Portland. In 1974, she and her schoolteacher husband emigrated to Nova Scotia and settled on Brier Island at the mouth of the Bay of Fundy.

If the growing family liked the breathing room they had in the sparsely populated state they had just left, the semi-isolation of their new home must have been heavenly.

Mrs. Norwood became a Canadian citizen and worked in her career as a small town journalist until late 1989, about the time she became involved with Legere. And she also served on the municipal council, and became a member of the local hospital board.

Southern Nova Scotia is a picturesque tourist mecca of small towns, national parks, game sanctuaries, forests, and fishing. Halifax and the province's other larger cities are two hundred miles north, or even farther away. St. John, New Brunswick, was closer, about a hundred miles across the Bay.

And it was only a few hours' scenic drive from St. John to the Miramichi. Barely a decade after emigrating to Canada, Mrs. Norwood would be driving along a tangle of roads to the three-year-old six million dollar prison at Renous. Constructed deep in the east central New Brunswick forest country, the prison is hundreds of miles from Brier Island.

Norwood and the killer were allowed to visit, although regulations limited them to talking by telephone as they faced each other on opposite sides of thick, protective glass windows. The two-hour visits were permitted every Wednesday.

In a telephone interview with the author, Mrs. Norwood revealed that she managed to get a contact visit with Legere during the Christmas holiday in 1990 after telling the warden she was Legere's fiancée. But even contact visits with maximum security prisoners at Renous are limited to a brief embrace and kiss under the watchful eyes of two or three guards.

Mrs. Norwood said she was firmly convinced of Legere's innocence, and claimed other people could have been the killers during the dreadful murder spree in the Miramichi after his escape.

Even Legere's murder conviction for the slaying of the elderly storekeeper was accomplished through use of a legal loophole, she insisted. She blamed powerful oil interests in New Brunswick for unfairly influencing the press, and helping create a media monster of the convicted killer.

According to her description, Legere was a sensitive and loving man, witty, well-read, and a talented artist. When Legere went on a hunger strike at Renous to press his demand for separate trials in the four Miramichi murders, and the court's permission for him to question potential jurors, she talked to the press about him.

Several days after he began refusing any food except for a tepid concoction of tea with milk, she reported that when she had last seen him he was weak and in poor spirits. "He finds it difficult to understand why he is punished so severely," she explained.

The imprisoned killer's outspoken advocate disagreed with people who believed he was malicious, and claimed there was nothing in his past record to indicate he was a vicious killer.

"If people would get to know him through his writing and also through his artwork they would realize this is a gentle person and this image that's been created of him. . . . It isn't there," she declared. She said she would reveal the real Allan Legere in a book she planned to write.

She attended as many of the hearings preceding his trial for the Miramichi slayings as she could, and Legere frequently turned from the prisoner's dock to smile at her as she watched and listened to the proceedings.

But she wasn't his only admirer. Several other women scrambled for places in the packed spectator's gallery, where they smiled and waved at him. One of them, in addition to Mrs. Norwood, was already deeply involved in a spirited campaign aimed at winning his freedom.

But as his reputed fiancée, Mrs. Norwood was his most prominent, and boldly loyal, defender.

She demonstrated her faith in his artistic ability by standing outside the courthouse when his new murder trial at last got underway, and peddling his pen-and-ink sketches. Some were from Legere's "Dorchester period," she explained of his artwork during the years he was locked in the federal prison at Dorchester, New Brunswick.

Inside the courthouse in the village of Burton, the proceedings weren't going well for Legere. He didn't help his own case by the tantrums he threw, or with the crude insults he hurled at the judge, whom he once called "just a prejudiced old fart."

Despite the fact that a dozen or more RCMP constables and local police officers were stationed inside and outside the courtroom, and his feet were chained to the floor, his behavior was so outrageous that he was finally ordered to be taken back to a cell. As court officers led him out of the courtroom to watch the proceedings on closed-circuit television, he snapped, "Up yours, judge!"

The so-called "Monster of the Miramichi" wound up at the conclusion of the gruelling marathon trial being convicted on four counts of murder, and was sentenced to four concurrent twenty-five-year prison terms. He was sent to a prison at St. Anne-des-Plaines, Quebec, near Montreal, hundreds of miles from the Miramichi.

By the time Legere's trial began in late August, 1991, the wedding had already been called off. Legere announced in February that he was no longer planning to wed Mrs. Norwood. The collapse of the marriage plans occurred by mutual agreement, she later said.

Talking by telephone from her home on Brier Island, she reported that her husband had undergone open-heart surgery. And she was spending much of her time fishing.

Asked about her links to Legere, she replied, "Let's say we still have a relationship."

But she stressed she also hadn't given up on her efforts to help him. "He's a very honest person, and I've gotten to know his family," she said. "The things he is concerned about, I am concerned about."

She indicated that one of those things is the long years in prison he has been sentenced to serve. She complained that it was unfair to sentence someone to such a long term behind bars for fatally knifing someone, when a drunk driver who killed might be ordered to serve only a fraction of that time.

The inequity of the treatment bothered her.

"Death is death, and it's gruesome," she said.

Chapter Eighteen

Veronica Lynn Compton,
Shirlee Joyce Book Bianchi
and
Kenneth A. Bianchi

There was something about men imprisoned for murdering strings of women that pretty and talented Veronica Lynn Compton simply couldn't resist.

In fact, murder and violent sex fascinated her. The dark-haired, twenty-three-year-old divorcee was an aspiring actress, poet, and playwright, whose creative efforts reflected much of the dark side of humanity.

She was hard at work attempting to write a play about a female serial killer when she decided to get in touch with Kenneth A. Bianchi. A former security guard, Bianchi was a sexual sadist who was behind bars after murdering or helping to murder at least twelve young women.

The sexy Latin beauty wrote to Bianchi for what she later described as part of the research for her play. Bianchi responded with a telephone call, and they set up a face-to-face interview at the Los Angeles County Men's Central Jail.

Bianchi was being temporarily held there after agreeing to testify in the upcoming trial in the Los Angeles County courts of his cousin, Angelo Buono, Jr. The cousins were accused by authorities of carrying out a string of grisly sex slayings in the Los Angeles area attributed to a mysterious killer the press called the Hillside Strangler.

Veronica first met behind bars with Bianchi a few months after his arrest in Bellingham, Washington, for the murders of two coeds from Western Washington University. Good detective work on the part of the small town police chief there had then tied him to the unsolved serial murders that raged through the Los Angeles area in 1977-1978.

When Veronica got her first look at the confessed serial killer in the visiting room at the jail, he seemed like the prototypical boy next door, she later recalled.

Soon, as they compared family background and made small talk about such subjects as the artistic talents of both their fathers, she began to feel that they were destined to be together. The amateur poet and playwright and the serial killer were soul mates, she realized.

The professional motivation for Veronica's contact with Bianchi quickly took a backseat to a rapidly growing personal and romantic interest. She was in love.

* * *

Soon she was visiting him twice-a-day at the jail, writing him long letters, and exchanging lovers' confidences in telephone calls. They had much in common. Although Veronica had never committed murder, she shared many of her new sweetheart's sadomasochistic fantasies.

Fantasy was a big part of her life, and while dreaming of fame and success she had combined her first and middle names to coin a glamorous new name for herself, "VerLynn." But somehow, she allowed her dreams to drift to the dark side where fantasies became nightmares.

The interests that VerLynn and Kenneth shared were not those of the typical girl or boy next door. The more common and conventional heady chats about such things as wine and roses, wedding dresses and babies, were given short shrift by the excited lovers. They talked, instead, of murder.

Bianchi had a plan that he believed could spring him from jail and bail him out of the trouble he was in. All he needed was Veronica's help.

According to the imaginative scheme he outlined to his love-struck sweetheart, she could help clear him of the twin-slayings of the Washington coeds by traveling to Bellingham and committing a copy-cat murder.

Years later Veronica would claim that she initially balked at the suggestion. But when Bianchi began bawling and got down on his knees to beg, she relented.

With the question of her cooperation settled in

his favor, Bianchi proceeded to demonstrate his strangulation technique to Veronica during one of their meetings in the jail visiting room.

Then he provided her with a sample of his semen. Veronica smuggled it out of the jail in the finger of a surgeon's rubber glove. The plan called for her to strangle a woman in Bellingham, then plant the semen inside the victim's body.

The devilish scheme was hatched years before genetic fingerprinting (matching suspects with samples of semen, blood, and other bodily fluids through their DNA) became an important tool in police work and forensic science.

Consequently, it seemed to the conspirators that the scheme had a good chance of working. The plan called for creating the impression that a sex killer with the same blood type and other features similar to Bianchi's was still at large in the Bellingham area, and was responsible for the slayings of the coeds.

Dutifully, Veronica padded the waistline of her dress in order to mimic pregnancy, pulled on a wig, and boarded a flight for Bellingham. It was the beginning of the biggest adventure of her life.

There had been some talk between the lovers of murdering another coed from Western Washington University. But after Veronica arrived in Bellingham and checked into a motel, she selected a waitress at a local cocktail lounge as the victim. Veronica lured the woman back to the motel.

But the would-be murderess had made a bad choice. The twenty-six-year-old waitress was an outdoorsy woman. She was athletic, strong, and bigger than her hostess. The woman was seated on a chair when Veronica padded up behind her and looped a cord around her neck. Startled, the waitress dug her fingernails into Veronica's arms and doubled over in the chair. Taken by surprise, Veronica was vaulted over the woman's head, and landed against a table, knocking herself temporarily senseless.

The frightened waitress sprinted from the room, climbed into her car, and escaped.

On October 2, 1980, police knocked on the door of Veronica's trailer home in suburban Los Angeles and arrested her for the assault.

Although she had failed to successfully carry out the murder, she still hadn't given up on the idea of clearing her sweetheart of accusations that he was a serial killer. She told Los Angeles police that they were in bed together when each of the murders had occurred.

According to the lovers' original scheme, she was to repeat the claims in court, so that the full blame for the Hillside Strangler slayings would be thrown onto Buono. But no one believed her story when she told it to the police. And by the time she was called to testify in Buono's trial, she had a far different story to tell.

Bianchi himself was among the disbelievers when she announced during a press interview at the jail that he was going to marry her, and they were planning to become parents of a daughter.

Although Veronica continued to write to Bianchi for months after her arrest, the man she had settled on to become her second husband had lost interest in her following the failed murder attempt. Other women were writing to him, and he had apparently decided that it was time to seek out new conquests.

His rejected sweetheart was returned to Bellingham, and a few months after her arrest she was sentenced to a life term in a Washington state womens' prison for attempted premeditated murder. According to sentencing guidelines, she wouldn't become eligible for parole until 1994.

Bianchi ultimately pleaded guilty to the murders in Bellingham, and admitted teaming up with Buono in some of the Hillside Strangler slayings. As part of a deal with the prosecution to escape the death penalty for the Hillside Strangler slayings, Bianchi pleaded guilty to five of the California murders and agreed to help prosecutors convict his cousin.

Meanwhile, authorities were continuing with the trial of Buono's sinister partner in the strangler slayings. The trial would eventually drag on for two years, and became the longest criminal court proceeding in U. S. history at that time. It was incredibly complex, and the testimony about kidnap, rape, sodomy and torture was gruesome and horrifying.

The murders tied by police to the Hillside Strangler killings began late in 1977, shortly after Bianchi travelled across country from Rochester, New York, and moved in with his cousin in the Los Angeles suburb of Glendale.

The son of a reputedly promiscuous and hard-drinking teenage mother, he was three months old when he was adopted by a loving couple. By the time he moved to California, however, he had run through a series of girlfriends. His efforts to carve out a niche for himself as a police officer were even less successful than his attempt to forge a lasting romance. He was rejected for a position on the Monroe County Sheriff's Department in Rochester, and had lost a couple of jobs as a security guard. In California he was turned down again after applying for jobs in law enforcement.

Bianchi's cousin was the divorced father of several children, and operated an auto upholstery business. But Buono had a second enterprise that was as much hobby as it was business. He sexually exploited teenage girls, some of them runaways, after luring them to his home.

The cousins quickly formed an easy partnership based on exploitation of the teenagers. They began forcing the girls to go out on calls to private homes and businesses as prostitutes. When two of their prostitutes ran away, the murders began. Yolanda Washington, a nineteen-year-old black prostitute and part-time waitress, was apparently the first to die. The mother of a two-year-old daughter, her naked body was dumped in Universal City.

After the prostitute's murder, the nude, violated bodies of teenage girls and young women began showing up dumped on hillsides in a half-dozen Los Angeles suburbs. The victims were runaways, prostitutes, aspiring models, college students, store clerks and bank tellers. All except Yolanda Washington were white.

* * *

By the time Veronica was called to testify in Buono's trial, her romance with Bianchi had been completely shattered. Instead of attempting to throw the full blame on Buono, she told the jury that Bianchi admitted to her that he committed the Hillside Stranglings by himself. She explained that she had benefitted by psychiatric treatment from prison doctors, and was telling her story because she did not want to see a man, who might be innocent, convicted of a crime he didn't commit.

Despite Veronica's concern, Buono was convicted of participating in nine of the murders. He was cleared of complicity in the Yolanda Washington slaying.

Both men escaped the death penalty and were sentenced to life terms in prison. Bianchi escaped because of his plea bargain; Buono because jurors thought it would be unfair to sentence one of the homicidal cousins to death and not the other.

Long before the trial was over, however, Veronica had become infatuated with another imprisoned serial killer.

Douglas Daniel Clark had trolled the same streets cruised by the Hillside Stranglers in his search for young prostitutes, runaway teenagers, and other victims for his necrophiliac pursuits. The skinny, ne'er-do-well son of a retired Navy Admiral, Clark liked to wear women's underclothes. And he liked to murder young females, then have sex with their dead bodies.

The sadistic pervert teamed up with Carol Bundy, a dumpy, weak-eyed nurse, while prowling

Hollywood's Sunset Strip in 1980 in a kinky sex and murder spree that claimed the lives of at least six young girls. Carol carried out another murder on her own, shooting a former boyfriend in the head after a sexual tryst in the back of a van, then decapitating him with a boning knife.

Clark also shot some of his victims in the head, usually as they were performing oral sex on him. Then he would decapitate the corpses, and have Carol pretty up the heads with lipstick and eyeliner so that he could continue necrophiliac sex until putrification forced him to get rid of them.

Soon after the accused serial killer called "The Sunset Slayer," by the press, was jailed, a fifteen-year-old girl began attending his pretrial hearings, visiting and writing letters to him. The visits and the letters stopped after Carol heard about what was going on, and sent her a personal note.

The smitten teenager was barely out of the picture, however, before Clark initiated a steamy exchange of love letters with Veronica. At that time, she was still awaiting trial for the attempted murder of the waitress and had her own press nickname as "The Copycat Strangler." The couple's bizarre correspondence was filled with talk of murder, necrophilia, and mutilation.

Clark was eventually convicted of six counts of first-degree murder, and sentenced to die in California's gas chamber at San Quentin. Veronica was called as a defense witness in the trial, but when an attorney attempted to question her she pleaded the Fifth Amendment, and refused to testify, citing her constitutional protection against self-incrimination.

(Veronica made news again in the summer of 1988 when she and another prisoner cut through four wire fences with pruning shears and escaped briefly from the Purdy Corrections Center for Women near Gig Harbor, Washington.)

Carol pleaded guilty to murdering her ex-lover and to helping Clark kill one unidentified prostitute. She was sentenced to twenty-seven years to life in prison on one count, and to twenty-five years to life on the other. The judge ordered the sentences served consecutively.

Bianchi meanwhile was narrowing down his list of favored female admirers to one. Imprisoned at the Washington State Penitentiary at Walla Walla where he was serving two life sentences, he had become infatuated with a pretty blonde from Monterey, Louisiana.

Shirlee Joyce Book had begun writing to Bianchi at the prison in Walla Walla in 1986 after she saw a news photo of him crying in a California courtroom. They exchanged letters and audio tapes and chatted by telephone for more than two years before he proposed marriage. She accepted, and he mailed her an engagement ring.

The prospective bride was thirty-six, and had a teenage son. The thirty-eight-year-old Bianchi had never been married, although he fathered a son with a girlfriend he had dated in California, then followed to Washington state a few months before his arrest.

The pen pal lovers first saw each other during a thirty-minute meeting in a small room inside the prison on the day before the wedding.

Nevertheless, on September 21, 1989, eleven years after the serial sex-slayer was locked in the maximum security prison, the couple was married in a fifteen-minute ceremony behind the walls. The petite bride wore a traditional white wedding gown and veil, and the convict groom was clad in a rental tuxedo.

Bianchi's parents, two convict pals, the bride's mother and an attendant assembled in the tiny prison chapel for the morning ceremony. A few minutes before 11:00 A.M., the minister pronounced the couple man and wife. Bianchi lifted the bride's veil, bent over, and gave her a wedding kiss.

The wedding couple refused to talk with anyone from the media except a reporter for the *National Enquirer*. The bride told the reporter she was looking forward to a honeymoon thirty days later in a trailer set up for conjugal visits on the grounds of the prison. And she revealed she was planning to move to Washington state to be closer to her husband. She said visits were allowed every three days, and use of the trailer would be permitted less often.

Prison authorities later confirmed that the trailer was outfitted with a television, a microwave, and a bed. And they said Bianchi fit the criteria for a trailer honeymoon.

After the story about their plans for the honeymoon trailer were reprinted in the weekly tabloid and in the *Los Angeles Herald-Examiner*, however, the state corrections officials were besieged with a storm of protest from outraged letter writers. A corrections department spokesman told the press that although Bianchi had asked for permission to honeymoon in the trailer, the request was rejected the day after he applied.

The spokesman said the prison superintendent made an administrative decision against allowing what they referred to as extended family visits to Bianchi because of the especially violent nature of his crimes. No appeal of the decision was allowed.

In a follow-up story in the *Enquirer*, the bride was quoted as saying the decision was unfair. She observed that her husband was studying law, and she said they would continue fighting to realize their dream of being together as husband and wife.

Chapter Nineteen

Dawn Pepita Hall Simmons
and
Lemuel Warren Smith

There was no question that the chilling twilight world of Lemuel Warren Smith was strange.

Locked up at various times in some of New York state's most secure prisons, he was a killing machine who raped, ripped, and mutilated his victims with no more remorse than if he was discarding toilet tissue.

The muscular, six-foot, four-inch psychopath was already in prison for a murder when a psychic linked him to two other brutal unsolved killings that had stymied police for months.

But the dreadful saga of the serial killer whom a federal judge once labeled, "the most dangerous man in the state of New York," became even more bizarre when the news media announced that Dawn Pepita Hall Simmons was in love with him and they planned to marry.

Public curiosity wasn't linked to the fact that Smith

was a product of America's violent black ghettos, and Dawn was a married white woman, who had emigrated to the United States from England, via Canada. Nor was his status as the last man on New York state's Death Row the primary source of the interest.

It wasn't even the fact that Dawn was a successful biographer of famous women who was adopted by one of the world's most renown actresses, Dame Margaret Rutherford. Dame Rutherford starred in a series of popular films as Agatha Christie's crime-detecting heroine, "Miss Marple," and as "Mme. Acarti" in Noel Coward's *Blythe Spirit*, as well as in a host of other major roles on stage and screen.

The curiosity was tied to a reputed dream message from the dead; and to press reports that Mrs. Simmons had changed her sex years earlier before marrying another black man — then given birth to a daughter.

It was shocking news in 1968 when the leading newspaper in Columbia, South Carolina, *The State*, announced in a blaring headline: "British writer changes sex to marry Charleston Negro."

The author of biographies of former U. S. First Ladies, Jacqueline Kennedy Onassis, Ladybird Johnson, and Rosalynn Carter, as well as novels and juvenile books, was born in 1937 in Sussex, England, as Gordon Langley Hall. No doctor was present, and the sixteen-year-old unwed mother was attended by a midwife.

According to the writer's account in a biography of her adopted mother, *Margaret Rutherford: A BLYTHE SPIRIT*, the baby's clitoris was so enlarged that the confused midwife mistook her for a boy. The mistake and lack of expeditious surgery to correct the condition led to a childhood marked by misery and confusion.

Hermaphrodites, who have both male and female sexual characteristics, or what are sometimes called "ambiguous genitalia," account for about one in every twenty-five thousand live births, say doctors who specialize in diagnosing and treating such infants. The exact physical characteristics of babies considered to be hermaphrodites vary, but many, like Gordon, may appear to be male when they are born, although they have ovaries, wombs, and vaginas.

Misidentified and raised as a boy, Gordon nevertheless looked like a girl and preferred playing with dolls rather than toy guns, soldiers, or miniature cars and trucks. The child's parents were married while he was still an infant, but his chauffeur father showed little interest in him. Gordon was raised by a loving grandmother and her twin sister.

Finally, as a teenager, he emigrated to Canada and took a job as a teacher on an Ojibway Indian reservation. After a stint as obituary editor of the *Winnipeg Free Press,* he moved across the border to continue his pursuit of a career as a journalist and writer in the United States. For awhile he was society editor of the *Nevada Daily Mail,* then moved on to New York City where he operated the Gordon Langley Hall News Service & Syndicate.

During that period he covered Queen Elizabeth's trip to Nigeria, and chronicled Princess Margaret's Caribbean holidays and her marriage in Westminster Abbey. A few years later he wrote *Princess Margaret: An Informal Biography.*

He had already launched a successful career as an author with publication in the late 1950s of the book,

Me Papoose Sitter, when he was adopted by Dame Rutherford and her husband, J. Stringer Davis. The Davises visited Gordon in New York after the actress read the book and decided she wanted to play the part of an Indian grandmother in the proposed movie. Dame Rutherford and her husband had no children of their own.

In the meantime, Gordon had churned out several other books, including the biography of Princess Margaret, and purchased an old Southern mansion in Charleston. He was living there when he began hemorrhaging, and during his treatment learned that his lifelong gender dilemma could be solved through simple surgery.

The surgery was performed a few months later at the Gender Identification Clinic at Johns Hopkins Institute Hospital in Baltimore. Gordon Langley Hall became Dawn Pepita Hall.

In 1969 she became engaged to John-Paul Simmons, a black auto mechanic she met when he arrived at the mansion for a date with her cook and was stood-up. Simmons was also a skilled sculptor.

Although, the well-known author's sexual surgery had created little stir in the United States outside her own personal circle of friends and acquaintances, her shocking relationship during the racially turbulent late 1960s with a Southern black man and their impending marriage was a different story.

In the country of her birth, London's cheeky tabloid, *News of the World,* headlined a story, "Royal Biographer To Marry Her Butler." In the United States, *Newsweek* covered the event by reporting that she had "rocked the Cradle of the Confederacy."

The couple was married by a black Methodist

minister in the drawing room of her mansion in Charleston after the pastor of a black Baptist church reportedly backed out following a reputed bomb threat. Dawn later wrote that a police bomb squad searched the basement during the ceremony.

At the request of her adoptive mother, the rites were repeated a few months later at the eight-hundred-year-old St. Clement's (Anglican) Church in Hastings, Sussex.

As Dawn Hall Simmons, wife of a black man, she was no longer as popular as she had once been with white Charleston society. She later claimed that the underhanded machinations by enemies led to loss of her mansion, and that she was advised by another author acquaintance that Mafia hit men had been hired to kill her.

Despite her sudden ostracism from the inner circles of Charleston society and the reputed threats from strangers, the dark cloud that suddenly descended over her had a silver lining. The marriage produced a daughter, Natasha Margienell Manigault Simmons who was born in 1971 on her mother's birthday, October 16.

According to the author's preface and other references in *A BLYTHE SPIRIT*, however, she finally fled with her family after she was beaten and hurled off a third-floor porch of the run-down house they had moved into by a mysterious intruder she found menacing her baby daughter with a knife. Mrs. Simmons wrote that her left arm, shoulder, nose, and two toes were broken in the assault.

The family retreated to upstate New York and settled in the little mountain town of Catskill. Her husband deserted her and the baby there, she wrote. By the time the couple divorced in 1982, the author and her daughter had moved across the Hudson River and into a stately old home known locally as the Paddock Mansion in the adjacent town of Hudson.

Although Mrs. Simmons was virtually penniless when she arrived back in New York state, she managed through her writing to support herself and her daughter and to buy their new home. She used the publishers' advance from *A BLYTHE SPIRIT* for the down payment on the mansion. Among other books turned out by the prolific author were the intensely personal, *Man Into Woman,* published by Icon Books in London. Another, *All For Love,* specifically traced her controversial marriage and its turbulent aftermath.

With the move to upstate New York and the breakup of her marriage, Mrs. Simmons and her daughter settled down to a quieter life.

But two days before Christmas in 1983, the British born writer was in the headlines again — in New York City and in Hudson.

In classic tabloid-style, the *New York Post* announced: "Sex-Change Writer Wants To Be Wife Of Triple Killer." The more subdued headline in Hudson's *Register-Star* reported: "Hudsonian offers to marry Smith."

The *Post* "exclusive," written by Jerry Tallmer, quoted her as saying, "I am going to marry Lemuel Smith, the last man on Death Row in New York state."

The interview also drew heavily on a tape filmed by video producer Dena Crane the previous May that traced a visit between Mrs. Simmons and the convicted serial killer in a Dutchess county courtroom. Smith's legs were chained to a chair, and guards kept close watch on the dangerous prisoner as the unlikely couple talked of love, poetry, and prison.

On the tape, Mrs. Simmons queried Smith about his ability to "express love so eloquently" in his poetry and other writings when, as she put it, he had been "treated so badly by life."

Smith replied that everyone wants somebody to love, wants to be needed, and wants somebody to need. Prison walls didn't change that, he said.

"And I come to the conclusion I want to love somebody, want somebody to love me, right?" he said. "And that's the most important thing in life."

Mrs. Simmons was reportedly so touched by the statement that she got up, walked over to his chair, and kissed him.

When Lemuel Smith was first locked up at Green Haven, he had already been convicted of murdering two people, had pleaded guilty to another kidnap-rape, and was indicted but never put on trial for two other slayings. He had benefitted from the reluctance of New York state politicians to restore the death penalty for especially heinous crimes, when he killed again.

His last victim was Donna Alice Payant, a rookie prison guard and mother of three children. Her gruesome rape and mutilation murder was typically vicious, indicative of the kind of savage brutality the killer had used on victims so many times before.

The thirty-one-year-old mother was the first woman corrections officer murdered by an inmate while on duty since females first became guards at prisons housing males in New York state in 1976.

Mrs. Payant joined about fifty other women on the 543 guard force at the maximum security Green Haven Correctional Facility in 1981 a week after her graduation on April 8 from the New York State Correctional Services Training Academy in Albany. Her husband, Leo, was already a guard assigned to the Clinton Correctional Facility in the small Adirondacks mountain community of Dannemora.

On May 15, 1981, she disappeared while she was on duty at the prison. Other officers reported seeing Mrs. Payant at about 2:00 P.M. in a corridor between two cellblocks, but she wasn't seen again. She wasn't even reported missing from her job at the twenty-nine-acre prison until nearly 4:00 P.M., when she failed to report for tear gas duty at the mess hall. Two hours after that, at 6:00 P.M., the 1,884 inmates at the prison were put on lock down.

Corrections officers twice searched the yards and the more than twenty buildings at the huge prison without finding the missing woman. They even looked inside garbage dumpsters, but there was no trace of her.

Her body wasn't found until the next day twenty-five miles away, dumped in a landfill near the town of Armenia. Guards assigned to transport dumpsters there made the grisly discovery. Two plastic bags had been slipped over her upper body, and another over her hips and legs.

The dead guard's shirt had been ripped open, and her bra pulled up above her breasts. Her hands were tied behind her back by a length of strong cord knotted on the other end around her neck.

She had apparently lain in the landfill since the previous afternoon when another load of dumpsters was driven there from the prison.

An autopsy, including detailed laboratory tests, disclosed that the pretty guard had been beaten, strangled, and sexually mutilated. The nipples of both breasts were bitten nearly off, and other bite marks inflicted with human teeth scarred her body. A bulldozer had further mutilated the corpse at the dump site, breaking several bones during compacting.

While more than two thousand corrections officers were attending memorial services in Dannemora for the victim, three prisons, including Green Haven, Great Meadow at Comstock, and Bayview, a medium security prison for women in New York City, were put under lock down. Meanwhile investigators were closing in on a suspect.

Considering Smith's horrendous record of violence and sexual assault, there was little question in the minds of investigators probing the prison slaying that he was capable of the kind of attack that led to Mrs. Payant's death.

When questioned, he claimed that the rookie guard was murdered by another corrections officer. He contended that he was the victim of an underhanded frame-up to protect New York state's Department of Corrections.

Smith attracted big-time legal representation for the high-profile trial and later proceedings, including the well-known death penalty opponent and social activist William M. Kunstler.

But the evidence against the defendant was too powerful to ignore.

Dr. Lowell Levine, a dentist who during an earlier court proceeding had identified Smith's teeth from a cast made by authorities in 1978 as matching the bite marks on the body of Maralee Wilson, one of his earlier victims, was called on as a forensic expert in the trial for the guard's slaying.

After examining photographs of the bite marks just above Mrs. Payant's right breast, he said they matched the cast of the defendant's teeth. He also recalled that they appeared to match the bite marks found on the body of the murdered woman in Schenectady.

The prosecutor told the jury he believed Smith lured the guard to the Roman Catholic chaplain's office by telephoning her and pretending to be a corrections officer with a message that she was wanted there.

At the conclusion of a four-month trial in Poughkeepsie, the Dutchess county jury returned a conviction for first-degree murder. Prosecutors demanded the death penalty, pointing out that no other significant punishment can be ordered for prisoners already serving life terms, visited only by members of their immediate family, their lawyers, doctors, and the clergy.

But less than a year later, New York state's higher courts overturned the provision of the statute under which Smith had been sentenced to death.

On March 28, 1985, in Poughkeepsie, Judge Rosenblatt, who had presided at the murder trial, resentenced Smith to a term of twenty-five years to life in prison for the guard's slaying.

The account in the *Register-Star* was based on an interview reporter Joe Kilcoyne conducted in Hudson with the biographer. Kilcoyne wrote that she said she wanted to marry Smith. She was quoted as saying Smith had changed the lives of herself and her daughter, and had influenced her to move from the Anglican church and begin studying to join the Roman Catholic Church. The son of a Baptist minister, Smith had converted in prison years earlier to Roman Catholicism.

During the interview Mrs. Simmons also told the reporter that the *Post* account of a sex-change operation was incorrect. She was not a transsexual, a person who believes they are a man or woman trapped in the body of the opposite sex.

Perhaps most startling of all, however, in her interview with Kilcoyne, she traced her relationship with the multiple killer to a message that her adopted mother gave her in a dream the previous January 23. She said that when Dame Rutherford, who died at 80 years old on May 22, 1972, appeared, she was dressed in a large hat, dangling necklace that was blowing in the breeze, and the cape worn in the role of "Miss Marple."

"Go and help Lemuel," she quoted the actress as commanding. "He's innocent."

Mrs. Simmons admitted to being puzzled by the cryptic message. She explained that the only man with that name she recalled was a Biblical Lemuel.

Five days after the mystifying dream, however, the *Register-Star* published a photo of Smith as he was being led in chains out of court.

". . . that led to our meeting and subsequent feelings for each other," she told Kilcoyne.

The author had experienced other ghostly visitations from her adoptive parents. She credited their advice from the grave during dreams on three consecutive nights for leading her and her literary agent in London to a deceased relative's steamer trunk filled with a treasure trove of biographical information used in compiling information for the book tracing the life and career of her famous adoptive mother.

After seeing the picture and reading about Smith, she began writing to him at the Green Haven Correctional Facility a few miles away in the Dutchess county community of Stormville, where he was the only person in the state under sentence of death in the electric chair at the time.

The news story was illustrated with her photo and a crudely sketched pen-and-ink drawing Smith created for her on Death Row showing her face, and smaller figures of them in each other's arms in the foreground. She was quoted in the picture caption as saying the drawing symbolized their love transcending prison walls.

A few years later in a letter to this author, she repeated her denial that she was a transsexual. She also denied that she was ever in love with Smith or planned to marry him. Mrs. Simmons branded the marriage stories as ridiculous, and nothing more than gossip. She was merely investigating his case in an effort to help him, she said.

Mrs. Simmons also disputed a report in the 1983 *Post* article that indicated she was eight years older than her true age. The author explained she was only seventeen when she left Europe for Canada, and had lied about her age by a few years so that she could get a job.

Chapter Twenty

Sharon Paul
and
Roger Keith Coleman

When rape-slayer Roger Keith Coleman placed a classified ad in a student newspaper at the University of Virginia inviting pen pals to correspond with him on Death Row, Sharon Paul was one of a dozen students who wrote replies.

Nine years later when the handsome and articulate onetime coal miner became the darling of the liberal news media and was facing imminent execution, she had outlasted all Coleman's other correspondents and become his girlfriend.

Coleman was a master manipulator. He manipulated individuals, and he manipulated much of the national press into believing his claims of innocence.

He became the subject of sympathetic stories by some of the most powerful elements of the national media, that led the prosecutor who sent him to Death Row to refer to him as "America's capital punishment poster boy."

The convicted sex slayer was featured in stories in the *Washington Post,* the *New York Times,* made the cover of *Time* magazine, and he and his supporters appeared on television's "Donahue" and on CNN's blockbuster show, "Larry King Live," to plead his case.

The thrust of the media message was that police, prosecutors, the jury at his trial, and a plethora of physical and circumstantial evidence was, or might have been, wrong; and he deserved a new trial. Coleman, his girlfriend, and the media knew better than the courts, the juries — and it would seem — the overwhelming majority of Americans whom, polls show, strongly favor the death penalty.

Sharon was one of the clean-cut-appearing Death Row inmate's most loyal and industrious supporters. And she worked tirelessly with the media and other anti-death penalty activists to keep the bespectacled killer out of the electric chair.

In 1983, she was a sophomore at the University of Virginia when she saw Coleman's ad in the *University Journal.* The wording had been carefully calculated for dramatic impact, and the ad read: "13 steps to eternity. Prisoner on Death Row seeks correspondence and possible visits. Sincerity is what counts."

Coleman later explained that the death watch cell at the prison in Richmond, where condemned prisoners were taken at that time to spend their last hours before electrocution, was supposedly thirteen steps from the execution chamber.

He also claimed that at the time he placed the ad, he didn't care whether or not his correspondents were male or female.

Somehow, however, within a year after the ad appeared, the attractive, dark-haired coed was the only one of those who had replied, who was still corresponding with him.

According to a report in the *Richmond Times-Dispatch,* written nine years after the college girl and the sex-slayer began corresponding, she wrote her first letter on a weekend and mailed it on a Monday.

In the note, she reportedly chatted about her classes in biology and childhood growth and development, her affection for folk music, and the bands she liked. She also told him she was a Lutheran, and asked about his religious links.

On the Thursday after she dropped her first letter in the mail, she had a reply. Coleman told her that he was innocent of the crime he was convicted of committing. She told him she believed him.

Several months after beginning the correspondence, Sharon's roommate drove her to the Mecklenburg Correctional Center for her first face-to-face meeting with Coleman.

While Sharon was becoming better acquainted with her pen pal, her roommate took the opportunity to chat on a visiting room phone with James Briley, a multiple killer who raped a pregnant Richmond woman, then murdered her and her five-year-old son. Briley was executed in 1983.

After her first meeting with Coleman, Sharon began studying the voluminous transcripts of his trial, which were on file at the university's law library. She also continued visiting two or three times per year. The visits didn't end, even after she graduated and took a job with the New Jersey Division of Fish,

Game, and Wildlife, turning out salt-marsh maps on computers.

According to Sharon's statements to reporters, soon after initiating her relationship with Coleman, she stopped her efforts to share her enthusiasm for him with other students. They had the unsettling habit of asking her questions about such unpleasant subjects as what she would do if Coleman was released some day and came after her.

Coleman was smitten with the young college idealist, and pressed his awkward courtship as best he could from behind bars. He earned a few dollars a month at Mecklenburg by performing prison chores, and spent some of the money on catalogs. Alone in his cell, he would flip through the catalogs, pick out clothing he thought she would look good in, and mail his selections to her, suggesting she narrow down the choices to her favorites. But the final selection was up to him.

She responded with gifts of her own, carefully selected to comply with prison regulations.

Sometimes family members or other friends bought magazine subscriptions for him, but he wasn't permitted to keep the premiums offered by some. So he passed some of them on to Sharon.

Coleman eventually suggested they marry. One of the benefits would be regular contact visits, an opportunity to face each other across a table for an hour at a time and hold hands under the watchful eye of guards, he pointed out. A kiss and a hug are permitted at the beginning and at the end of contact visits.

294

But she replied that she wanted to marry him in a church wedding in the presence of her family and friends, the prisoner later revealed. The public demonstration of affection would be proof of her love. But their plans never materialized.

Nevertheless, Sharon and Coleman were at last permitted a contact visit in March, 1992. That was only a few weeks before a new execution date that had been set for May 20.

Coleman wasn't about to go to the death chamber quietly, and he dug in his heels for the fight of his life. Sharon, his mother, Mary Huslander, and anti-death penalty organizations, including Amnesty International, were supported by a deluge of sympathetic stories in the print and electronic media questioning his conviction and guilt.

The shy nineteen-year-old housewife who was so savagely murdered in her modest one-bedroom home, beside a mountain creek in Grundy, Virginia, seemed to be almost forgotten during the press frenzy.

Wanda McCoy was home alone on the night of March 10, 1981, when she was raped and slashed to death with a knife by her brother-in-law, Roger Coleman. The Buchanan county homemaker's sister was married to the killer.

Coleman was scheduled to work a night shift at the southwestern Virginia coal mine where he was employed, but the work project was cancelled and he left the mine at about 10:00 P.M. He didn't return to his home, which was only a few minutes from the mine entrance, until after 11:00 P.M.

In the meantime, his sister-in-law was raped and murdered. Her husband, Brad, found her mutilated body when he returned home after completing his shift at the mine at 11:00 P.M. Her neck was slashed so viciously that she was nearly decapitated.

Coleman was one of the pallbearers at her funeral. But he also quickly became a primary suspect in the shocking crime. When he was a high school senior he was convicted of attempted rape, and had also been accused at various times of other sex crimes.

And when forensic tests were conducted on semen found on the body, police learned that it had come from someone with a "B" blood type. Only thirteen percent of the population, including Coleman, shared that blood type. Brad McCoy had type "A" blood.

Tests on a speck of blood found on a pair of blue jeans Coleman turned over to police showed it was type "O." Mrs. McCoy's blood was type "O." Although another speck of blood was found on Coleman's pocketknife, it was too minute for laboratory technicians to determine if it was human or from another species of animal.

But police said they believed the pocketknife was the murder weapon. Two loose pubic hairs found on the woman's body were also found to be consistent with Coleman's hair.

Investigators arrested Coleman and prosecutors later contended in court that he had driven his truck to the creek after getting off work, waded across to the house, and attacked his sister-in-law.

He was convicted at a jury trial on March 18, 1982, of rape and murder. The next day he was sentenced to death.

* * *

The nation's unofficial death penalty lobby launched a highly organized and sophisticated crusade in the court and in the press to save Coleman from the electric chair. But by early May, 1992, his time was running out. A federal judge who reviewed the case announced that the evidence against Coleman was even stronger than that which the jury was permitted to hear.

Coleman had lost key appeals in the federal courts when his last hopes were dashed. He volunteered to take a lie detector test to prove that he was telling the truth about being innocent of the murder. Although lie detector tests may not be introduced in trials as evidence, he and supporters reasoned that a good showing might influence Virginia Governor L. Douglas Wilder to provide him with clemency.

The test was performed by a Virginia State Police polygraph operator, and Coleman failed — miserably. He was pale and shaken, and could hardly speak after his crushing performance.

Gov. Wilder carefully reviewed the court record, as well as claims by Coleman's attorneys that new evidence raised serious questions about his guilt, and turned down the clemency request.

"I have to be guided by facts, not be concerned with emotions or hype," the governor explained his decision. "It wouldn't be fair to other persons who did not have the same degree of media campaign mounted for their case."

The condemned man, Sharon, and his mother appeared on "Donahue" in the last-ditch efforts to win a reprieve. His lawyer, Kathleen A. Behan, told the national audience watching NBC's "Today Show" that she had new evidence which undermined "the prosecution's entire theory of the crime."

Arnold & Porter, a high-powered Washington, D. C. law firm, which was representing Coleman, organized the flurry of Death Row interviews.

Sharon told reporters that he was innocent, and deserved to live. They hadn't yet given up hope, she said.

He was transferred to the Greensville Correctional Center in Jarratt, about fifty miles from Richmond, where the electric chair is kept.

When he wasn't busy with interviews, he tried to read some science fiction. He said he thought the *Time* magazine article about him was great. But at Greensville he was permitted twenty-four-hour-a-day telephone privileges. Consequently, he continued to spend much of his remaining time conducting interviews. He could talk with his friends in the press whenever he wished.

But he told reporters his most difficult moments were watching Sharon sob on the other side of the heavy glass window during their visits.

Coleman spent most of his last day and early evening at Greensville in a final visit with Sharon. She had taken a week off from her job, and visited a couple of days earlier for six hours. They talked, as usual, by telephone while peering at each other through the thick glass window in the visiting room.

* * *

During the earlier visit, he explained that he had changed his mind about wanting to be buried in Grundy, next to his grandparents. He said he had realized he would be only a few yards from Mrs. McCoy's body and was afraid that would cause Sharon to worry about his grave being desecrated.

Consequently, he suggested a choice for her: either bury him in New Jersey, or have him cremated so she could keep the ashes. She replied that she wanted to go to Grundy and spread his ashes.

While she was inside the prison visiting her boy-friend for the last time, a Monday night memorial service for Mrs. McCoy was being held outside the Buchanan County Court House.

Finally, at 10:59 P.M.. the U. S. Supreme Court voted seven to two to reject his last appeal for a stay of execution.

Sharon had bid her final goodbye to Coleman a few hours earlier, and he had choked down his last meal. He chose pepperoni pizza, fudge cookies, and a Seven-Up.

At about 11:30 P.M. he walked the approximately two-dozen steps from his cell to the death chamber and was strapped into the electric chair. He was pronounced dead at 11:38 P.M.

His lawyer, Ms. Behan, responded to the execution by predicting that the case would be remembered as "the Dred Scott of death penalty law," (the 1857 U. S. Supreme Court decision that upheld slavery).

* * *

Ted J. Smith, III, of the Virginia Commonwealth University department of journalism, had a different response when he was interviewed by the *Washington Times* about the dramatic case and the media circus it engendered.

"It is a grotesque and frightening spectacle," he was quoted. "Grotesque because we see the transformation of a vicious murderer into a victim. It's frightening because it further erodes public confidence in our legal system."

HE'S THE LAST MAN YOU'D EVER
WANT TO MEET IN A DARK ALLEY . . .

THE EXECUTIONER

By DON PENDLETON

*Available wherever paperbacks are sold, or order direct from the
Publisher. Send cover price plus 50¢ per copy for mailing and
handling to Pinnacle Books, Dept. 702, 475 Park Avenue South,
New York, N.Y. 10016. Residents of New York and Tennessee
must include sales tax. DO NOT SEND CASH. For a free Zebra/
Pinnacle catalog please write to the above address.*

WALK ALONG THE BRINK OF FURY:

THE EDGE SERIES

Westerns By GEORGE G. GILMAN

Available wherever paperbacks are sold, or order direct from the Publisher. Send cover price plus 50¢ per copy for mailing and handling to Pinnacle Books, Dept. 702, 475 Park Avenue South, New York, N.Y. 10016. Residents of New York and Tennessee must include sales tax. DO NOT SEND CASH. For a free Zebra/ Pinnacle catalog please write to the above address.

SCALE TO THE HEIGHTS OF ADVENTURE WITH

MOUNTAIN JACK PIKE

By JOSEPH MEEK